Begin the Begin
R.E.M.'s Early Years

ROBERT DEAN LURIE

Verse Chorus Press

For David and Susan Lurie

Verse Chorus Press
Portland, Oregon
info@versechorus.com

Front and back cover photographs © Joanna Schwartz

Design and layout by Steve Connell Book Design | *steveconnell.net*

Author and publisher wish to thank all those who supplied photographs and gave permission to reproduce copyright material in this book. Every effort has been made to contact all copyright holders, and the publisher welcomes communication from any copyright owners from whom permission was inadvertently not obtained. In such cases, we will be pleased to obtain appropriate permission and provide suitable acknowledgment in future editions.

Printed in the USA

Library of Congress Cataloging-in-Publication Data

Names: Lurie, Robert Dean, 1974- author.
Title: Begin the begin : R.E.M.'s early years / Robert Dean Lurie.
Description: Portland, Oregon : Verse Chorus Press, [2019] |
Identifiers: LCCN 2018054807 (print) | LCCN 2018055301 (ebook) | ISBN 9781891241697 (e-book) | ISBN 9781891241680 (pbk.)
Subjects: LCSH: R.E.M. (Musical group) | Rock musicians--United States--Biography. | LCGFT: Biographies.
Classification: LCC ML421.R22 (ebook) | LCC ML421.R22 L87 2019 (print) | DDC 782.42166092/2 [B] --dc23
LC record available at https://lccn.loc.gov/2018054807

Contents

*Do these people realize that this is pure impressionism?
I close my eyes and all I see are pastels, and I listen and
all I hear are gliding blocks of tone.*

—Betty Hendricks Carlton Minder (Ort's mother),
on hearing R.E.M.'s "Harborcoat"

*I reveal self sparingly and deliberately so people can
really do what they want, and it clearly is mysterious.*

—Jonathan Omer-Man

Author's Note

Several books have already been written about R.E.M., a few of which—
Fiction by David Buckley, *Perfect Circle* (previously published as *Remarks*
and *Remarks Remade*) by Tony Fletcher, and *Reveal* by Johnny Black—are
very fine examples of music journalism and near-definitive treatments of
the R.E.M. saga as a whole. But most of the R.E.M. biographies to date
(including those listed above) were written by British authors and, first and
foremost, for UK audiences. Perhaps inevitably, they tend to overlook many
significant details about Athens and the American South. I get the sense that
their depictions of the region have been largely shaped by the comments
of the band members themselves. But since the claims of Bill Berry, Peter
Buck, Mike Mills, and Michael Stipe to authentic Southernness are (as we
shall see) tenuous at best, to attempt to appraise this unique locale through
their eyes can be a bit like squinting at a blurry photo of a blurry photo. The
people and places of the South are crucial to the R.E.M. story in ways far
more complex and interesting than have been presented thus far, and it has
been my intention in what follows to provide a more thorough assessment. I
make no claim to factual infallibility, but I do bring to this task the benefit of
having lived in Athens specifically, and the South generally, for a significant
portion of my adult life.

There is another major reason why I feel this book needed to be written.
I have been aware for some time that several local figures who were pivotal
in the band's early history have been underrepresented in previous accounts,
even completely omitted in some cases. All biographers must be selective,
of course, and there are plenty of personalities *I* have left out due to space
considerations, lack of interview availability, heavy coverage elsewhere, or
my own blind spots. But I'm proud to have incorporated Ort, Pat the Wiz,
Velena Vego, Jeff Walls, Chris Edwards, Billy Holmes, and others into the
R.E.M. saga. They all deserve to be here.

I also believe there is value in returning to people and events with the
benefit of knowing the full arc of the R.E.M. story. Many, though not all, of

the earlier books were written and published in the thick of R.E.M.'s mainstream success. The ending of the story was not yet known, and because the band were still a going concern, some interviewees were reluctant to divulge personal details. Such reticence has dissipated considerably in the years since R.E.M. disbanded in 2010.

I would be remiss if I did not single out one writer who *has* gotten the details mentioned above absolutely right. Rodger Lyle Brown's book *Party Out of Bounds* covers the early Athens scene as a whole. He has both the Southerner's gift for colorful detail and the luck of having been present at (and participated in) the inception of said scene. *Party Out of Bounds* has been invaluable to my understanding of these events, and I recommend it without reservation. (And yes, Ort features in that one.)

Like any dutiful journalist I have attempted to obtain the participation of the members of R.E.M. themselves. Traditionally, their approach to biographies has been hands-off (with the exception of the various versions of Tony Fletcher's book and the occasional single-member interview). In response to my enquiries, Bertis Downs, R.E.M.'s manager, explained, "The band doesn't really take a position—people are welcome to write [biographies], and we don't generally have much to do with them." This is understandable, particularly now that the band is no more. It could even be argued that the members of R.E.M.—especially Peter Buck—have been overinterviewed by the press through the years, and as a result have developed standard responses to most biographical questions. It is more interesting to the long-term fan, I would argue, to offer the stories the band members *haven't* told, as well as alternative interpretations of the well-worn mythology. This book attempts to explore those threads whenever possible.

Prologue

A needle drops on a record. The static crackles and pops. And then, emerging from a space between the speakers, the galloping of horses' hooves—in the form of guitar arpeggios, bass harmonics, tom-toms—pounding the riverbanks, heralding an arrival. Then a shriek—not the kicked-in-the-groin yelp of Robert Plant or Steven Tyler, more the startled exhalation of a young Confederate soldier caught in the chest with buckshot. Then:

> *Suspicion yourself, suspicion yourself, don't get caught.*
> *Suspicion yourself, suspicion yourself, let us out.*

This is the illusion, and the truth. Dispatches from a South that never existed, from Southerners who were not really Southern. Who reinvented pop music without having any credentials for the job. Four young men of middling talent who left the door ajar and were just as surprised as anyone when scattered fragments of genius blew in. Perhaps they wanted to sound like the Velvet Underground but didn't have the patience to stick with that "Heroin" drone. Maybe they wanted to mimic Television but none of them had the chops of a Tom Verlaine or Richard Lloyd. The singer wanted to be Patti Smith, but his fondness for Tammy Wynette kept getting in the way. Through no fault of their own, and against all logic, they ultimately upstaged many of their influences. And they arrived at their "accidental" stardom via a series of carefully calculated steps.

> *In a corner garden, wilder lower wolves!*

Huh?

I arrived in Athens, Georgia, in 1992, a decade late. I missed all of the events described in this book. But the ghosts of the town's fabled music scene—the loose collective of college students and sundry misfits that had birthed the

B-52's, Pylon, and R.E.M.—still lingered. Like Ross Shapiro, a wiry, dark-haired guy of indeterminate age who regaled customers at the Gyro Wrap with tales of that seemingly long-ago time. "By 1986 I was already talking about the old days," he'd say wistfully as he carved thin slices of meat off a rotating spit.* And there were the members of R.E.M. themselves—who were not ghosts at all, really, but not exactly corporeal either. In 1992 they all still lived in the Athens area and were striving mightily to hang on to the notion of being a small-town band. They navigated the waters of their recent international fame a little shakily, doing their best, at home, to ignore the dropped jaws and wide-eyed stares of newly arrived University of Georgia (UGA) freshmen who were unschooled in how to handle sudden close proximity with celebrity. R.E.M.'s supposedly reclusive singer, Michael Stipe, hit the town just about every night and could typically be found hovering on the periphery of the audience at the 40 Watt Club—checking out performances by new bands (the Daisy Group) or old friends (Bob Mould, Robyn Hitchcock), or ambling out the front door of the Globe, always unshaven, always wearing a hat, and usually rolling a cigarette. On rare occasions the entire band might be glimpsed ensconced in a booth at this or that bar, their animated discussions of their next move blending into the innocuous chatter all around them.

The unspoken rule around town was to leave them alone, and apart from some of those overeager freshmen, or the frat boys who periodically hassled Stipe, people abided by it. Still, when you've got a lot of people in a cramped space, all keenly aware of the identities of the men in the corner, all trying mightily not to look, not to stare, the air itself takes on a nervous energy: the electricity of expectation, of anticipation, the loading up on stories to tell later.

These were the years when Athens pretended to be jaded about its most successful musical export. In 1992 the rest of the world was fawning over the band's new album, *Automatic for the People,* many declaring it their best yet. But you wouldn't have known that in Athens, where the old-timers still talked about the 1981 shows at Tyrone's and most everyone else seemed to draw a line after the Reconstruction tour of 1985. Even though R.E.M. were *still there,* ever-present, people spoke mournfully of a vanished era. They spoke of R.E.M. in the past tense because *their* R.E.M.—Athens's R.E.M.—was long gone. Perhaps it had been that way ever since the release of the band's first LP, *Murmur,* and their first out-of-state tours in the early '80s. The irony is

---

*Shapiro ultimately started an excellent band called the Glands, which unfortunately never quite caught fire like those groups from the "old days."

that during those fabled glory days—particularly during that now legend-ary run of gigs at Tyrone's O.C.—these same kind of people (sometimes the exact same people) berated the young band for being too conventional, too conservative . . . *You know, they sure as shit weren't Pylon.* "Golden eras" tend to be moving targets, never recognized as such at the time, constructed and mythologized after the fact.

I was one of those University of Georgia freshmen shamelessly gaping at Stipe and company; at the same time, I was largely unaware of the signifi-cance of much that surrounded me. When I took up residence in Reed Hall, at the time (1992) virtually unchanged from the late 1970s, I had no idea that I may have been living in the fourth-floor room that R.E.M.'s drummer Bill Berry had inhabited 13 years earlier. And when I hung out with residents of the subbasement—a claustrophobic space full of young bodies with very little adult supervision—I knew nothing of its significance as an incubator for the legendary Athens music scene.

Reed Hall was still a wild, happening place in my day. Friendships were forged there, hearts broken, bodies entwined and decoupled in a feverish waking dream. Most of that was due to the natural, combustible energy of hundreds of young adults gathered under one roof, but perhaps part of it came from the spirits still clinging to the beer-stained walls—the psychic imprints left by some crazed girls raising hell a generation earlier, bursting out of the confines of their suburban lives, parading their outrageousness before the openly longing stares of Bill Berry, Mike Mills, and other soon-to-be movers and shakers in the nascent scene—young adults still growing into their own bodies, thinking, *My God, I don't know if this is heaven or some kind of irresistible hell, but I'm going to throw myself into it.*

A few months into my time at UGA, I found myself quite accidentally at a loft party hosted by Michael Lachowski. A girl I was interested in had already managed to insinuate herself among the Athens old guard and had gotten herself invited. I tagged along, though I knew nothing about Lachowski or his band Pylon.

So there I was, a fresh-faced 18-year-old, bobbing my head to the techno music Lachowski spun on his turntables, getting drunk as several of the char-acters in this book danced around me. There was Michael Stipe, gaunt and wiry, winter cap pulled low over his forehead, throwing his body around the dance floor with unselfconscious abandon; twitching, jerking, shaking his hips almost violently, he was at this moment among perhaps the only people in the world—apart from his family—who truly knew him.

I didn't know it then, but this book had its inception in that moment. In one sense, this was a group of equals: the *inner* inner circle of the Athens scene. Pylon had, in fact, exerted a major influence on R.E.M. There appeared to be no hierarchy and no resentment within this group of friends. And yet . . . the following morning they all headed off to their various jobs—one managing a restaurant, one clocking in at a factory, one building houses. Except for Stipe. If he worked that day at all, he did so as a member of a multimillion-dollar-earning, Grammy Award–winning rock band. What was that like for this close-knit group? How did they navigate through, and accommodate, such disparities in fortune? Who remained in the circle and who was left out in the cold? Athens is not like New York City, or Los Angeles, or even Minneapolis. How do you contain something as big as R.E.M. in a place so small? Is it even possible, or was the attempt doomed from the start?

R.E.M.'s gradual takeoff intrigued me. Theirs had not been an overnight success, but rather a slow, seemingly careful ascent, each successive album improving on the sales of the previous one. Perhaps that's how the band members had managed to hang on to their old friends and community for so long: from day to day the slow walk toward fame may have been barely perceptible to those around them. Everyone knew that R.E.M. were going somewhere, but no one knew where exactly, or when they would be getting there. In the meantime, here's Mike, Bill, Michael, and Peter. Want to go grab a beer?

An Australian songwriter I profiled in my first book once said of R.E.M., "They're a bunch of boring people who make boring records." While that assessment is neither charitable nor true, the first half of his statement plays into a common prejudice about how rock stars should behave. As they ascended to the public stage, the members of R.E.M. appeared to lack the feral, dangerous edge of the early Rolling Stones or Led Zeppelin (or, for that matter, the punk bands they admired and sometimes emulated). Even Michael Stipe's much-ballyhooed "eccentricity" appeared, at times, painfully contrived. Yet this clean image belied a wild and woolly truth: this band that supposedly held itself to a higher standard of ethics (whatever that means) had, in fact, gone through copious amounts of drugs and groupies in its day—a revelation that ought to come as a goddamned relief to everyone.

Yes, in those early years R.E.M. was a raucous and unpredictable band, gloriously ragged onstage and correspondingly unhinged off. Seasoned road warriors, they held their own in just about any crappy venue in any given "flyover" state. On a seemingly never-ending circuit of the blue highways of America, they blew the roof off many a pizza joint and dive bar. They played the places no one else cared to play and won fans—even if only in the single digits at times—at all of them. And no matter how insufferable their singer might have seemed, even to members of his own band, no one could deny that he was one of the most compelling front men to tread the boards in many a year.

The *real* R.E.M.—the R.E.M. held so dear by those Athens scenesters of yore—drank, popped pills, snorted stuff, got laid, and worked their asses off. This is the story of *that* band, and of those who loved them and lifted them up.

Atlanta Civic Center, December 31, 1984. Photo © Joanna Schwartz.

Chapter One

There are not many allusions to sex—even to romantic love—on those early R.E.M. albums. Not that the four band members were cloistered ascetics— far from it; it's just that Michael Stipe was trying to get something else across in those days, something to do with two-headed cows, Man Ray, a drunk named Pee Wee, and Brer Rabbit. So it may come as a surprise to learn that R.E.M. was born of an old-fashioned instance of boy-meets-girl physical infatuation.

When Kathleen O'Brien first laid eyes on Bill Berry at the beginning of 1979, she had already been a student at the University of Georgia for several months, having taken up residence at Reed Hall in fall 1978. Situated directly alongside the gargantuan Sanford Stadium on the north side of campus, Reed Hall was a paradoxical place: a dump by any conventional standards, yet fondly remembered to this day by generations of alumni for the very qualities that made it seem so inhospitable at the time: lack of air-conditioning; small, cramped rooms; loud, clanking pipes; the very same horrendous carpeting that must have lined the rings of Dante's Inferno (you know, the type where the threads have been ground down into the rubberized base so the whole surface is smooth and sticky, the color of Georgia red clay mixed with shit). And the men's wing had communal shower rooms reminiscent of those found in prisons. Such adverse conditions really brought people together, and during the early fall and late spring months, it was impossible to survive in that building without leaving your door wide open; otherwise you'd have suffocated in the stale, humid, cigarette smoke–saturated air.

The consequence of all those open doors was dorm-wide conviviality. Let's say you're walking down the hall of the first-floor men's wing, you casu- ally glance in one of the doorways, and, hey, wait a minute, that guy's pulling a Clash record out of its sleeve. And you thought everyone here only listened to Southern rock. Lifelong friendships were kindled by such chance encoun- ters. If you had, say, a fondness for marijuana, you could discern pretty quickly which rooms were occupied by fellow enthusiasts. Some believed that if they exhaled into a poster tube stuffed with socks they could mask the smell, but in those cramped surroundings they weren't fooling anyone. Everybody was in everybody's business, and for a certain concentrated period in a person's life, that can actually be comforting.

The Reed Hall I'm describing here no longer exists. With the best of intentions, the powers that be overhauled the building in the late 1990s and equipped it with all the modern conveniences—air-conditioning and individual shower stalls, for instance—that tuition-paying parents expect for their children. Now those kids sit squirreled away in their little climate-controlled dens. Doors remain closed, and the soul of the building is gone.

But back to Kathleen and Bill.

After catching that first glimpse of young Mr. Berry, Kathleen told her friend Sandi Phipps that Bill was a "fox." It's easy to see the appeal. He had a feral, wolfish appearance: wiry body; thick, tousled hair; hooded Robert Mitchum eyes; a complexion that looked slightly Mediterranean; and thick eyebrows that stretched across his forehead in a nearly unbroken line—a feature that would have been distinctly unattractive on just about anyone else but on Berry served to accentuate his uniqueness.

That initial encounter occurred in the Reed Hall mail room, right off the first-floor lobby. Few, if any, words were exchanged, but Kathleen ascertained through the grapevine that Bill had recently arrived at UGA from the central Georgia town of Macon, home of the Allman Brothers. To this day, nearly everyone who has known Bill characterizes him as "a good old boy from Macon," even though he actually hails from Duluth, Minnesota, and did not set foot on Georgia soil until the age of 14. Something of the South got into his blood, though. Some years later he would tell an interviewer that he and his bandmates were "not ashamed of being Southerners; we're proud of the fact . . . Like most Southerners, we're easygoing and don't usually get uptight." Berry had fully internalized this mind-set by the time he arrived at UGA. He even had a slight drawl.

Nineteen-year-old Kathleen was lean and long-legged (her friend Diane Loring Aiken reckons she had the greatest legs of anyone ever). Her sleepy green eyes, perpetually arched eyebrows, and devilish grin hinted at a worldliness that most of her peers did not yet possess. She had already lived on her own and was more self-sufficient than many of her friends in Reed, most of whom had come straight from their family home and were accustomed to being taken care of (and cleaned up after). And she was often the instigator of some seriously high-octane blowouts that transpired in Reed's previously mentioned subbasement (or "subwastement," as she calls it), of which more later.

Kathleen O'Brien grew up in the Atlanta suburbs during an era of significant racial upheaval. Government-mandated integration was in full swing, and for the first time in Georgia's history, a robust black middle class was emerging. Half a century later, few would argue that this was in any way a bad thing, but any great social transition carries with it considerable tensions. The newly affluent black families did what anyone in their position would have done: they began to move into the more upscale (read: historically white) neighborhoods. Kathleen's family lived in one of those neighborhoods, in southern DeKalb County.

"We stayed," she recalls now.

We didn't really have a problem with [integration]. But massive white flight ensued and we were one of the few white families left in the neighborhood. By the time I got to seventh grade, pretty much all of my friends had already moved. I had plenty of black friends at that point, but what I experienced was that some of their parents didn't really want their kids hanging out with a white girl.

Once she reached high school, Kathleen herself became an involuntary white flighter. "The high school I was supposed to go to had become predominantly black at that point," she says.

This happened over a period of, oh, maybe three years. It went from pretty much lily white to completely black, and it was a very strange time. My brother ended up going there but he had been mugged a couple of times. And my mother was afraid that if I went to that high school, something horrible would happen to me because of my tint of birth, you know, since I wasn't going to put up with any bullshit.

Because of these concerns, Kathleen's parents devised an elaborate plan that would enable her to attend high school close to where her mother worked at the CDC, then known as the Center for Disease Control. They rented an apartment off Claremont Street that they proceeded to furnish and stock with food. "It was basically a little high school pad for me and my brother," Kathleen says. The family held on to the apartment for a year—long enough to convince the county that they really had moved. Then they ditched the apartment while continuing to use the address for school documentation.

From our current vantage point, it's easy to ascribe racist motives to those parents who pulled their kids out of schools en masse in the 1970s, although most of them acted out of genuine, if often exaggerated, concern for their children's safety. The "white flight kids" themselves by and large accepted racial equality as a given. Many of the protagonists of this book came from such a background, and, as we will see, they mostly developed markedly progressive political and social views. Had their parents all been virulent racists that would likely not have been the case.

Georgia-based lawyer and sportswriter T. Kyle King grew up in a section of Atlanta where the transitions were not quite so extreme as they were in Kathleen's neighborhood (his family did not feel the need to uproot, for instance), but his views reflect those of the majority of white kids who grew up in Atlanta in the 1970s and early '80s: "In the 1970s, metro Atlanta still felt like 'the South,'" he says.

> But it was changing, though we didn't know it at the time. Race was as ancillary an issue as it ever is; the South had come through a tumultuous time in the '50s and '60s, so the tone of race relations was subdued in the '70s and early '80s. I know I never thought much about the rather remarkable fact that I was going to school with black kids my own age, and, in retrospect, it's noteworthy that the reality of integration no longer seemed noteworthy. Atlanta had passed from a period of having white mayors to a period of having black mayors, which again, from a kid's perspective, seemed rather unremarkable, given the swiftness with which we moved from Ivan Allen, who presided over the civil rights era, to Maynard Jackson [Atlanta's first African American mayor, who took office in 1974].

As King's comments indicate, integration in urban Georgia was fairly successful—at least compared to the much rockier experiences of adjoining states. By the time of the 2010 Census, DeKalb County, which included Kathleen's former home of South DeKalb, had become the second most affluent majority-black county in the United States. The path to that outcome was rocky and generated the collateral damage of many self-uprooted white families, but the outcome was one that most of the white flight kids supported.

It is the first of many ironies in our story that the politically incorrect phenomenon of white flight played a part in the birth of one of the most liberal rock bands in history: the O'Briens' flight to what Kathleen's parents perceived as the more hospitable environs of Druid Hills High School led directly to her first meeting with a towering, stick-thin record store clerk named Peter Buck, who was at that time working two doors down from the restaurant where Kathleen waitressed in the evenings. Buck was—and still is—loud, gregarious, opinionated, and, according to at least one of his friends, "kind of obnoxious." As such, his character is trying mightily to insert itself into our narrative at this point and dominate the proceedings. But let's keep him in the wings a bit longer. Suffice to say for now that Kathleen was exposed to Buck's personality and forceful opinions on music during her many visits to browse the latest releases at his store in Emory Village. These chance encounters created the first strands of a tangled web of relationships that would ultimately beget R.E.M.

Another important strand came in the form of Kathleen's friendship with Paul Butchart, who, like Buck, was tall, opinionated (though a bit more reserved in his delivery), and fiercely loyal. Paul worked with Kathleen's brother at a steakhouse and shared with Kathleen interests in the German language (they had first met at German camp one summer) and, of course, music. Paul, too, would become a pivotal player in the genesis of R.E.M.

By the late 1970s, Kathleen was listening to music that, as she says, "pretty much no one else had heard of at Druid Hills." This included such now-mainstream artists as Tom Petty, Elvis Costello, and Blondie, all considered very much "alternative" at the time. What's more, she says, "I already had a reputation as being weird because I read weird poetry and I dressed strangely."

Frictions with her mom prompted Kathleen to leave the family home and live on her own at age 18, giving her that crucial taste of independence (and lack of adult supervision) before she moved into Reed Hall the following fall. No sooner had she arrived in that charmingly dilapidated building than she became involved in a seemingly nonstop party in the girls' subbasement. The rotating cast of characters in this bacchanal included several Kathys (Russo, Fain, and another that Kathleen simply remembers as "Kat"), Sandi Phipps, Linda Hopper, and a Patti Smith–emulating interloper from the fourth floor named Carol Levy. In *Party Out of Bounds*, Rodger Lyle Brown (Phipps's boyfriend at the time, and a frequenter of these "subwastement" parties) describes their activities thusly:

> The girls were rowdy. They knocked out ceiling panels just to see the dust fly. They broke windows to hear the glass shatter. […] Mark Cline, who would form the band Love Tractor, lived on the fourth floor of Reed, and when he came down to the subbasement he and the girls pasted pornography on the walls and sat smoking cigarettes, carving genitalia into Barbie dolls.

Where were the dorm authorities, you may be wondering? Well, the subbasement was apparently too small to warrant its own dedicated RA (Resident Assistant), so the girls who lived there fell under the jurisdiction of the already overworked main-basement RA, who never came down because, Kathleen says, "everybody was so afraid of us."

It was perhaps inevitable that Bill Berry would get drawn into this crowd. (Hard partying, sexually provocative young women with a taste for cool and edgy music? What's not to love?) But his engagement with the subbasement scene was initially shy and tentative. For that first month or so after Kathleen saw him, the two would pass each other only occasionally on the Reed quad or in the mail room. Bill was on the exact opposite side of the building, his fourth-floor room facing out over the parking lot. And despite the wildness she displayed when in her own environment, Kathleen was too shy—or too cautious—to venture up to the men's wing on her own. But she did begin to piece together Bill's backstory from what she gleaned through the grapevine.

She learned that Bill was a drummer, though he maintained a strangely ambivalent attitude toward playing music, or at least toward the idea of a performing career. "I'd like to say that playing the drums and being a rock 'n' roll drummer were big dreams I had for as long as I can remember," he told an interviewer years later. "But they weren't. I never considered the possibilities of being a musician. Back then I thought that was what others did." Despite this reticence, he did exhibit a simple joy at playing for its own sake, spurred, no doubt, by the enthusiasm of his best friend and frequent musical partner, Mike Mills.

The story of how Bill Berry and Mike Mills became best friends and bandmates is one of the most oft-told tales in all of R.E.M. lore. It has a neat-and-tidy fairy-tale quality to it, though it lacks any corroborating sources. If it's true, it is something that could only happen to kids.

The story goes like this: In high school, Bill Berry was a self-described "juvenile delinquent," heavily into alcohol, pot, and general malfeasance. Mills is on record saying that Berry ran with a "rough crowd" in Macon and was "on the wrong side of the law" (Marlon Brando and his *Wild One* gang spring to mind). Mills, who at the time resembled—there's really no other way to put this—an endearing rodent in glasses, was a straight-A student and all-around overachiever. R.E.M. biographer Johnny Black lays it on perhaps a bit thick in describing the young Mills (a future hellraiser par excellence) as a "clean-living, hard-working lad," and the young Berry (a future teetotaling recluse) as a "wayward youth," but it does appear that the teenaged Mills and

Berry were opposites in several ways and that some low-level hostility may have existed between them because of this.

Along came music to smooth over their differences. Sometime early on in high school, Berry got invited to take part in an afternoon jam session with a friend's fledgling band. He duly arrived at the designated house and began setting up his drum kit. In walked Mills, his supposed nemesis, who had been recruited to play bass. (Berry has stated that he would have left at that point if he hadn't already set up his gear.) They began playing, and sometime during that afternoon Berry's musical instincts overrode his thuggish instincts and he came to realize that he'd stumbled into something pretty special—not this nascent band, per se, which would go on to play under the names Shadowfax and, later, the Back Door Band—but this effortless groove he had going with Mills. They were in the pocket, as the saying goes.

And just like that, they became best friends forever. Or something along those lines.

Mike Mills did present himself to the world as a nerd, that much is true. The California native wore thick glasses, styled his hair in a manner that resembled a muddy toupee, had the pallor of someone who spent a lot of time indoors, and was generally out of step with his peers sartorially. Compounding this uncool appearance was the fact that he played tuba and sousaphone in the school band.

But beneath the contrasts in Mills's and Berry's exteriors lay some notable similarities. For one thing, both could play a variety of instruments. In addition to the aforementioned horns—and bass, of course—Mills was proficient on piano and guitar and had a solid grasp of music theory. Berry, too, could navigate the piano, guitar, and ukulele, though his approach to music was more intuitive and less schooled than that of his new friend. Both young men came from households in which music was appreciated. Mills's father, Fred, had been an operatic tenor and instilled in his son a love of melody from an early age. Bill Berry's passion for music had been sparked by an older sibling. "I was five or six when my older brother bought *Meet the Beatles* and listened to it incessantly," he told reporter Erin Rossiter in 2007. "Well, I met the Beatles all right, and it was a magical revelation." Both listened to a wide variety of musical genres and paid little attention to what their peers considered to be cool. They liked what sounded good to them. For Mills this included Seals and Crofts, Harry Nilsson, and even a bit of Yes. For Berry it included Gene Krupa and all things Motown. Mills and Berry were, in fact, kindred musical spirits. They were both highly unorthodox players: Berry a self-styled "basher" more interested in the overall structure and cohesion of a song than in innovating on his particular instrument, Mills favoring a high-on-the-neck lead bass style (think Paul McCartney's noodly bass line on the Beatles' "Rain"). In light of these philosophical bonds, then, it becomes easier to understand why two supposedly opposite personalities became the fastest of friends and decades-long bandmates.

Berry and Mills, like Kathleen O'Brien, Paul Butchart, and others in their future peer group, were affected by the wave of desegregation policies that had begun in the 1960s and escalated sharply with the Supreme Court's 1969 order that all US public school districts desegregate "at once." The court had offered no practical instructions for achieving this aim, which threw open the door to all manner of well-meaning (but not always successful) social experiments. One of these was busing, which involved transporting kids to schools outside their own (typically segregated) neighborhoods in order to create a more even racial mix. In the South this meant that some black students found themselves bussed great distances in order to attend school with white students, while some white students found themselves getting bussed in the opposite direction. Both Mike and Bill ended up attending a high school that was 80 percent black. For the most part they navigated these circumstances about as well as teenagers could be expected to, though Bill did run afoul of some of the black male students over his perceived interest in a black girl. "(She and I) would sit around the lunch room discussing things," he said. "But it wasn't long before she suddenly stopped paying attention to me. The day after she wouldn't even talk to me, six black guys jumped me and beat me up."

This episode underscores the complexity and ever-shifting nature of race relations in the South in the 1970s. Forcibly putting kids of different backgrounds together for their daily schooling didn't automatically erase the deep-seated tendencies toward tribalism and self-segregation that many white and black students had inherited from their parents. And it would not prevent some of them from continuing to self-segregate into the future. And yet, around the same time that Bill Berry and Kathleen O'Brien's brother (in Decatur) found themselves the unwitting victims of racially motivated violence, and countless black students continued to receive the same, or worse, treatment from their white peers, younger students like T. Kyle King began making their way through grade school blissfully unaware of the remarkableness of their newly desegregated classrooms. Bill Berry himself harbored no discernible racial prejudice (as is probably clear from the behavior that got him into his predicament) and the beating seems to have done nothing to instill any such feelings in him. If anything, the incident may have reinforced his distaste for segregation.

Bill and Mike continued to hone their groove as members of Shadowfax—the band that had emerged from their fateful jam session.* After a few lineup changes, the group would eventually mutate into the Back Door Band. Their musical style was solidly mainstream rock 'n' roll, or what is now referred to as "classic rock": they played covers of songs by Bachman Turner Overdrive, Foreigner, the Doobie Brothers, and the ubiquitous Allman Brothers. The Back Door Band introduced more straight blues into that mix, along with some original compositions in the vein of the artists listed above. In subsequent years—in the wake of the punk and postpunk revolutions— Berry and Mills would feel compelled to distance themselves from their musical endeavors in Macon, but in truth both men continued to harbor a fondness for this style of straightforward, foot-stomping rock 'n' roll.

Regionally, the Back Door Band was quite successful. They played Atlanta's Great Southeast Music Hall, no mean feat for a group of high school students. Yet any dreams of further glory the other members might have harbored were squashed when Mike and Bill quit the band on graduating high school in 1976. In *It Crawled from the South: An R.E.M. Companion*, Marcus Gray characterizes Mills and Berry's decision as the result of the pair being "heartily sick of the Capricorn roster's domination of the local scene with the likes of Marshall Tucker and the Allman Brothers, and bored with a public that discouraged anything straying too far beyond the Doobies and Lynyrd Skynyrd." Whether this is supposition on Gray's part or actually derives from interviews with Berry and Mills, it's hard to see it as anything other than a retroactive attempt to impose rarefied tastes on two teenagers who probably didn't possess them at the time. The two friends would not be exposed to the more challenging music of punk and various underground ancillaries until the following year, so it seems a stretch to imagine these "good old boys" attempting to push their high school band in directions they were not yet aware of.

The real reason the duo briefly abandoned their musical calling seems to have been more prosaic: the band was doing well, but not well enough. High school was over and so were the eighteen years of free room and board that came with living under your parents' roof. It was time to go out and get real jobs. The two moved into an apartment together and proceeded to do just that.

From our current vantage point, with the vaunted Athens music scene still going strong alongside a thriving hip-hop community in Atlanta that has

---

* Discerning readers of a certain bent will recognize the *Lord of the Rings* origins of the band's name. Shadowfax was the preferred steed—the "lord of all horses"—of the wizard Gandalf. Perhaps this tells us something about the nature of the music we're dealing with here.

produced artists such as Outkast, Ludacris, Arrested Development, and Cee Lo Green, it's easy to forget that Macon was unquestionably *the* music hub in Georgia in the 1970s. The establishment of Capricorn Records by Macon natives Phil and Alan Walden in 1969 was crucial in this, but so was the fact that the Allman Brothers Band, the label's enormously successful group, were a local act. The Capricorn roster also included such disparate artists as Wet Willie, the Marshall Tucker Band, Dobie Gray, and Kitty Wells. It surely did not go unnoticed by Berry and Mills that the Walden brothers had chosen to establish their thriving music empire right in their sleepy Southern hometown, rather than decamping for Nashville, New York, or Los Angeles. Had Bill and Mike truly wished to become professional musicians in 1976, they were already geographically well positioned to do so.

Yet Berry continued to believe that the life of a musician did not constitute a legitimate career. He did, however, harbor an interest in the business side of music. (It's unclear what Mills's career ambitions were at this point; we only know that the type A, overachieving impulse that had so distinguished him in high school seemed to have evaporated upon graduation. He took a job at Sears.) Bill was the recipient of an unbelievable stroke of luck: he landed a job with Paragon, the booking arm of Capricorn Records. "Get this," he later told Rodger Lyle Brown, "[the Back Door Band's] guitarist's girlfriend's brother had this . . . great job at Paragon, but he couldn't keep it since he was going to become a cop, so he said to me, 'You want the job?' And I said, 'Fuck!'"

The work was a combination of menial paperwork-oriented tasks during the day and the opportunity to chauffeur big-time rock stars at night. "I would have paid to do it," he told Brown. "Here's this 18-year-old kid who got double-time to go spend the night out with rock stars."

Although he didn't realize it at the time, Berry's career received a further boost with the arrival of the London-based agent Ian Copeland in 1977. Copeland had been brought in at the behest of Paragon head Alex Hodges to introduce a new, more modern musical sensibility into the organization. The timing could not have been better for the once and future musical duo of Berry and Mills. Ian Copeland and his brothers Stewart and Miles were on the verge of becoming serious players in the music industry: Stewart would soon be enjoying international success as the drummer for the Police, and Miles was putting together an independent record label he would name I.R.S.

We can say with some degree of certainty that when Bill Berry arrived at the Atlanta airport in his chauffeur cap to escort the new agent back to Macon, he had never met anyone quite like Ian Copeland. For one thing, while Berry had halfheartedly aspired to the role of juvenile delinquent in high school, Copeland had been a full-on renegade in his day. The fact that his father, Miles Copeland II, had been an active CIA field officer involved in engineering coups d'état in Egypt and Iran (among other places) seems to have inspired some spectacular acts of defiance on Ian's part. In his teens, Ian had: 1) fallen in with a biker gang in Lebanon (where Copeland Sr. was stationed for a time); 2) become a serial car thief (a perilous vocation in an Arab country); 3) run away from home, crossing several countries in the process; 4) dropped out of school and volunteered to fight in the war in Vietnam. According to his memoir *Wild Thing*, Copeland had "mostly fond memories" of his time at war, which coincided with the Tet Offensive. He was, in other words, a bona fide badass. He also happened to be more passionate about new and interesting music than just about anyone Berry had ever met. This last detail must have seemed surprising given that Ian was a decade older than Berry and, with his long hair and shaggy beard, appeared an otherwise perfect addition to the hirsute, Southern boogie–loving Paragon staff.

Ian took an immediate liking to his new chauffeur. He later characterized the young Berry as a "compulsive talker" who "probably knew more about Paragon than anyone else on the payroll."

> [He] explained that he was not only Paragon's chauffeur, but also the gofer, mail clerk, tea boy, messenger, and odd-jobs man. He gave me a full run-down on all of the people who worked there . . . Before long I knew the whole company's chain of command and all of the players.

Additionally, Bill—himself a transplant from another region—was perhaps the ideal person to ease Copeland through the culture shock he was about to experience. Despite looking the part, and even though his father hailed from this part of the country, Copeland had little familiarity with the people and history of the American South and knew next to nothing about Southern rock. Berry helped fill in the blanks.

It's a toss-up as to which of the following factors was more transformative in the lives of Mike Mills and Bill Berry: their newfound friendship with the well-connected Ian Copeland or the record collection he had brought with him. It's probably not true that Ian single-handedly introduced the city of Macon to punk rock, but he does seem to have been the first person to turn Bill and Mike on to the new sound, exposing them to such bands as the Damned, the Ramones, the Dead Boys, Chelsea, and the Sex Pistols. Mills credits this adrenaline shot of raw rock 'n' roll with inspiring in him a renewed interest in playing. "We would play along to the Ramones' first record," he recalled later. "And the first Police single, which was 'Fall Out' and 'Nothing Achieving': That was huge. That was the sort of stuff that got us playing again."

Bill and Mike were essentially hearing this stuff in a vacuum. Outside of Ian's apartment, there was no punk subculture in Macon. There were no clubs where the music could be heard live. And any fashion aesthetic had to be gleaned solely from the album covers. Thus they missed out on much of UK punk's Cultural Revolution–style emphasis on demolishing the past and rebuilding from scratch. They either missed or disregarded the Clash's declaration of "No Elvis, Beatles, or the Rolling Stones in 1977!" For these two, the lean, hard-charging sound of this first wave of punk was simply an exciting new chapter in the ongoing narrative of popular music. Mike still loved Harry Nilsson and Bill still loved Motown. Punk for them functioned as a renewal rather than any kind of ground zero.

Ian's attitude was much the same, even though he had been to the punk clubs in London and had spent time with the progenitors of the movement. A '60s kid at heart, he retained his earlier love of classic and progressive rock and very quickly grew to appreciate the Southern rock bands he was initially tasked with booking. Still, this new music invigorated him with its leanness and ferocity, and he longed to bring it to the United States.

The rest of the Paragon office did not initially share his enthusiasm. Alex Hodges had told Ian, "I want you to sign bands I can't stand," and that's exactly what happened. In January 1978, Copeland talked his co-workers into attending the Sex Pistols' debut US concert at the Great Southeast Music Hall in Atlanta. He figured that if any group could turn his colleagues on to the new sound, it would be the flagship band of British punk. This turned out to be an overly optimistic goal: "Not to put too fine a point on it," he later wrote, but [the Sex Pistols] sucked."* For a time afterward, he found himself socially ostracized by virtually everyone at Paragon except for Bill Berry. But things turned around when he once again managed to drag everyone out to the Macon performance of a band he himself had booked, a new wave band from London called Squeeze, who were signed to A&M Records. Their tight musicianship onstage and friendliness offstage softened the hearts of the

---

* It's interesting, given Copeland's recollection, that virtually every musician and scenester I interviewed for this book pointed to this particular concert as a watershed moment in the formation of the Athens music scene. This probably had less to do with the Sex Pistols' performance and more with the fact that the event opened everyone's eyes to the existence of a hitherto hidden, robust subculture of seekers and misfits dissatisfied with the musical status quo.

Paragon staff. From that point forward the company got on board with the new wave program.*

The Squeeze tour turned out to be a major game-changer, not just for Copeland and Paragon but for the music industry as a whole. Circumventing A&M's lack of financial support for their own band, Ian lined up a series of dates at small clubs mostly off the beaten path and booked the musicians into the cheapest motels possible—the whole band often had to cram into a single room.

Bill Berry and Mike Mills were heavily involved in Ian's guerrilla promotional tactics for Squeeze's Macon show. As Ian wrote:

> Bill and Mike hung me upside down over a bridge where I spray-painted UK Squeeze† (with the e's the wrong way round) on the overpass to the interstate. Then we climbed up on an enormous billboard out by the airport as you come into town, and sprayed it in big letters on top of where they had just freshly painted it white. It stayed there for several months . . .

The combination of such "outside the box" marketing techniques with Ian's many cost-cutting measures enabled Squeeze to turn a decent profit at the conclusion of the tour. Perhaps even more significantly for posterity, Copeland had single-handedly cobbled together a club circuit that could be utilized and adapted by subsequent under-the-radar bands. Ian himself reused this template when booking the first American tour for his brother Stewart's band, the Police, in October–November 1978. This was an even more audacious endeavor, given that the band had decided to tour prior to the release of their debut album. But the Police's incendiary live performances created a word-of-mouth buzz that preceded them wherever they went. Bill Berry was on hand throughout the planning and execution of this tour and, perhaps unbeknown to Ian, absorbed all its details and lessons.

Bill put in only two years at Paragon, though he might have remained in Macon had it not been for an eventful phone call between Mike Mills and his father in the fall of 1978, during which the elder Mills berated his son for squandering his excellent SAT score by hanging around Macon and working at Sears. This prompted Mike to talk with Bill about pulling up stakes

---

* Ian Copeland claimed to have coined the phrase "new wave" as a less-fraught descriptor for the new bands he was bringing in.

† The band was required to add the "UK" prefix because another band was already using the name "Squeeze" in the US.

and enrolling at the University of Georgia together. Bill didn't need much of a push; he continued to nurse dreams of working on the management side of the entertainment industry, or as an agent or manager for professional athletes. In either case, he would need some type of higher degree, an MBA perhaps. His departure from Paragon turned out to be well timed; the company, along with Capricorn Records, collapsed into bankruptcy shortly thereafter.

The two friends arrived in Athens in January 1979. The town was not altogether different from Macon in appearance, but its massive preponderance of young people gave it a different temperament. Athens is often described as a sleepy little college town, which does it a disservice. Yes, it has always been a college town: it was actually willed into being by the Georgia State Legislature for the express purpose of hosting a "college or seminary of learning"—what became UGA. And yes, relative to Atlanta, New Orleans, Birmingham, and the large cities of the South, it is small, even little. But sleepy? As far back as anyone can remember, the place has had a reputation for hedonism and alcoholic excess.

Perhaps the "sleepy" label is due to the impression the town gives of being enclosed; long branches of Darlington oaks and other towering trees arch over many of the streets. Back in the 1970s, the only way to get to Athens from Atlanta was via a two-lane road, the "Atlanta Highway" later immortalized in the B-52's' hit "Love Shack." For long stretches a driver could feel like Moses parting a sea of Georgia pine. After miles and miles of this, Athens would appear seemingly out of nowhere—an oasis of buildings and street lamps at the end of a long, lonely road. Yet the impression of a great canopy of vegetation—a second sky of branches and leaves—persisted throughout the town. This was by no means unique to Athens; many Georgia towns, including Macon, had nearly identical blueprints: the central courthouse, the post office, and streets lined with sturdy old trees. But downtown Athens was certainly different from downtown Atlanta, which was dominated by large, modern, impersonal buildings and obsessively manicured tracts of "green space" that seemed soulless and antiseptic.

Some residents of Athens, particularly the art school students who harbored (usually New York–centric) dreams of recognition and success in the big city, felt hemmed in and stifled by the town. But many other artistic people felt cradled and supported both emotionally (as we will see, there was a growing community of like-minded souls ready to support all kinds of creative ventures, provided alcohol was somehow in the offing) and physically (a person could just about rest in the palm of this town, or wrap it around themselves like a blanket).

In one respect, Athens may have seemed like a step backward to Bill and Mike. Although the University of Georgia was integrated at the classroom level, the students still tended to self-segregate in other settings. Black students had their own fraternities and sororities and gravitated toward certain residence halls, and so did their white peers. Outside the university, the color line was even more pronounced. The town was divided into white neighborhoods and black neighborhoods, with very little overlap. This dynamic would remain in place throughout the following decade with only marginal changes.

Having submitted their names to the school's lottery-style dorm assignment system, Berry and Mills ended up in different buildings. Bill, as we have seen, landed in Reed, and Mike took up residence in Myers Hall, at the time a virtual clone of Reed, further south of the stadium, a modest walk or short bus ride away. Bill believed he had left music-making behind him. Mike, however, brought along his bass.

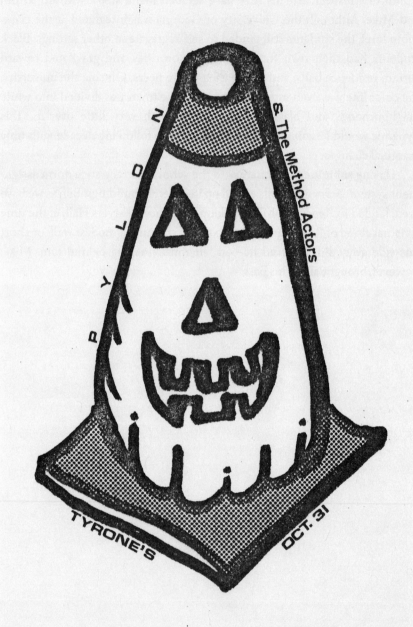

Poster for Pylon's Halloween show with the Method Actors at Tyrone's O.C., 1979

Chapter Two

The Clermont Lounge occupies the bottom floor of a condemned hotel in downtown Atlanta. Somehow the lounge, billed as "Atlanta's oldest strip club," remains open in spite of the mold, bedbugs, and (in the words of the *Atlanta Journal-Constitution*) "black water spilling from faucets" that plague the building that houses it. I arrive on a Saturday night, better known to the locals as Disco Funk Night, ten-dollar cover charge in my hand. The DJs this Saturday—every Saturday, for that matter—are an oddly mismatched pair who bill themselves as "the Illuminaughty." First up, at 10 p.m., is an affable young party animal known as Quasi Mandisco. He plays hits of today and the recent past such as "Dick in a Box" by Justin Timberlake and the Lonely Island, and "Sexy MF" by Prince. Then, at 11:30, the proceedings get turned over to Quasi's mentor: a shadowy, semi-legendary local figure known as Romeo Cologne. Cologne makes no concessions to the present day; his clock is turned back to 1977. He's the man I'm here to see.

The Clermont Lounge is the type of strip club you'd expect to see in a David Lynch movie: cramped, dimly lit, and filled with a menagerie of characters who don't seem quite real. A short, slightly overweight black stripper with burning candles protruding from her nipples sways awkwardly on a very thin walkway. She looks to be in her late sixties. A tall, big-haired white stripper who looks vaguely like the woman in the old Whitesnake videos (you know, the lady writhing on the car) dances across the bar. Male and female patrons gaze up adoringly.

Romeo Cologne, meanwhile, works his magic in a small booth beside the dance floor. He sports a black fedora, an ascot, and a carefully sculpted mustache that gives just the right accent to his narrow, kind face. His sloping, spidery fingers gingerly pick through a booklet of CDs, searching for the perfect track to play next. Among his selections for the evening: "Take Your Time" by the S.O.S. Band, "Early in the Morning" by the Gap Band, "Let It Whip" by the Dazz Band, and "Get Off" by Foxie. He's immersed in the music, mouthing the words and jabbing his index finger at some vague destination beyond the confines of the room, somehow managing to get the room dancing while at the same time remaining entirely inside himself. In this last respect he reminds me very much of his old friend Michael Stipe.

As you may have guessed, "Romeo Cologne" is not the mysterious DJ's birth name, though in this day and age he answers to no other. When he first arrived in Athens, Georgia, he was David Hannon Pierce, a recently discharged Air Force vet eager to pour himself into a more carefree civilian life. It was 1976, the year of the bicentennial. Pierce had served stateside during the Vietnam War, working as a medic in an Air Force unit set up specifically to treat former POWs returning from the conflict. He may not have seen combat himself, but this was nevertheless emotionally wrenching work. The most he'll say about it now is that "a lot of the POWs were in pretty bad shape."

That first visit to Athens, then, was a welcome change. Pierce's brother was working his way toward a drama degree at UGA, and as soon as Pierce took stock of the surroundings, he decided this was where he needed to be. "I loved it," he says. "There were three girls to every guy. And I was like, 'Yes, I'm staying here!'" Although he initially failed the preliminary entrance exam, as a veteran Pierce qualified for night school. He spent the next couple of years completing his core curriculum requirements and began attending day classes at the art school in 1979.

Athens underwent some pretty significant changes during those years. When he first arrived, in 1976, the mainstream culture at the University of Georgia still centered almost entirely around football. That year fell smack in the middle of Vince Dooley's long and storied career as head coach, and in that year the Georgia Bulldogs—"the Dawgs," as they are affectionately known—were in contention for the national title, which ensured a season of particularly heavy partying all across town.

Not that Athenians waited until football season to throw a party. Through-out the academic year and beyond, the social calendar was dictated from the ostentatiously columned fraternity and sorority houses that lined Milledge Avenue. There was not yet much of a bar scene, apart from a popular hangout called the Station, so students vied eagerly for invitations to the fraternity blowouts. And these parties did not disappoint: kegs arrived by the truckload, the music got cranked pretty loud, and sometimes a live band would play. Everyone lost their minds pretty quickly, and a lot of fucking ensued.

There was a dark side to this, as there is any time alcohol and hormones mix freely. Given the long list of incidents that were documented in later years, it seems probable that the sex at these parties was not always consensual. And sometimes ancillary violence was inflicted on those who were seen as not fitting in. Fraternities were regularly suspended or expelled for various infractions, but others always popped up to take their place.

Over time an alternative to these frat parties emerged—one that seems almost pathetic by comparison. Rodger Lyle Brown describes the hippie parties of the time as "a dozen guys in flannel shirts . . . listening to the Grateful Dead or old Rolling Stones; smoking joints and waiting in teeth-gritting rough-house futility for stray good-smelling girls to show up."

This would all change in 1977, when this long-suffering hippie scene bumped into Athens's heretofore below-the-radar gay scene and begat a band called the B-52's. The group consisted of former flower-girl hippie Kate Pierson on vocals, Keith Strickland on drums, Ricky Wilson on guitar, Cindy Wilson on vocals, and a flamboyant gay man with a bullhorn voice named Fred Schneider. The band seemed to have been willed into existence in order to facilitate some honest-to-god *parties* for all the weird kids who didn't fit in with the "Dawg" culture.

As it happened, many of those weird kids were art majors at UGA, and so the arrival of the B-52's initiated a symbiotic relationship between the University of Georgia Art Department and the fledgling Athens music scene. For those first few years, the former would feed the latter with both talent and an audience. The connection solidified with the second major band to emerge from the scene: Pylon, all four of whose members—Randall Bewley, Michael Lachowski, Curtis Crowe, and Vanessa Briscoe—were art students.

There are a number of people out there who believe to this day that Pylon was the greatest band ever to come out of Athens. Millions of R.E.M. fans would dismiss that statement outright, yet it deserves serious examination. Certainly, Pylon was unique among the first wave of Athens bands. Virtually every aspect of their sound—from the minimalist, trancelike groove laid down by Lachowski and Crowe, to Bewley's jagged, atonal guitar textures, to Briscoe's yelps and guttural grunts—was unlike anything the Athens party crowd had heard before. And only in the Athens art community could such a pointedly anti-mainstream ensemble have become that community's "resident dance party band" (Brown's description). But there it was. Something in that locked-down rhythm section and those stuttering guitars got people moving, jerking their bodies across living-room floors.

Much of Pylon's genius can be attributed to the fact that the band was built from scratch by people with no preconceived notions about what they were doing. Lachowski and Bewley had begun writing songs together almost immediately after purchasing their instruments (at a yard sale and a pawn shop, respectively). Crowe had been playing drums for less than a year.

Briscoe had apparently sung in her high school chorus, but you wouldn't know it; seemingly unschooled in the rudiments of rhythm and intonation, she created her own alternative parameters. Pylon were cluelessly overconfident art students coming at rock 'n' roll from the outside. They rebuilt it in their own image and lo, it was great.

The success of Pylon inspired many other art school kids, few of whom had any previous musical training, to form bands of their own. They threw themselves into the endeavor with naïveté and passion. When I get him to step out of his Romeo Cologne persona and think back to those days, David Pierce recalls:

> The whole Athens scene was against all the virtuosity that was prevalent in rock music. You know, the prog-rock thing. In a way, the art school confronted music with no feelings of pressure or sense of duty to tradition. That was the basis of much of the Athens music. People were experimenting and creating—not just their own music but in some cases their own instruments too. There might be situations where you'd say, "I've got you and me in the room, so let's just play this. We don't need a guitarist. We don't need a keyboard." People would try to work their way around all of that.

The art department occupied a unique place—both physically and spiritually—at UGA in the 1970s. During the period when David Pierce and Michael Stipe were attending classes, the department was housed in a white, angular, futuristic-looking structure nestled incongruously among the classical 19th-century buildings that made up most of the university's North Campus. This building, constructed in the 1960s, was often derisively referred to as "the ice plant," and it certainly stuck out in an area of the campus that prided itself on its antebellum Southern aesthetic. (The South Campus, which housed most of the science, math, and agricultural departments, was a different story altogether; its buildings were distinguished by their fealty to the worst architectural fads of the 1960s and '70s).

Taken on its own terms, the Visual Arts building was quite striking. The emphasis was less on discrete classrooms than on open studio space and abundant utilization of natural light. Its flat, blocky exterior clearly owed much to Frank Lloyd Wright's visionary late period (exemplified by Fallingwater and the Robie House). The building's modern aesthetic was an appropriate outward manifestation of the art department's deeply subversive character. This was a dense cluster of fre-thinking individuals planted smack in the middle of a student body obsessed with football and alcohol and not much else. And yet perhaps these two populations were not as dissimilar as they first appeared. If one strolled across North Campus on a football Saturday, one would encounter grown men decked out in red and black (the Georgia colors) dancing around coolers and transistor radios, willing their team on to victory with shaman-like intensity. And despite these football fans' conservative hairstyles and general antipathy to both the hippies and the art school crowd (the only viable subcultures at the time), in their fervor they would often attain a "derangement of the senses" that would have given Rimbaud pause.

By 1979, the year that Bill Berry and Mike Mills arrived on campus and David Pierce began taking classes at the art school, the Athens music scene was beginning to assert itself at the national level. Through a combination of grit and Southern charm, the B-52's had secured a gig at the Manhattan nightclub Max's Kansas City and had used the performance as a sort of beachhead to insinuate themselves into the New York nightlife scene. Their outrageous costumes and wigs, along with their catchy, ultra-positive music, caught on like wildfire with jaded New York audiences. Their infectious debut single, "Rock Lobster"—produced and released independently by an aspiring music impresario named Danny Beard—further solidified their success and led to a major-label record deal.

Pylon quickly followed in the wake of the B-52's, playing the same New York clubs and working the same connections. They secured a slot opening for British postpunk band Gang of Four in both New York and Philadelphia and duly impressed audiences and critics alike. In the magazine *New York Rocker* and elsewhere, a buzz began building about the mysterious Georgia town that kept producing great bands.

Meanwhile, the town in question remained largely oblivious to the new music it had incubated. One of the reasons the B-52's and Pylon had hightailed it to New York was the lack of available local venues willing to host new music. Very few of the eateries and clubs that now make up so much of the heart of Athens were in existence back in the 1970s. The exceptions were the Mayflower Restaurant—a traditional meat-and-two-veg establishment that gives the impression of predating the Confederacy; the Last Resort—now a restaurant but back then a nightclub; and the Georgia Theatre—primarily a movie theater in the '70s, but now one of the city's premier concert venues. Sidewalk dining was not allowed at the time due to the city government's concerns about garbage; the downtown consisted mostly of department stores such as Belk, Davison's, and Woolworth's, and a Five and Ten that had a diner inside. Apart from the Last Resort, there were just a few bars scattered on the edge of downtown, among them T.K. Harty's Saloon and Tyrone's O.C. Perhaps the biggest difference between those days and now was the fact that the art scene—and by that I mean the parties, the associated bands, and the various other "happenings" and projects that had their origins in the art school—was confined almost exclusively to individual houses and neighborhoods; very little of it penetrated the downtown area.

That was all about to change. Against a backdrop of creative possibilities and social and artistic experimentation within the growing scene, David Pierce—who *did* have a musical background—met and befriended Michael Stipe in a survey-level art class. "We started gravitating toward each other because everybody else was so preppy at the time," Pierce says. "We just kind of hung out. He was just a guy from St. Louis."

Stipe most certainly was not preppy. For one thing, he wore his hair in a style some of his friends have affectionately called a "reverse mullet": it was cut short in the back but in front it hung down over his face. Not only did this serve notice of Stipe's individuality, it also had a practical function: the young Stipe suffered from severe acne and his long bangs obscured this affliction.

John Michael Stipe first enters the historical record via grainy 1970s video footage from a St. Louis TV station. In the segment, two newscasters of the Ron Burgundy school awkwardly pontificate over the then-new phenomenon of young people dressing up as characters from *The Rocky Horror Picture Show* when attending screenings of the movie. Cut to some footage of the costumed audience waiting outside the movie theater, with the newscaster's voice solemnly intoning, "No, these people are not crazy. Yes, all of their decks are completely stacked. They're here to see a movie. The characters in the movie are dressed like these people . . . which explains why these people are dressed as they are." At the 1:25 mark we see the young, leather-clad Michael Stipe, heavily made up in an approximation of the character Frank N Furter, his five feet nine inches considerably enhanced by platform shoes. A Blue Öyster Cult medallion dangles from the lapel of his leather jacket. While another fan is being interviewed, Stipe cuts in to declare, in a slight Midwestern accent, "This is an excellent movie. It really is. And we're all quite normal, really."

This version of Stipe—flamboyant, confident, attention-hungry—seems on the face of it to stand in marked contrast to the carefully cultivated image he would present to the world just a few years later: that of the introverted, fame-shy art student who just happened to blunder his way into fronting a major rock band. In truth, all these aspects seemed to coexist in his personality. His attempts at extroversion would always carry the awkwardness of an imperfectly tailored jacket hanging off a diminutive frame. At the same time, the pose of extreme shyness came with an almost imperceptible wink and a slight whiff of bullshit. From an early age, Stipe wanted to be noticed—but he wanted to be noticed on his terms.

Stipe was born in 1960 in Decatur, Georgia. Athens is little more than sixty miles away, but his route to the city in which he would establish himself proved to be a circuitous one. His father was a career military man, and Stipe had the typical childhood of an Army brat: being frequently uprooted and having to reassert himself in a new, not always friendly social environment. Like many children thrust into such a situation, Stipe developed especially close ties to his siblings—Lynda and Cyndy—and his parents. The family was a solid foundation in an ever-shifting outside world. This solidity held even during the long periods when his dad left to pilot helicopters in the Vietnam conflict. Stipe has since characterized this upbringing, which dropped him in Germany, Alabama, Texas, and Illinois, and finally took him back to Georgia, as "enormously happy."

Of the four members of R.E.M., only Michael Stipe can lay claim to being Southern by birth. Even though he spent almost all his youth about as far from the South as you can get, he came from solidly Southern stock. "My people," as he has referred to them, were from Georgia. The Stipes were a churchgoing Methodist family complete with a preacher grandfather. And since Michael spent much of his youth in such a tight-knit family, he picked

up the Georgia influences, even if they are sometimes only discernible in trace elements: the accent, the religion, the values, the music. But this was a theoretical Southernness, acquired far from actual Southern neighbors, from the Southern landscape—and from the complicated racial negotiations that were and are such a prominent aspect of daily life in the South. It was at once more closely held and less tied to reality than the day-to-day culture of resident Southerners.

This is not to say that the Stipe children sat around mourning the Lost Cause. Rather, Michael Stipe's "South" consisted of his grandparents' stories, an accent that set his family apart, a collection of country records, and some books—including, apparently, the fiction of Joel Chandler Harris, whose Brer Rabbit character would later be referenced in a number of Stipe's songs.

If there is one man whose life illustrates the complexities and contradictions of the post–Civil War South and its refusal to fit neatly into the "black" and "white" categories the rest of the world continually foists upon it, it is Harris. A pale, kindly-looking man with a shock of bright red hair, he became the unlikely ambassador of African American folklore to the world at large. The Brer Rabbit stories, first published in a series of columns in the *Atlanta Journal-Constitution*, were allegedly transcriptions of fables Harris had heard from the slaves at Turnwold Plantation, where he had lived as a teenager in the early 1860s while working as a printer's apprentice for plantation owner Joseph Turner, who also owned the newspaper the *Countryman*. Harris made painstaking efforts to render the slaves' dialect as phonetically accurately as he could, and for several decades the stories, collected in several books, were embraced by white and black readers alike. Harris's views on race relations were, in the context of his times, progressive verging on radical; in his editorials he enthusiastically cited W. E. B. Du Bois and Booker T. Washington, who was a personal friend. Viewed through a modern lens, however, Harris is a problematic figure, not just due to the paternalism that permeates the Remus stories, but also because of his nostalgia for the institution of slavery, the realities of which, he felt, "possess a romantic beauty and tenderness all their own." He maintained this view even while championing racial reconciliation in the aftermath of Reconstruction.

What did the young Michael Stipe get out of these stories? Most likely he was oblivious to their racial complexity, and at any rate, he probably didn't encounter a whole lot of racial diversity during his early years. But if his later lyrics are any guide, he was apparently much taken with the crafty, anthropomorphized animals who populated the fables—particularly the trickster Brer Rabbit—and also with the enduring image of the Tar-Baby, derived from one of the most popular Uncle Remus tales, in which Brer Rabbit finds himself physically stuck to a tar-and-turpentine doll that has been cunningly laid in his path by his nemesis, Brer Fox. The harder Brer Rabbit fights to extricate himself, the more deeply stuck he becomes.

Almost all of the information we have about Michael Stipe's childhood comes from Stipe himself, and it is not a great deal. As for his young adult years, until very recently those remained largely obscure. For much of the duration of R.E.M.'s existence, no one who knew him prior to his move to Athens surfaced to corroborate or contradict the singer's recollections, fueling a rumor—perpetuated in print by both Rodger Lyle Brown and Marcus Gray—that Stipe had sworn all of his pre-Athens friends to secrecy. But in the age of the Internet the blanks are slowly being filled in.

If I may break the fourth wall for a moment, let me say that you are going to meet some unusual people in this book. You've already met Mr. Cologne, so perhaps you've picked up on this. Sometimes the outlandishness of the supporting cast has given me the impression—wrongly, it turns out—that the members of R.E.M. might actually be the least interesting characters in their own story. Certainly they've happened to bump up against some pretty colorful individuals. But the freaks and head cases waiting for you in later chapters will have a hard time competing with Mike Doskocil of St. Louis. If this were a novel I would save him until later in the story and give him a more prominent role, but I have to play the nonfiction hand as it is dealt. In truth, Doskocil was never more than a passing acquaintance—barely even that—of the teenaged Michael Stipe, but he happened to be in the right place at the right time, and he has some interesting things to say.

First, some background: Doskocil is remembered in St. Louis for his role in two 1980s bands. White Pride was intended as a parody of white supremacist hardcore groups—the fact that one of the members was part Chinese should perhaps have made this obvious, but the earnest neo-Nazis of the day missed the sarcasm and embraced the group, ensuring that White Pride's reign was short-lived. Doskocil's next effort, Drunks with Guns, for which he served as vocalist and primary songwriter, attempted to do the same thing for beer-swilling troglodytes. Songs such as "Dick in One Hand" (featuring the refrain "I got my dick in one hand and a rope in the other"), "Punched in the Head," "Hell House," and "Wonderful Subdivision" have an appealing primal energy and purity of intent.

The many rumors surrounding Doskocil suggest the same bad-taste prankster energy that is readily apparent in his music. Many of them imply criminal activity, and I can't in good conscience print them. But there is one widely circulated story to the effect that he once told all of his acquaintances that he had AIDS—just so he could see how they would react. I have no idea if the story is true, but it would certainly be consistent with his musical MO.

Given the punishing abrasiveness of Doskocil's singing, the many stories of antisocial behavior, the White Pride thing, and the hints of a criminal past, I was a little nervous going into our interview. But Doskocil is actually an extremely friendly, funny, thoughtful guy, albeit one who sometimes begins sentences with the words, "So, when I got shot during the carjacking" or variations thereof. When I tell him I've been listening to Drunks with Guns, he says, "Oh, I'm sorry to hear that."

Mike Doskocil first met Michael Stipe in the late 1970s. Stipe was a few years older and had just begun attending classes at Southern Illinois University, while Doskocil was still in high school. Both men's music careers lay well ahead of them. They had both drifted into the *Rocky Horror Picture Show* subculture. "Everybody would go down to the Loop in U City and hang out till midnight to see the film," Doskocil recalls.

> I remember we used to go down there and hang out, because for somebody who'd just discovered the Sex Pistols, that was pretty much the only alternative thing to do, go and sit on the wall. The hipsters with spray-painted hair would do their catwalk down Delmar Boulevard in their homemade stacked-heel tennis shoes.
>
> There was the Underground FM radio* and then there were the weirdos, and the weirdos predated the punk-rocky. In the mid to late '70s, St. Louis was a pretty redneck town, and—you've got to remember—you just needed to drive ten miles south of the city into Jefferson County and you were in Klan territory. White chicks got beaten up for dating black dudes; white guys got beaten up for being suspected of being homosexual. To a certain extent, it still is a really tough town. There's a reason I live in Ohio. There's a reason why I've lived in ten major cities—because I couldn't get out of St. Louis fast enough. And I think Michael was also one of those people. He couldn't get out fast enough either. That was obvious.
>
> One of the first nights I remember him being there, he was

---

* Washington University's student-run station, KWUR 90.3 FM, calls itself "St Louis Underground Radio."

sitting on the wall. He was a spindly little guy and he had a book of poetry and he was trying to grow his hair out, you could tell, and he was dressed up as one of the *Rocky Horror* people. But just the fact that he had brought his journal with him, that was really out of place. And I remember that made an impact on me. When three, four, five years later I see the guy on *David Letterman*, I was like, "That's the guy with the goddamn journal, oh my God."

I ask Mike if there had been any indication back then that Stipe had musical ambitions. "Absolutely none," he says.

Because back then, any guy with an earring I would approach to find out if he also had a guitar. If Stipe was talented as a lyricist, if he was a great singer, he wasn't then and he certainly gave nobody the impression that he ever wanted to be. Because if he would have, we'd be talking about all the deep conversations I had with the guy I almost started a band with instead of that weirdo who carried a spiral binder drawing the one-footed head people on it.

This would seem to contradict a story Stipe has told about his St. Louis years: that he sang in a new wave band called Nasty Habits (or Bad Habits) and they even played a few shows. If I only had Doskocil's impressions to go on, I'd be inclined to conclude that this group only ever performed in Stipe's imagination. But wait—here's a 2004 post on Murmurs.com (a fan-run message board dedicated to R.E.M.) from someone calling himself Polyman31* claiming to have played in a band with Stipe over two years prior to the formation of R.E.M. When asked by the other forum members to elaborate, he said, "Our band had different names since it was very loose, Nasty Habits, the Jotz (both Michael's ideas), and the Band, even though there was already a band called 'the Band'—like it really mattered. Most of the time [it] was just jam and try to play a few songs all the way thru." He mentioned that he and Stipe liked to talk about "punk rock, skinny people, beer, girls (respectfully)."

Further research revealed that Polyman31 is one Craig Franklin, a former longtime resident of Austin, Texas, and current Minnesotan who continues to write and record music to this day. Like Doskocil, he's happy to talk. Franklin's relationship with Stipe actually predates Doskocil's run-ins with the singer, and

---

*Just to be clear, the "poly" in this nickname refers to complex polymers (the person in question is a chemist), not to polyamory.

was far more substantial. They first met in Collinsville, Illinois, some twenty minutes east of St. Louis, in the summer of 1976, when Stipe was heading into his junior year at Collinsville High and Craig was about to become a freshman. The Stipes lived adjacent to the only major public swimming pool in the town, Town N Country, which has long since been filled in and built over. Michael's backyard was on the other side of a four-foot chain-link fence. Craig was introduced to Stipe through a mutual acquaintance. He was immediately struck by Stipe's hair, which he describes as "big, bushy, and curly"—the kind of hairstyle you'd see on a rock star like Roger Daltry. When they parted after their casual "hello," Franklin's friend muttered, "This guy is kind of weird." But Franklin was intrigued. Being a budding musician, he could sense that Stipe was something of a kindred spirit, and the two became friends—though Stipe's shyness initially presented a challenge. "He's probably the shyest person I've ever met," Franklin says. "The difference between him and all my other friends was that he was very slow to talk and to respond. You'd ask him a question and it's like he would think of everything he was going to say, and *then* say it. And it was just different. He was very quiet, but he also had a very good, bizarre sense of humor. He was a funny guy, once the ice was melted."

As will become clear, it's quite likely that R.E.M. fans owe a major debt of gratitude to Craig Franklin, because it was Franklin who cajoled a reluctant Stipe into singing in public for the first time. But first, we need to deal with the Patti Smith angle . . .

Perhaps Stipe's most oft-told story concerning his teenage years—one that, to be quite honest, I thought was a complete fabrication until I met Franklin—is that of his dramatic discovery of Patti Smith's music. Supposedly, at the end of 1975, Stipe had an epiphany. The story goes like this: he purchased a copy of Smith's debut album, *Horses*, and stayed up all night listening to it on headphones while absentmindedly munching from a bowl of cherries. Then, apparently stricken by some sort of cherry poisoning, he vomited. The deeper significance of this story is that he allegedly made a vow the following morning to become a rock star.

While there is no reason to doubt the key details here, the reality may not be nearly so clear-cut as Stipe remembers it. For one thing, there is the question of the date. Craig Franklin relates a story that seems to pin Stipe's discovery of Smith not to the release date of *Horses* in December 1975, but to the following school year.

> He calls me up and says, "Craig, you got to hear this record." I think
> it had already been out awhile, but I said, "Okay." I still didn't have

Collinsville High, 1978. L to R: Scott Jentsch, Michael Anthony Edson, Craig Heimback, Michael Stipe. Photo by Sandra Casson.

my driver's license, so I had my mother drive me over to his house, you know, the one by the swimming pool. And he was so excited. I remember him standing outside the house eating a big ball of cheese; you know, the cheese that you get during Christmastime where it's a ball and it's got all those nuts or whatever on it? He was eating one of those like an apple.

Anyway, I pull up and tell my mom, "Okay, I'll call you when I'm done." I went into his house. His parents had a big stereo, but in a cabinet—a console stereo. So he put this record on and it was just so different. I was like "What?" because at the time I think I was listening to Peter Frampton, Kansas, Boston, Styx—highly produced, very smooth, glossy types of music, a lot of keyboards, a lot of strings, and all kinds of stuff like that. This was very raw. And I looked at him and I said something like, "This is terrible." And he looked at me like I had just killed his two poodles in the kitchen or something. Later on I found out that this record was his epiphany. It was Patti Smith's *Horses*. At first listen I just didn't get it . . . Because you didn't hear it on the radio, for sure . . . And then later on I got it.

Mike Stipe

Craig Franklin

Top and bottom left: **Collinsville High yearbook photos of Michael Stipe and Craig Franklin;** top right: **Michael Stipe and Craig Franklin;** bottom right: **the former Stipe family home in Collinsville in 2015, photograph by Craig Franklin.** All images courtesy of Craig Franklin.

That was his thing, and then he showed me . . . he got this magazine from New York in the mail called the *Village Voice*. He really was into that.

Franklin is quick to point out that his account doesn't necessarily contradict Stipe's story. It's not unthinkable that the teenaged Stipe purchased the record earlier, had his epiphany, then got fired up later about sharing the discovery with his new friend.* Regardless of when he discovered Smith (and in either scenario he was an early adopter of Smith's brand of punk ethos), Stipe quickly began to model his fashion sense on the photos he had seen of Smith and her sometime boyfriend/muse/photographer Robert Mapplethorpe. Franklin remembers Stipe tying his shirt at the waist "almost like a girl would tie it at the beach," mimicking a well-known picture of Mapplethorpe.

> He started wearing a blue, and sometimes red, bandana out of his left back pocket and had some very large safety pins he would attach to the black vest he would wear to school. That drew a lot of comments from classmates. Then he started having a few friends that were kind of copying him and kind of had this punk rock thing going, whereas, in the Midwest in 1976, my typical outfit would have been blue jeans and a Rush T-shirt.

There were other fashion influences too, not all of them from the realm of music. One afternoon not too long after the Patti Smith revelation, Stipe asked Franklin if he'd like to go see a movie. When Stipe appeared at Franklin's house that evening, Franklin's mother said, "Craig, there's a girl here to see you." When Franklin acted surprised, his mother scrutinized the impish figure decked out in a vest, white collared shirt, baggy pants, and hat, and corrected herself: "Oh, it's a boy." Franklin felt sheepish; Stipe had gotten dressed up for the movie, and here he was in his Rush T-shirt. Michael also brought along his two sisters, who'd been waiting in the car. Later, as the movie began—Woody Allen's *Annie Hall*—Franklin realized with a start that Stipe seemed to have patterned his wardrobe after the style Diane Keaton

---

* One possible explanation for Stipe's delayed communication of his epiphany to Franklin is that he had just been fired up all over again after seeing Patti Smith's rendition of "Gloria" on *Saturday Night Live*, on April 17, 1976. The show had a huge youth audience, so it seems quite likely he would have seen it, and Smith's incendiary performance would certainly have reinforced the impact of her album on the young Stipe.

adopted for the title role. "If you look at early R.E.M. photos," Franklin says, "they were trying to be like Patti Smith as far as their dress and their attitude, especially Michael, but Peter Buck and the other guys too. But that look of the black vest with the white shirt and all that—that was really Annie Hall."

A number of journalists and R.E.M. biographers have concluded that it was Stipe's discovery of Patti Smith that inspired him to become a singer, but that does not seem to have been the case. It's true that he began singing around this time, but he had to be cajoled into doing so, it seems. The impetus was a high school talent show. Franklin had a loose band ready to play, but he needed a front man. He stopped Stipe in the hallway between classes one day and said, "Michael, we're going to do a talent show. Would you like to sing?"

Stipe's response: "I don't sing."

"But you look like a rock star," Franklin said. "I've got microphones and amplifiers. Come on over to the garage."

Stipe began going over to Franklin's house, where the two tentatively ran through some songs together. "The first time he came over," Franklin says, "I remember he had two books of sheet music—one of them was the Who, and the other was the Rolling Stones." After a couple of these informal sessions, Franklin introduced Stipe to his classmates Andy and Danny Gruber, the rhythm section of his hypothetical band, and rehearsals began in earnest. The most pressing task was to select two songs for the talent show. Franklin recalls:

> We did "Working Man" by Rush—which he [Michael] probably would never admit; I've never heard him talk about it—and "Gimme Shelter" by the Rolling Stones. Actually, that was his choice. "Working Man" was my choice because that was one song we all knew pretty well as far as the drums, bass, and my lead guitar. So those were the two songs. I knew he was not too excited about singing the Rush stuff, but, you know, you got to do what you got to do!

I ask Franklin if Stipe's singing voice circa 1977 was anything like the distinctive, gravelly voice listeners fell in love with during the subsequent decade. "I think you would definitely recognize it," he says. "And here's something I remember: the first time he came over and brought that sheet music book and all that stuff, he brought along some of that stuff you spray in your throat that's for sore throats. I don't know what that's called. It's a red spray. And every time we'd stop, he'd grab that spray and he's like, 'My throat is kind of rough.' And I told him, 'That's fine. It sounded good.' I was encouraging him because he was really self-conscious."

Franklin's recollection of the talent show itself is that it came off quite well. "My mother and an older brother were there," he says. "My brother told me, 'It sounded pretty good but that singer is kinda different.' That would prove to be an understatement. We received second place behind a pianist and a classmate singing Bette Midler's 'The Rose,' if I remember correctly." Right before the group went on, someone asked Franklin what the band was called. Various names had been discussed, including Nasty Habits, but nothing had been decided, so Franklin just said "the Band." When the *Collinsville Kahokian* 1978 yearbook arrived at the end of the school year, it contained a single photo from that night—a close-up shot of the drummer. The caption read, "The Band plays punk rock."

It's difficult to tell how seriously Stipe took his singing at the outset. Franklin recalls that Stipe did sing for a brief spell in another covers band (perhaps also called Nasty Habits, or Bad Habits) while still living in Collinsville, and it's true that upon his arrival in Athens Stipe joined the Southern rock–oriented Gangster. But he harbored a strong desire to become a visual artist, and his choice of major at UGA reflected that ambition. His subsequent career as a rock vocalist was therefore by no means assured. And if we look back to the St. Louis years, it would seem that Stipe also toyed with the idea of being a poet. "He wanted to be a writer," Mike Doskocil recalls. "Who didn't want to be a writer? There were only two options in 1978. You were into the Clash and the Sex Pistols and the Dickies and all that other shit. You were going to be a musician, or you were going to be a writer."

Stipe initially presented his Patti Smith epiphany to journalists as the start of his interest in music. He later amended this account to acknowledge an earlier love of David Essex's "Rock On" and Elton John's "Benny and the Jets." But this still left out his mid-'70s love of solidly mainstream rock, as betrayed by that telltale Blue Öyster Cult medallion* and an affection (presumably pre-Smith) for REO Speedwagon and Boston. Stipe finally fessed up to his classic rock predilections in a May 2006 interview with *Death & Taxes*, in which he stated, "What I've never told anyone, and this is an exclusive, is that I also bought four other albums that day [of the *Horses* purchase]. One of them was Hall and Oates, one of them Foghat: *Fool for the City*. I gravitated towards one over all the others. But the others were still there, and still in my consciousness."

---

*Patti Smith was in a long-term relationship with Allen Lanier of Blue Öyster Cult in the mid-1970s, which underscores the fact that many musicians of the period were not nearly as concerned with the divide between punk and classic rock as fans and critics were.

Going further back, Stipe had a particular fondness for the country music that had constituted much of the sonic background in the Stipe household during his upbringing—Tammy Wynette, Patsy Cline, and Glen Campbell in particular—and for such '60s stalwarts as the Kinks and the Who.*

So it's likely that the Patti Smith moment may not have been quite the road to Damascus conversion that Stipe has made it out to be. Yet it's also clear that Smith had a tremendous influence on Stipe's personality and visual aesthetic. She served as a model for how an outsider like Stipe might move through the world.

What was it about Patti Smith's music and persona that spoke so strongly to the young Michael Stipe? Beyond stating that her debut album "tore my limbs off and put them back in a whole different order" (whatever that means), he hasn't given much by way of specifics. Certainly, *Horses* would have sounded quite unlike anything a teenager had heard on mainstream radio at the time. On December 13, 1975, the day the album was released, KC and the Sunshine Band, the Bay City Rollers, Barry Manilow, and the Bee Gees ruled the US pop charts. Compared to those artists' precision-engineered hits, the John Cale–produced *Horses* sounded like something recorded in a cave. Smith herself could barely carry a tune and preferred to yelp and growl when she was not sing-speaking. At its best, the album has a hypnotic, incantatory quality, with Smith—arguably more talented as a poet than a musician—building elaborate cathedrals of language atop crashing, plodding, drone-like rhythms.

The lyrical content would have stood out to Stipe. Smith had a crowded lexicon of left-of-center influences and idols, and referenced them liberally in her songs: characters like Wilhelm Reich, the radical psychoanalyst pursued by the FBI and FDA throughout the 1940s and '50s because of his "unorthodox sex and energy theories" (in the words of *Time* magazine), who died in prison; and the renegade 19th-century poet Arthur Rimbaud, famed for his incendiary verse, his scandalous affair with fellow poet Paul Verlaine, and his renouncing of all literary pursuits by the age of 21. These figures make spectral appearances on Smith's "Birdland" (cited by Stipe as a pivotal track) and "Land," respectively. Also in "Land," a character commits suicide by slitting his own throat, which Smith describes by intoning, "His vocal cords started shooting like mad pituitary glands . . . No one heard the butterfly flapping in his throat."

---

* He has repeatedly claimed to have disliked the Beatles. "I've always referred to the Beatles as elevator music, because that's exactly what they were," he told *Rolling Stone* in 1994. "Those guys just didn't mean a fucking thing to me."

In contrast to Stipe's other alleged purchases that day (Hall and Oates, Foghat, and two more whose identity we can only speculate about), *Horses* offered a window into an enticing and somewhat frightening world of brutal rhythms, surrealistic imagery, and streetwise attitude. Then there was the cover itself: a stark black-and-white photo of Smith taken by Robert Mapplethorpe, in which she looks almost as inscrutable as the Mona Lisa. Is that a defiant stare or merely a pretension to world-weariness? Is "Patti" female or male? Her slender figure and gender-neutral attire of white blouse, undone tie, dark pants, and dark coat slung over her shoulder make it difficult to tell. There's something darkly attractive about the young Patti Smith as portrayed in this photo, something outside the "normal" parameters of sexual attraction. There is very little skin on display and nothing in the way of feminine curves, and yet there is nothing overtly masculine either. In short, there is nothing in the photo that would normally excite either heterosexual or homosexual onlookers, and yet it is an undeniably sexual cover. This is a different sort of sex appeal, one based primarily on attitude and intellect. Smith looks smart in this photo; she seduces the observer with her intelligence—and her otherness. This would have been a key difference between Smith and the other musical acts Stipe was listening to at the time. Hall and Oates, Foghat, R.E.O. Speedwagon, and even Elton John all invited the listener in with songs that appealed to a wide demographic. Their lyrics spoke to the concerns of the common listener, and their straightforward melodies sealed the deal. Smith's appeal, on the other hand, lay in her alienness. No one sang quite like her. No one looked quite like her. And certainly no one juxtaposed lyrical imagery like she did. No one since Rimbaud, anyway.

Smith was heterosexual, but her perceived lack of conventional feminine beauty had prompted her to play up her tomboy side to an extreme degree—so much so that early on she had attracted the amorous attentions of the poet Allen Ginsberg, who mistook her for a fetching young man. Smith's deliberately ambiguous image, and her determination to define herself by her own rules, would almost certainly have struck a chord with the teenaged Stipe, who was then in the process of working out his own sexual identity.

When asked in 2011 by journalist Sean O'Hagan if he had been troubled by his sexuality while growing up, the singer claimed, "Not troubled, no."

> Not confused either. But I just felt there wasn't a place for me . . . I never identified with [the term] "gay," that's all. I will always honor anyone who had to make a different choice, then stand by them, and I would hope that honor would extend to me and my choices as well.

I'm talking about how one chooses to define oneself, the community within which one feels comfortable.

These words were spoken with the advantage of 36 years of hindsight. It is difficult to believe that the 15-year-old Georgia-born Stipe was really so serene about his nascent sexuality, when virtually every other young person throughout history has, at one point or another, been troubled and/or frightened by the sudden onset of sexual desire that comes with puberty. But perhaps we're getting overly caught up in semantics here. Stipe's frustration at there not having been any place for him sounds an awful lot like what his interviewer probably meant by "troubled," whether Stipe wants to use that term or not.

One key to Stipe's apparent sereneness on this subject may lie in his discovery, in eighth grade, of the novel *Dhalgren* by science fiction author Samuel R. Delany. "Where I learned," Stipe later told the *New York Times*, "that in the future you could have unbridled sci-fi sex with every man and woman within reach, without guilt, fear or weirdness, and have great end-of-times adventures." Indeed. The sexual encounters depicted in *Dhalgren* are varied and explicit, and take place in a post-apocalyptic city in which traditional authority has vanished, along with its attendant social mores—a handy metaphor for the post-revolutionary society wished for by '60s radicals. To be fair, Delany does not shy away from the inevitable violence and chaos that would accompany such a scenario, and the novel is surely tempered by its author's observation of the hippie movement's decline in the late 1960s and early 1970s. Even so, there is a giddy exhilaration to its depiction of unconstrained sexual possibilities.

It is unclear if Stipe learned anything about Delany's personal life after discovering this book, but the parallels in the two men's approaches to sexual identity are striking. Like Stipe, Delany came to accept his sexuality in adolescence, but nevertheless went on to have a long-term relationship with a woman (as Stipe would do a number of times). In adulthood, both remained wary of labels and hard-and-fast definitions of something so malleable as sexuality. While generally homosexual in orientation, both could be strongly attracted to kindred spirits of the opposite gender. Whether or not Stipe knew any of this, *Dhalgren* itself—which was a sort of coming-out for this side of Delany—would surely have been a powerful confidence booster at such a crucial age.

One thing is clear: attempting to shoehorn Stipe's early predilections into separate categories of "gay" or "straight" is an exercise in futility. Stipe has said as much in interviews, time and time again, though when he first trotted out this line of thinking in the 1990s, many journalists and observers concluded that he was simply obfuscating because he didn't want to declare that he was gay. That is a view I also held until I began researching this book. Mike Doskocil's recollection of Stipe during the *Rocky Horror* days seems to further muddy the waters. Or, looked at another way, perhaps it clarifies them. "I remember that, at least to me, he seemed like he really wanted to be quite the player," Doskocil says.

> Come on, you walk around with a journal under your arm, especially in Missouri in 1978, somebody is going to ask you what the hell it is. And he was always ready, willing, and able to break it open for any piece of trim. I remember that myself and my friends that I spoke to, that I hung out with, we looked at Michael Stipe as a bit of a weirdo, because he didn't seem to ever score [*laughs*]. We were all getting hand jobs out back behind our VW bugs, and he never seemed to close the deal. He just didn't seem to be very successful at it. I remember thinking, "Boy, that guy is just never going to get laid." He needed to come up with something new, because his "Will Work for Pussy" sign just wasn't happening.

Perhaps the young seeker found, in the form of Patti Smith, a role model and a perceived kindred spirit—someone who provided an alternative to the confusing and maddening rituals of gender expression, teen courtship, and sex he saw all around him. Even as Stipe did his best to conform to the parameters of the world he found himself in, the strength that this newfound identification gave him would carry him through his bewildering first few years in the public eye.

No discussion of Michael Stipe's origins would be complete without an acknowledgment of his unusual speaking voice. We have no way of knowing what he sounded like pre-adolescence: whether he engaged his family and friends with a full dynamic range or employed a modulated squeak. We do know that from puberty until fairly recently he addressed the world in a deep, unvarying monotone: a flat tire of a voice, not unpleasant in its sonorousness, but difficult for the listener to latch onto.* It was as if he reserved

---

* Intriguingly, Stipe seems to have abandoned this modulated style of speaking since the breakup of R.E.M. In recent televised and audio interviews, Stipe's speaking voice is relaxed and dynamic; in other words, he now talks like a "regular" person. This either points to a personal evolution or

all of his emotion and dynamics for his singing voice, which is a different story entirely. His singing would evolve over time, but on R.E.M.'s earliest recordings the Patti Smith elements were firmly in place, to be showcased or modulated depending on the occasion. Yelps. Strange throat noises. Guttural grunts. An occasional dropping of consonants following an *o* (*more* becomes *moe*, etc.) He emphasized what he called the "acid *e*": an elongation and overemphasis on that vowel ("What noisy cats are weeeeeeeeeee..."), a technique that had more in common with the country and bluegrass he'd heard in his youth than with the punk and garage rock he was listening to in the late '70s. This vocal quirk alone set him apart from just about every other rock singer in his age group.

It is possible that the mumbling style that would become his vocal signature initially served a purely utilitarian purpose. Stipe began his musical career singing in cover bands and often had difficulty remembering other people's (and, later, his own) lyrics. The mumble, then, may have come about so he could fake his way through some of these songs, wrapping a hodgepodge of vowels and consonants in the cloak of the song's melody and just barreling through. That's certainly what he did when R.E.M. performed covers, and there's no reason to presume that the practice didn't begin earlier.

Gangster, the Athens-based band Stipe joined shortly after his family left Illinois and moved back to Georgia in 1979, was the brainchild of Derek Nunally, a local guitarist who had allegedly once been a roadie for Molly Hatchet. They had a shtick: all the band members wore zoot suits. Stipe took the stage name "Michael Valentine." According to Rodger Lyle Brown, the group played "all covers, from Tom Petty to Elvis." Stipe's sisters attended every show, cheering their brother on.

It's safe to assume that Gangster was not a huge draw for the nascent art-school party crowd. It seems, in fact, that very few people saw the band play other than Stipe's sisters and a big, fun-loving, hard-drinking loudmouth named Billy Holmes. Holmes, who was knocking around Athens playing in folk duos and hard rock outfits at the time, was decidedly *not* of the art school scene; his tastes ran more in the direction of classical music and the much-maligned genre of progressive rock (he counts Yes and Genesis as two of his favorite bands) than the primitivism of the B-52's and Pylon. What brought him to see Gangster perform at the Last Resort on Clayton Street was not any kind of premonition about the singer's future but rather

---

the possibility that what may have seemed like a vocal quirk during those earlier years was actually a deliberate choice.

his friendship with Gangster's bassist, Danny Bell.

"I just thought, poor Danny. There was nobody there," Billy tells me in his thick drawl.

> But that was the first time I ever laid eyes on Michael Stipe. I was really happy for him when R.E.M. did something years later, because *I* was sort of an outcast, and was eccentric, and had been picked on my whole life. And Michael—I did not really know him, but I had heard he had tried to get in bands with people, and people would not play with him. Nobody would give him a shot, and that is why he ended up singing Lynyrd Skynyrd covers with guys from Monroe. You know, he didn't really want to join a bunch of—quite frankly, let's just put it like it is—Monroe rednecks. But he had acne, and you never saw his face because he grew his hair out long and he would put his hair all over his face.

Michael Stipe has claimed in numerous interviews that he spent his entire first year in Athens not talking to anyone. This is surely an exaggeration, since it's awfully hard to maintain a vow of silence when performing live every few weeks in a rock 'n' roll band.* It's also not likely that his family, with whom he remained very close, would have gone along with a ban on verbal communication. But perhaps there is some emotional truth to the statement. Gangster clearly didn't represent the summit of Stipe's artistic ambitions, and his concurrent job at Steak and Ale was not exactly in line with any of his career goals. One source who knew some of the waitresses at the steakhouse says that the future rock star and sex symbol earned the name "Pigpen" from his female co-workers due to his (allegedly) slovenly demeanor. Given the shunning he seemed to be experiencing in his new hometown, perhaps he did feel as if he were not communicating with another living soul.

Compounding the feelings of alienation was the very real grief he felt at having been uprooted from his peer group in St. Louis. Earlier moves had not had such traumatic consequences, but this time he had really begun to find his voice—both figuratively and literally. Mike Doskocil might have found the place intolerable, but in St. Louis Michael Stipe had made friends and had been playing music. Consequently, Stipe viewed his family's abrupt move to small-town Georgia as a catastrophe. In at least one interview, he

---

*Stipe apparently continued to propagate this tale well into the 1990s. The poet Douglas A. Martin, in his fictionalized account of his four-year relationship with Stipe, *Outline of My Lover*, recalls the singer boasting of this ascetic phase.

has said that he remained behind in St. Louis for a few months, but finally caved and joined his family out of economic necessity. At that point, the familiar pattern of spending most of his time with his sisters reasserted itself. His youngest sister, Lynda, in particular, seems to have served as a sounding board and kindred spirit as Michael began exploring his artistic side in earnest. She was still in high school at the time, but she accompanied Michael practically everywhere.

"Lynda Stipe is an awesome gal," Billy Holmes says. "I worked with her, actually, at Sons of Italy pizzeria, up in Five Points. She is very creative, always has been, and I always thought she deserved more recognition than she got."

In several respects, Lynda bears a striking resemblance to her older brother: full lips, piercing eyes, extremely curly brown hair, and the same smile. She also shares with Michael an intuitive, almost childlike approach to creativity

Lynda and Michael Stipe, ca. 1985. Photo by Ingrid Schorr.

and artmaking, unencumbered by formal theory or over-intellectualization. Less is known of Michael's other sister, Cyndy (or "Cindy" or "Cyndi" as her name has been spelled in various accounts)—mainly because she went on to something resembling a conventional career (in education), started a family, and consequently faded from the Athens scene fairly early. But initially she was right there with the other two, running around town, checking things out. So when Stipe strode in to the Wuxtry Records store on Baxter Street sometime in early 1979 flanked by two attractive young women, it made an impression. The clerk behind the counter was a towering, mop-topped guy who carried himself with a jaded "I've seen it all" air. But the sight of this skinny reverse-mullet guy with a hot girl on each arm threw him for a loop. The clerk's name? Peter Buck.

So here we are at last. "Pete" Buck: the gangly, hawk-nosed motormouth and autodidact with idiosyncratic tastes and an encyclopedic knowledge of rock 'n' roll and more. He's seen every episode of both *The Monkees* and *The Man from U.N.C.L.E.* And he can drink you under the table.

Born in Berkeley, California, Buck moved with his family to Atlanta in his teens and graduated from Crestwood High School. He has, over the years, told extravagant, Beat Generation–tinged tales of a young adulthood filled with cross-country hitchhiking, sleeping in ditches, and taking odd jobs washing dishes and cleaning toilets. He stops just shy of saying he rode the rails and hung out with hoboes. Occasionally, he has also intimated some sort of dark criminal past. No evidence to substantiate these claims has ever surfaced.

It seems likely that Buck took a cue here from Bob Dylan, who told outlandish tales about his past in order to liven up a rather boring middle-class backstory. What is known for certain is that Buck attended Atlanta's Emory University for a time and was a member of the Delta Tau Delta fraternity. As we have already seen, he first came in contact with a young Kathleen O'Brien while working at a record store near the campus. He had the requisite childhood for a future rock star, which is to say he spent most of his adolescence sequestered in his bedroom listening to records and perusing the latest issues of *Rolling Stone* and *Creem*, dreaming of a wild on-the-road life while likely living a confined, isolated one. His early interest in the Monkees and the Beatles (in that order of preference) gave way eventually to the Velvet Underground, the Stooges, and the New York Dolls. He was aware of "punk" from the moment the term was coined. Oddly, though, this passionate interest in listening to music was not accompanied at first by a desire to *play* music. He had learned a few guitar chords from his younger brother Ken and occasionally noodled around, but that was the extent of his involvement with the instrument.

It was quiet, studious Ken who seemed destined for a musical career. Billy Holmes, who knew the younger Buck during the latter's time at the University of Georgia, says, "Ken is one of the best musicians I have ever known. He has a classical guitar degree from UGA. And he took his knowledge of classical guitar and he taught himself to play classical piano from it, which is astounding to me. He is a really good bass player and a really good singer. Like Lynda Stipe, he ended up getting overshadowed by his famous sibling."

The brothers Buck both arrived in Athens at roughly the same time, though by different means. Ken came as a student. Peter, whose vague ambitions of getting an education degree had fizzled at Emory, became aware of an open Wuxtry job via a contact at its sister store in Decatur. With his previous record store experience and his impressive storehouse of musical lore, he was a shoo-in. He reported for work in January 1979, around the same time that Bill Berry, Mike Mills, and Michael Stipe all arrived in town, and quickly established himself as something of an in-house oracle. He was immediately recognizable, due to his height and the purple high school letter jacket he wore like a second skin, and few customers made it through a visit without receiving a lecture on some aspect of music history.

"He listened to or had in his collection pretty much everything," says Billy Holmes,

> from John Coltrane to Karlheinz Stockhausen. Dunno if he listened to it all, but he had it, and would gladly tape copies. If he had something he thought was cool, he would tell you all about it and ask if you wanted a copy. He wanted to share his finds. He was a big fan of James Bond and spy shows and stuff like that. He made me VHS tapes of [the entire run of] *The Man from U.N.C.L.E.* . . . We both would buy and swap those little paperbacks that you used to buy in grade school: *Monkees Go Mod, Love Letters to the Monkees* . . . all of that stuff.

This is the den of geeks that Michael Stipe began frequenting, sometimes in the company of his sisters, sometimes alone. He was fronting Gangster at that point, and his musical knowledge remained spotty; mainstream rock from the '70s, country music from his childhood, Henry Mancini soundtracks, and Patti Smith made up the bulk of his diet. But in his reading of *Creem* and other music periodicals he was beginning to note certain names that kept popping up: the Velvet Underground, Big Star, the Stooges. It was Stipe's attractive sisters who first piqued Peter Buck's interest in his new customer, but what *kept* Buck's attention was Stipe's tendency to purchase records that Buck had earmarked for himself.

It quickly emerged over the course of their conversations that both men harbored musical ambitions. Buck was by now chomping at the bit to write music of his own and make some kind of contribution to the ongoing rock 'n' roll dialogue. Stipe, while already actively fronting a band, appreciated the fact that Buck had a more expansive musical palette than his Gangster bandmates. That seemed to override any apparent lack of practical musical ability on Buck's part. They decided they would try their hand at writing some songs together.

Here, like a comet, is where Kathleen O'Brien comes back into view. She had begun drifting into Wuxtry around the same time as Michael Stipe. Throughout much of the 1978–79 academic year she had hosted a new wave show on WUOG (the university's radio station) called *Purely Physical*. "I knew everybody at the record stores," she says, because that's what we DJs did. And the musicians and everybody that was into the music thing were all at the stores because there was so much coming in. There was the early rap coming out of New York and then there was—not real garage bands, but what had evolved from the B-52's.

The people following these developments were, O'Brien explains, "the same group that just kept coming together and coming together and coming together." They included many of the characters from the raucous "subwastement" parties: Mark Cline, Rodger Lyle Brown, Sandi Phipps, Kurt Wood (another WUOG DJ), Paul Butchart, Carol Levy, Linda Hopper, and more.

Kathleen had tried her hand at music-making herself, albeit in what she referred to as a "mockery band" called the Wuoggerz: a train wreck of an ensemble consisting of O'Brien on vocals and tambourine along with several of her colleagues from WUOG. They performed, as she puts it, "horrible obscure bad covers" of punk, alternative, and classic rock songs. At the time, the thing that distinguished the Wuoggerz was their outlandish costumes. What distinguishes them in the annals of Athens music history now is the fact that they elicited Bill Berry's return to the drum kit for the first time since his Macon days, thereby ending his supposed swearing-off of rock 'n' roll.

Bill and Kathleen were still circling each other at that point. Whether it was due to shyness or just a general attitude of circumspection, Bill hadn't responded—at least overtly—to Kathleen's obvious interest. And yet, when she asked if he would drum for her ragtag group, he accepted without hesitation. His actual words: "Hell yeah!"

Bill's connections with the Copelands enabled the Wuoggerz to land a plum opening slot for the Police—then in the lift-off stage of their meteoric rise to stardom—at a campus May Day concert. During the gig, Bill clearly had eyes for the gyrating Kathleen. But nothing happened—for now. The Wuoggerz fizzled out, since none of the band members were all that interested in actually playing music. It was only ever a rambunctious group of friends anyway, and those friendships persisted.

Fall 1979 found Kathleen on the hunt for a new place to live, having finally outgrown Reed Hall in spite of its ineffable charms, and at some point she got to talking with Dan Wall (the owner of Wuxtry Records) about her predicament. Wall had been living in a room in a converted church on Oconee Street but was in the process of moving out and needed someone to take over the lease.

"Hey, I'd like to move into the church," she told him. "So who's the landlord? Who do I talk to?"

"Well, I kind of promised it to one of my employees."

"Oh well," she said. "They might need a roommate. Who is it?"

"Well, it's Pete Buck."

"I know Pete Buck!"

And so it was that Kathleen and Peter moved into the old church. And, being young, heterosexual, and living in such close quarters, they also became romantically involved for a brief period of time. So Kathleen was on hand to witness some of Peter Buck and Michael Stipe's earliest songwriting sessions. "Michael was coming over frequently," she says, "and they were writing songs. It was more like Pete sitting around with the guitar and Michael doing the lyrics. They had good stuff, and they were also doing covers together. Pete was still kind of rough around the edges on the guitar, but it was interesting. It was fun."

Regarding the church—it had become known as Steeplechase—where this all transpired, Peter Buck has said, "[It] has been romanticized beyond all belief. It was just a rotten, dumpy little shithole where college kids, *only* college kids, could be convinced to live." Buck is often given to hyperbole, but in this instance there is no reason to doubt his appraisal. If the place wasn't already on the verge of being condemned when Dan Wall moved out, then Buck, O'Brien, Stipe (who moved in shortly after the songwriting collaborations began), and their rotating cast of roommates—who included a drug dealer at one point, and later the other two future members of R.E.M.— surely hastened its demise. In many ways it was the subwastement writ large: one nonstop party. And it's saying something that Kathleen O'Brien, who certainly knew how to turn a place upside down in the name of a good party, was apparently the tidiest person in the bunch.

So yes, the place was a dump. No one who set foot there has ever suggested otherwise. Nevertheless, there are a number of valid reasons why Steeplechase has been "romanticized beyond all belief," all stemming from the fact that it became the birthplace of R.E.M. There was the metaphorical significance of it having been a house of worship—with its exterior still intact. Lots of bands have started out in garages or basements, but very few have begun in churches, and it's fitting that a band such as R.E.M., which would come to be distinguished by its gnomic lyrics and—at least early on— its out-of-focus, not-quite-there public image, had its genesis in such a place.

And yet this wasn't really a church. It was the shell of a church with a two-story bunker built inside. The tale of how such a structure came to be has been lost to history. Did the developers have superstitious reservations about destroying a church to make way for their planned rental units, and therefore decide to build the apartments *inside* the church? Or did they simply think that a church-on-the-outside, wood-grain-paneled-"house"-on-the-inside was a neat idea that gave the place an edge over traditional apartment complexes?

In either case, the execution was half-assed at best. Even without the 24-7 hell-raising of its inhabitants, the place would have been in bad shape. The exterior windows had either been deliberately removed or had fallen out over time; they'd been replaced with wooden shutters. It was clear that no one had laid a paintbrush on the place in decades. Also, there was the small matter of the gaping hole in Kathleen's bedroom closet, which led to the still-intact sanctuary of the original church—which, incidentally, made for a killer rehearsal space for a fledgling band. But not yet, not yet.

Across town, Billy Holmes had made the acquaintance of Mike Mills and Bill Berry. Paul "Crumpy" Edwards, Holmes's bandmate in the Red Scare, had known Mills and Berry in Macon and introduced them to Holmes. The four of them (and others) often congregated around Express Pizza on Baxter Street to play video games and avail themselves of the two-dollar pitchers of beer on offer. What most struck Holmes at the time was Mills's brown bomber jacket ("like a fly jacket") that, much like Buck's letter jacket, never seemed to leave its wearer's body. As musicians, though, the duo didn't strike Holmes as anything other than dilettantes.

"I was a snob," Holmes says, laughing. "I was a long-haired hippie type and I had been heavily into all the seventies prog music. A buddy of mine named Richard Marlow swears up and down that Mike and Bill told me over beers one night in Express Pizza that they were going to start a band and asked me if I was interested in playing with them. And I said, 'I don't know. I'll get back to you.' So . . . I may have blown my shot at playing with R.E.M." He pauses, then adds, "I would have just screwed them up anyway!"

Holmes describes Bill Berry—the man who just two years earlier had struck Ian Copeland as a motormouth—as "always kind of quiet. I don't remember Bill as being all that talkative. The main thing that stuck out to me about Bill is that he had a warped sense of humor, which I liked. Sometimes he would crack jokes, and he was trying to be funny, and people wouldn't get it. The other thing was, we all made fun of Bill because he had one eyebrow."

Billy Holmes, then, has the distinction of being one of the few people who knew all four members of R.E.M. prior to the formation of R.E.M. But he never thought to put the guys together. And why would he? Here was a so-so rhythm section from Macon, good for a couple of beers and some jokes on any given night, but not too promising musically, and there was the singer from Gangster with the reverse mullet—you know, the Steak and Ale guy, Pigpen—who did the Thin Lizzy covers. And Pete Buck? Are you kidding me?

It took a twisted sort of genius to see that these elements could be mixed to create some kind of radioactive cocktail. Only Kathleen O'Brien could make that leap.

Chapter Three

Her fling with Peter Buck notwithstanding, Kathleen still harbored a strong interest in Bill Berry. A year is a pretty long time to carry a torch at that age, particularly when there are so many other potential companions available. So that probably says something about both Berry's appeal and O'Brien's ardor.

Meanwhile, Michael Stipe and Peter Buck found themselves in need of a rhythm section. They had already played with a few other people in the sanctuary—most notably Dan Wall—but nothing had clicked. To Peter's way of thinking, they were just fucking around, but Michael had latched on to some kind of vision. It was a blurred vision, but it was his. "These are dangerous times / I don't want to get old," began one of those early songs. Two lines, both heartfelt expressions, but they don't seem to have anything to do with each other. Or do they? "I don't want to get old" is not typically a statement that would flow out of musings on the precarious state of the world; it would be much more likely to indicate a desire to remain in the present. But if the present is so dangerous, as indicated in the preceding line, why would one want to do that? An alternative explanation is that the prospect of growing old is, in itself, what makes these times so dangerous— maybe not physically (aging from 20 to 21 is not going to slow someone down) but perhaps the danger in growing old is the possibility of giving in to convention and losing one's present identity.

My tortured attempt here to make sense of lyrics that are—let's face it—a bit off, somewhat misshapen, is a microcosm of what a generation of listeners and critics would end up doing with Michael Stipe's words. It was never clear—then or for a while later—if the "offness" was a calculated effect, or if Stipe's unintentionally awkward phrasing had opened a space of ambiguity into which people could read all kinds of meanings. In either case, opaqueness was a component of Stipe's writing from the very outset, and it set him apart from most other fledgling songwriters.

Musically the duo worked the same handful of chords over and over. Buck harbored no illusions concerning his ability on the guitar, but he had enthusiasm and a willingness to learn. Plus, he already looked and acted the part, with his shaggy hair and penchant for wearing vests and carrying knives around. He was a rock star minus the fame and success, which may be the purest sort of rock star there is. Still, the pair needed a bassist and a drummer, no two ways about it. They would not be playing folk gigs at T.K. Harty's as "Buck and Stipe." They wanted to play—oh, never mind where; they hadn't thought that far ahead. But they wanted to play loud—electric.

It should come as no surprise to the reader that Kathleen O'Brien immediately thought of Bill Berry as the solution to the new duo's quandary. Sure, she had an ulterior motive—she wanted to bring Berry into the band for the same reason she had recruited him for the Wuoggerz: to be closer to him. But she also knew from that earlier experience that Berry could play, and that he came with an added bonus: Mike Mills.

What happened next is a matter of some conjecture. We know for certain that Kathleen introduced Michael and Peter to Bill at a party and that Michael was rather taken with Berry's unusual appearance—particularly his eyebrow. But Kathleen vaguely remembers also introducing the duo to Mike Mills at that same party, whereas the version of the story told by the band members over the years has Berry introducing Buck and Stipe to Mills at Tyrone's O.C. nightclub a few weeks later. Whatever the exact circumstances, Michael Stipe was initially adamant that Mills not be part of their fledgling band. It wasn't the fact that the bassist was drunk off his ass that evening, crawling around the floor in his bomber jacket; it was simply that Mills didn't look cool. No matter his musical talent, his bowl haircut and penchant for bell-bottoms were violently at odds with the mental image Stipe had constructed of his hypothetical ensemble. Buck had some initial concerns too, though his were of a more practical nature: based on the state Mills was in that evening, Buck worried that he might be too out-of-control to shoulder the commitment of being in a band.

Fortunately for posterity, Berry was equally adamant that he wouldn't participate in any new musical undertaking without Mills. Since Stipe and Buck had immediately warmed to Berry and desperately wanted him to be in the band, they had no choice but to acquiesce.

Kathleen still remembers the first rehearsal vividly: "It was just *there*. You know, the dynamics between the personalities—what Peter and Michael had been doing and then what Mike and Bill already had established from years of playing together . . . it just immediately fit. I had thought it would, but it was one of those things where I was like, 'Oh, this is perfect. This is *perfect*.'"

Lynda Stipe [facing camera], **Carol Levy** [behind Lynda Stipe], **Cyndy Stipe** [back to camera], **ca. 1982. Photo by Ingrid Schorr.**

Mike moved into the church, followed in close succession by Bill. The as-yet-unnamed band rehearsed regularly, working up covers of songs by '60s garage bands (practically the only material that Buck felt competent— and confident—enough to play) along with full-band arrangements of some of the Buck and Stipe originals. With all four musicians now under the same roof, they made steady progress in laying the foundations of their sound. Many distractions surrounded the young men at Steeplechase, though, and it was not initially clear how far this new project of theirs would go.

One of the biggest challenges to having consistent, focused rehearsals was the increasingly wild partying going on at the church. A scene began to coalesce around Steeplechase that included many familiar faces from Reed Hall, such as Carol Levy, Linda Hopper, Sandi Phipps, and WUOG DJ Kurt Wood, a wiry, bushy-haired former Reed resident. Paul Butchart was there, as were a number of Stipe's acquaintances from the art school, including David Pierce and his professor Jim Herbert. So too were other future stars of the Athens music scene like Paul Lombard, Mark Cline, and Mike Richmond. (This is, by its very nature, a woefully incomplete list).

If Rodger Lyle Brown's account is to be believed (and he was there, too), many of these folks were fucking each other rather indiscriminately.

It was a heavily sexual time. Rutting in the dirt. At parties. In the bathrooms. Making somebody before passing out and then loving whomever you wake up next to, found groping from floor to couch. The worst thing to worry about was herpes, but that scare didn't really hit too hard until the next year. But even with that negligible fear you can still just do it anyway. You meet somebody and you can just see it in their eyes and in fifteen minutes you are out in the car.

This group of misfits may not have been breaking new ground, but like those crazy kids who gave the Summer of Love its name a little over a decade earlier, the Steeplechase crew celebrated their newfound sexual freedom with all the vigor and urgency that came with the belief that they had invented the orgy. In the reminiscences of Brown and others, one picks up on the subtle but very real melancholy of a post-party comedown—the impression, intentional or not, that nothing that came afterward burned quite so brightly or joyously as those days and nights in Athens in 1979 and 1980.

Inevitably, human nature interceded. Just because a bunch of young adults were high and horny didn't mean that jealousy and possessiveness could be staved off forever. And anyway, not knowing who you're going to bed with on any given night can be a little exhausting. Out of chaos came some kind of order—for at least some of the individuals involved. Peter Buck and Bill Berry, in particular, emerged as having slightly more conventional approaches to relationships than some of their peers. Buck drifted into what would become a long-term relationship with Ann Boyles. And Berry finally began dating Kathleen O'Brien.

"I was attracted from the very beginning," Kathleen says. "But once we started going out I was a goner."

It was just one of those feelings like he was a compatible soul or something. I thought he was incredibly talented and once you got to know him, he had a great sense of humor. He was a gentleman. He had a very cool sense of dress and style. I love his voice; I mean, you could just listen to him for hours. And even though he was quiet, he was very intense. He was real adventurous, which you wouldn't know if you didn't know him.

One particular incident remains embedded in Kathleen's mind. During a seemingly aimless car ride through north Georgia farmland, the two spotted a man on a tractor working his fields. That was when Bill confided to Kathleen that his ultimate ambition was not to be a rock musician but rather to own a farm and be a farmer. They parked their car and walked over to the guy on the tractor, and somehow Bill talked the man into letting him take a spin on the machine. They spent the better part of the afternoon riding the tractor over the man's fields, and Bill was about the happiest Kathleen had ever seen him.

Though not much of a hedonist (at least in relation to his peers), Michael Stipe was philosophically in sync with at least one aspect of the emerging Athens party culture, shunning conventional romantic relationships in favor of unburdened, no-fuss encounters. It's not that he flew though a succession of partners at this point in his life, but he nevertheless displayed an aversion to commitment. Stipe has claimed in recent interviews that he had never been in love or experienced a real relationship prior to becoming involved with the photographer Thomas Dozol in the late 1990s. He characterizes all partners prior to Dozol as simply "lovers."

Whatever the nature and extent of the relationships, in his early years in Athens he was involved most visibly with women. He obliquely acknowledged in a 2011 *Interview* profile that one of his early partners had been Carol Levy, the dark-haired provocateur Kathleen and others had known in their Reed Hall days. According to one of his friends from this period, Stipe was also involved at some point with another Reed Hall alum, Linda Hopper. This friend says, with a laugh, "I'm old enough to remember when Michael Stipe liked girls." In one respect she's kidding: she's not really suggesting that Stipe was once straight and somehow turned gay over time. But she is underscoring the fact that his relationships with women were not in any sense fraudulent ones. Stipe, by his own account, "enjoyed" having sex with women, and he chose partners who were kindred spirits. Both Levy and Hopper were artistic and "nonlinear" thinkers like himself.

For the first half of R.E.M.'s thirty-year run, journalists and biographers skirted the subject of Stipe's sexuality entirely. It's unclear whether this was due to some kind of direct mandate from R.E.M.'s management, or simply out of fear of libel suits. (Stipe, after all, did not make any public statement on the topic of his sexuality until the release of the *Monster* album in 1994.) By 2011, though, Stipe was ready to talk specifics. He told the *Observer*'s Sean O'Hagan, "On a sliding scale of sexuality I'd place myself around 80–20, but I definitely prefer men to women."

In 1979–80, Stipe seemed to be making the most of that 20 percent heterosexual side, and who can blame him? Despite the powerful influence of gay culture on Athens' burgeoning art and music scene, local attitudes toward homosexuality varied widely. Stipe's new songwriting partner Peter Buck didn't at first seem especially sensitive to the issue. (*Party Out of Bounds* contains a story in which the young Peter threatened Paul Lombard with physical violence after Lombard called him a "faggot": "How can he call me a fag? I sleep with ten times as many women as he does!" Peter is quoted as saying.) In the larger culture, pop music itself seemed to be going back into the closet after a brief flirtation with open expressions of homosexuality in the 1970s. The dawn of the new decade saw David Bowie—previously the de facto spokesman for the more flamboyant side of gay culture—backpedaling from his earlier assertions that he was gay, or even bisexual. Queen's Freddie Mercury, despite a provocative onstage persona, remained firmly in the closet. Even Elton John wore a mask of heterosexuality. Fred Schneider of the B-52's aside, being openly gay must have seemed a career-threatening move for just about any aspiring rock singer at the dawn of the 1980s.

Many of Stipe's friends in Athens viewed him as quirky, shy, and emotionally guarded, but they seemed at first to have little inkling that he might be gay. Given Stipe's later statement that he had always been open about his sexuality to his closest friends and loved ones, that circle must have been small. Velena Vego, who got to know him a few years later, says: "At the time I was around [the mid-'80s], Michael wasn't out. He was dating Natalie Merchant from 10,000 Maniacs. So things did change over the years."

And yet Stipe didn't make himself out to be super-hetero either. His early lyrics, many of which had been jettisoned by the time R.E.M. began making records, represent perhaps his only attempt to put forward any kind of macho swagger. R.E.M. biographer Tony Fletcher has characterized this material as misogynistic, but that's a bit of a stretch—at least when judged by the usual rock 'n' roll standards. "Hey, Hey Nadine" (aka "Small Town Girl"), in which Stipe sings "Pretty blond hair singing as she walks / China-like smile bitchin' as she talks"* doesn't exactly threaten the Rolling Stones' "Under My Thumb" in the sexist anthem sweepstakes. No, these songs were merely exercises in rock 'n' roll affectation: an instance of Stipe trying on the ill-fitting coat of machismo on his way to abstract expressionism.

There will always be people who feel that an artist's sexuality has no

---

* Or something along these lines; as usual, his words are hard to discern.

relevance to an appreciation or understanding of their work. In one sense, that's probably correct: most artists, gay or straight, strive for universality. A song, poem, story, or novel that deals with the subject of relationships— even if those relationships are cast in an unambiguously homosexual context—is typically deemed successful if it connects with a wide audience of diverse backgrounds. The successful artist, in this scenario, is tapping into the human condition; his or her sexual orientation is deemed irrelevant when the art is viewed in that way.

But from another perspective, an artist's sexual orientation has *everything* to do with the work. I remember having a debate with a visual artist a few years ago, brought on by my reading of a biography of the composer John Cage. I said I found the biographer's refusal to address the topic of Cage's homosexuality beyond a few cursory sentences surprising and frustrating. I was taken aback when my artist friend retorted, "Well, whose business is it who he fucked?" I suppose the Stipean response to that question would be, "Only the business of Cage and the people he was fucking." (This is a paraphrase of something Stipe once said in response to a journalist's questions about *his* sexuality.) But at least one later Cage biographer found the subject of who the composer fucked—or their gender, at least—to be of great import. In *Where the Heart Beats*, author Kay Larson makes the argument that an "acute personal crisis" stemming from Cage's difficulty in reconciling his sexual orientation and politics with those of society at large led him to the study of Zen Buddhism, which, in turn, transformed his art. Perhaps there will come a day when it really won't make a difference to anyone whether a person is gay or straight, but during Cage's time, and during at least the first phase of Michael Stipe's career, straight people and gay people often led radically different lives. The former could air their preference openly and confidently, secure in the knowledge that their actions were sanctioned by mainstream society. The latter often felt compelled to lead veiled and compartmentalized lives. Straight people rarely stop to think of what that must feel like—to keep such an elemental part of one's psyche so closely under wraps. How could such a situation *not* affect a person's art, when just the act of being oneself in front of one's friends and co-workers—something that should be effortless and even mundane—requires great fortitude?

Given the above factors, Stipe's lifelong friendship with Charles Jerry (Jeremy) Ayers, who passed away in 2016, is significant. The son of a UGA religion professor, Ayers had already been to New York, participated in Warhol's Factory scene (assuming the drag persona "Silva Thin"), and returned to Athens by the time Stipe met him in 1979. Alongside friends Keith Strickland, Fred Schneider, Kate Pierson, and the Wilson siblings, Ayers played a key role in the creation of the visual and musical aesthetic of the B-52's. All of this would have been impressive enough to Stipe, but by 1979 Ayers had begun to move into a new style of dress, behavior, and performance that likely played a role in the formation of Stipe's public persona. "Jerry was quieting," Rodger Lyle Brown writes in *Party Out of Bounds*,

> now quitting the campy drag that had dressed the B-52's for their success. He was turning away from the audacious glitter fag assault and was now falling silent, retreating to mystery, a coyote trickster, but still pretty.... Michael Stipe saw Jerry Ayers . . . He watched him. He was intrigued.

Stipe, too, had passed through flamboyance on the way to something else. It seems significant that in *Volume 1*, Stipe's 2018 book of photography (described in its press release as "centering around [Stipe's] unconventional and deeply personal understanding of queerness"), Ayers appears more than any other figure, and over a larger span of time (from 1980 through 2015). He is depicted on both the first and last pages of the book.

With all that was going on around them, the four musicians' focus on band practice was scattered at best. But that was about to change. Kathleen had a birthday coming up, and she wanted all her musician friends—Paul Butchart, for example, her old friend from German camp, who had recently formed a band called the Side Effects—to play at the inevitable party.

O'Brien was just as insistent that her roommates' new band should play. They were reluctant at first, feeling they didn't have enough material. But when it became clear that she wouldn't take no for an answer, they buckled down and began rehearsing as if they were preparing for a high-profile concert (which in a sense they

The Side Effects: Paul Butchart (drums), Kit Swartz (guitar), Jimmy Ellison (bass), 688 Club, Atlanta, 1981. Photo by Margot Butchart.

were; having already experienced several bacchanals at the church, they knew that this would not be a small party). For Buck and Stipe, at least, the stakes were high. Given the abysmal attendance at pretty much every Gangster gig ever, Stipe might as well have never been in a band before—in fact, this was the image he liked to convey to his new friends. And everyone knew Buck as the opinionated guy from Wuxtry; it was time for him to show how *he* would do this rock 'n' roll thing.

The old church on Oconee Street, ca. 1980. Photo by Rick Hawkins, © Rick Hawkins 2010.

Chapter Four

Paul Butchart stands on a sidewalk corner in downtown Athens, gazing vaguely in my direction. Alone, he looks a lot taller than he actually is. I think the illusion is mostly created by his cascading white beard. As I will learn, he makes good use of this in the holiday season, suiting up every year as a professional Santa ("like his father before him," a mutual acquaintance tells me). He wears loose clothes that are hanging off him, has a mischievous glow in his eyes—and then there are his pointy eyebrows. He's *not* Santa, he's Jeremiah Johnson crossed with Merlin. An imposing presence, for sure.

Of the various people I've contacted up to this point, Paul has been the most guarded, and it has taken a while for us to get to this face-to-face meeting. During our first e-mail exchanges, he remained noncommittal about being interviewed, and he's still wary this afternoon. I had a backup plan in case he bowed out: I would simply figure out a way to tag along on one of his Athens Music History walking tours and jot down everything he said. For the past several years he has been showing paying customers the town's hidden musical landmarks: the old railway trestle from the back cover of R.E.M.'s first album, the cemetery where Ricky Wilson from the B-52's is buried, the various locations of the 40 Watt Club through the years, and the remains of that church on Oconee Street where R.E.M. formed and eventually played their first gig. That event, and Butchart's role in it, is what we are here to discuss tonight, and it is my great good luck that he has finally acquiesced. As I will learn, spending one-on-one time with Paul over a few beers is time to be treasured.

We shake hands on the street corner and he motions me into the doorway of the Globe. We make small talk as we step out of the cold, and I can sense that he's still on his guard, but his slow, syrupy Georgia accent undercuts that tension, and when he cracks the first of several broad smiles he will bestow over the course of the evening and the corners of his eyes crinkle, I know we'll be fine. I can't say we part friends, but our conversation is easy and relaxed.

Paul's towering shadow looms over our story at several key intervals. As we have seen, he met Kathleen O'Brien early on at a German-language camp for high school students. Like several of our principal actors he attended the Sex Pistols concert at the Great American Music Hall in 1978 and was galvanized by that event. ("By November," he says, "I had traded in my Styx and Boston albums for Richard Hell and the Voidoids and Talking Heads and the Ramones.") In Athens, he landed a job at the local Steak and Ale alongside prep cook Michael Stipe. ("He'd cut the vegetables and I'd cook them and serve them.") And, like everyone else, he got to know Peter Buck at Wuxtry Records.

It almost seems like fate might have been actively conspiring to put Paul Butchart in R.E.M., except that he misread the signals. Around the time Michael Stipe and Peter Buck began circling each other, Paul and his best friend, Kit Swartz, started writing songs together. They were not art students, but their efforts were very much in the primitive, anti-technique school of music-making that David Pierce described earlier. Butchart had never taken a drum lesson in his life and developed a style in which he accented the upbeat with the same emphasis as the downbeat. Kit Swartz, meanwhile, had developed a droney, surf-influenced guitar style that was, in Butchart's words, "like a mantra." Peter Buck caught wind of these experiments and invited Paul and Kit to come over to the church and jam with him and Michael. It seemed like a natural fit: all four were approaching music in the spirit of adventurous children, not quite knowing what they were doing and therefore stumbling into interesting sounds. But it was not to be; Paul and Kit never showed up that day.

How differently things might have turned out! Recall that at this very moment, across town, Billy Holmes was (so the story goes) drunkenly turning down an overture to play in a band with Mike Mills and Bill Berry. Perhaps, in a parallel universe, these two would-be bands—the trio of Holmes, Mills, and Berry, and the combo of Buck, Butchart, Swartz, and Stipe, are playing Athens clubs to this day. But instead of R.E.M. No. 1 and 2, they are called ... Well, we'll get to that.

Back in the real world—or, rather, the hazy dreamworld of Athens, Georgia, circa March 1980—Stipe, Buck, Butchart, Kurt Wood, and two women whose names have been lost in the sands of time decided to go on a road trip to New York City to see Pylon perform. Never mind that they could see Pylon play any given week in Athens—this was the Big Apple! And it was on this trip that the template for R.E.M.'s future road behavior was set: constant drinking and a complete disregard for the necessities of sleep and personal hygiene. This latter aspect made a lasting impression on the attendees of a party that was thrown for Pylon. According to Paul, there are people walking around New York to this day who refer to his band of interlopers as "the guys that smelled bad." (The women had broken away from the group a few days before). This event also doubled as a birthday party for music journalist Lester Bangs—a hero to all four young men for his iconoclastic, acerbic writing in *Creem* and *Rolling Stone*. The now-bloated, shaggy-haired Bangs spent much of the party slumped in a corner, drugged out of his mind. Butchart recalls Peter Buck keeping a respectful distance. As Buck explained to Butchart, "I don't want to talk to famous people because they'll ruin my image of them; they'll probably be arrogant or something like that." (Buck's oft-quoted version of the story includes Bangs calling him a "rotten cock-sucker" even as Buck attempted to keep a wide berth.) The hungry travelers had intended to load up on food at this party, but all that was on offer was cheesecake and jelly beans. They ate as much as they could stomach.

It would be some time before Stipe and Buck returned to New York City, but it's safe to say the place got in Stipe's blood—or more accurately, that it reinforced an obsession he'd begun to develop a few years back when he bought that *Horses* album. The trip also seems to have focused Stipe's and Buck's ambitions. They returned to Athens suitably inspired, and channeled this new energy into preparations for their upcoming debut.

Meanwhile, Butchart and Swartz filled out their own fledgling band with Jimmy Ellison—the ex-husband of Pylon's Vanessa Briscoe—on bass. "We both just naturally thought of Jimmy because he was this character around town," Butchart says. "And so we asked Jimmy if he wanted to play bass. He's like, 'I don't know how to play bass,' and Kit said, 'Don't worry, we'll show you what to do.'" Jimmy's lack of ability only accentuated the primitive surf-drone inherent in the music Swartz and Butchart had been working up. Butchart characterizes the Side Effects' resulting sound as that of "an instrumental band with vocals," Swartz's barked lyrics coming across almost as an afterthought.

As the fateful day approached, word of the party circulated throughout the larger UGA community. Kurt Wood remembers riding on a university bus down Milledge Avenue—the fraternity and sorority area—and over-hearing a girl telling her friend about the upcoming "party at that church place down on Oconee Street."

"I thought, man, word has really gotten out," Kurt says. The anticipation was probably augmented by the wild stories that had circulated about previous parties there, since Athens was a small town (its population in 1980 was around 40,000).

As a result of all this chatter, far more people showed up at the church on the night of April 5, 1980, than anyone had anticipated. Estimates put the attendance at anywhere between 300 and 600 people. Just about everyone remembers it as a hell of a party. Beyond that, details become hazy and contradictory; some people remember the band Turtle Bay (soon to be renamed Men in Trees) opening the show.* "They were kind of like a hippie hard rock band," Kurt Wood says. "They were OK. They were definitely experienced musicians but it wasn't really what I was there to see."

Next up were the Side Effects. "I think they did their first song, and it totally fell apart," Wood says. Which didn't seem to matter. Everyone loved the Side Effects. The party was roaring along by that point; a number of people remember the floorboards literally bending under the weight of everyone dancing. Kathleen had stationed the kegs outside, which helped keep the crowd dispersed, but there were still an awful lot of people inside that sanctuary, jumping around and sweating.

When their turn came, Berry, Buck, Mills, and Stipe took the "stage" fortified with booze, adrenaline, and take your pick of what else. Nerves ran high, and the performance certainly had all the shaky qualities of a debut. The band still hadn't even committed to a name. And yet something stood out. As Paul Butchart remembers, "They sounded more like a real band that was tight and everything. They were really good. I know they were better than us, but that didn't matter at the time."

Kurt Wood adds, "I thought they had the most . . . chops or whatever. It was still pretty loose. Everyone was pretty drunk."

Any partygoers who didn't lose track of time were probably surprised by the number of songs R.E.M. played. They did two sets, and included amid the generous quantity of covers were a number of songs that would remain in their set for years, a few of which would make it onto record: "Just a Touch," "All the Right Friends," and "Mystery to Me" among them. The covers included three songs that would become band signatures over the next few years: "There She Goes Again," "(I'm Not Your) Steppin' Stone," and "Secret Agent Man," along with crowd-pleasers by the Stones ("Honky Tonk Woman") and the Sex Pistols ("God Save the Queen").

By any measure it was a varied and impressive set list, all the more so for a band making its debut. Although no one could have predicted the turnout,

---

* Paul Butchart insists this is not the case. "Turtle Bay did *not* play the night of the first show at the Church. There was another party there earlier that year where they may have played." Paul's statement conflicts with the recollections of more than one other person present that night, but it carries weight because a) Butchart was in one of the bands that played; b) a flyer he had created for the event only mentions the Side Effects and Twisted Kites (an early R.E.M. name); and c) four bands seems like a lot, even for an epic Athens party. We are in *Rashomon* territory here.

the members of proto-R.E.M. clearly had had some kind of premonition that this would be an important performance and had prepared accordingly.

Perhaps the biggest surprise for those in attendance was just how animated Michael Stipe could get in front of an audience. Typically quiet and withdrawn, he turned into a spinning, vibrating maniac when performing the more aggressive songs. Almost no one in attendance had seen Gangster play, so almost no one had heard him sing before. In *It Crawled from the South*, Marcus Gray states that Stipe became virtually "incapacitated due to alcohol consumption toward the end of the band's set, necessitating the participation of audience members to help out on vocals." Gray suggests that the performance could have gone on longer but "the gig ended abruptly when half the group fell off the altar, the floor fell out, and Michael burned himself with a cigarette 'real bad.'"

That bit about the floor must have been an exaggeration. Or perhaps even the loss of the floor couldn't derail the event, since there was *another* band that performed later that evening: a trio of interlopers calling themselves the $windle$ who asked if they could play a few songs using the equipment the Side Effects and R.E.M. had been sharing. This group, so nearly forgotten except for the diligent efforts of the people who maintain the online R.E.M. Timeline, consisted of Chuck Connolly (known around town as "Chuxtry" due to his employment at, you guessed it, Wuxtry Records), his brother Paul, and a drummer named John Underwood. Paul Butchart remembers that "they sounded like a British cover band, right down to the fake accents." He also believes that it was the $windle$, *not* R.E.M., who performed "God Save the Queen"—an assertion that directly contradicts Bill Berry's own recollection, but, given the Dionysian nature of the evening in question, has at least as valid a claim to reliability. Or perhaps both bands played that song.

The $windle$ ended their short set with John Connolly yelling out in the snottiest Johnny Rotten impersonation he could manage, "Congratulations! You've just been swindled!"

No one had really gone there that night specifically to see R.E.M.; free beer was probably a much bigger incentive than any of the live music on offer. But clearly the new band had made an impression that would last beyond the hangover. As Kurt Wood drove away from the church in the early hours of the morning, his friend and passenger William Orten Carlton (known by everyone as "Ort") turned to him and said, half seriously, half tongue-in-cheek, "If they can keep this up, they're going to end up being bigger than the Beatles."

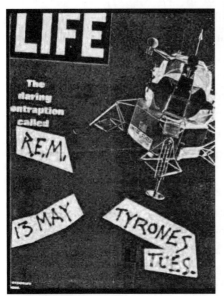

Posters for three Athens shows in 1980.
top left: **Tyrone's O.C., May 13;**
bottom left: **Tyrone's O.C., May 21;**
above: **Mad Hatter, June 30.**
Courtesy of Paul Butchart.

Chapter Five

On a late fall day way back in 1992, I sat nibbling on a quesadilla at Frijoleros while Ort, seated across from me, offered his theory on the origins of the name R.E.M.

"A lot of people think the letters stand for 'Rapid Eye Movement'" he said in his low, buttery voice. "That's not right at all. The band was actually named after Ralph Eugene Meatyard, the zen photographer. This man was largely unknown in his lifetime. He was married, had a family, and was an optician by trade. But on weekends and holidays he took these astonishing photographs and then, on one specific day each year, he developed them. He would say, 'Whatever develops develops, whatever doesn't doesn't.' And that's how it went, year after year."

Ort took a sip of his beer, sat quietly for a moment, and then added, "He was a member of the Lexington Kentucky Camera Club."

I don't remember how I first met Ort. I want to say it happened one evening not too long before the Meatyard conversation, at a popular downtown establishment called the Globe. ("The bar that wants to be a coffee shop," as one of my friends affectionately described it.) I had gotten to know the doorman—the drummer in a local band—and had somehow clouded his brain via flattery into believing I was of legal drinking age. On that particular night I saw Ort sitting by himself at the long bar and I walked over to say hello. Just about everyone knew Ort's face from the head shot that ran every week alongside his beer column in *Flagpole* magazine. Some also remembered his prominent role in the 1986 documentary *Athens, GA: Inside/Out*. As far back as anyone could remember, Ort had always looked the same: bespectacled, with slightly unkempt hair and a long, unruly beard, white T-shirt tucked into tight pants riding high up on his belly. He may have been born looking like that.

Ort was, and is, a storyteller par excellence, a de facto town historian and walking compendium of obscure facts and figures. He is what is commonly referred to in the South as a "local character." Historian and UGA alumnus Jeffery J. Rogers describes the Ort mystique like this:

Ort is one of those creatures that you'll only find in a place like Athens. If he were to go to a big anonymous city he'd probably have a tough time of it. I'm guessing he doesn't have a lot of money, and his employment record is probably spotty. But in Athens it's unlikely that he'll ever go without a hot dinner or friendly conversation. He's just part of the town.*

On that 1992 evening at the Globe, I found Ort sipping pale beer from a tall fluted glass with orange slices bobbing on the surface. He passed the glass over to me and said, "You should try this. It's called Hefeweizen. It's like drinking . . . flowers."

I raised the glass to my lips. Ort's description fitted the beverage just as perfectly as the nickname "Ort"—short, strange, forceful, unforgettable— fits the man. I've drunk many Hefeweizens since then, some of them at the Globe, but none of them has matched the one Ort handed me that night.

That was the beginning of our very casual association. I'm not sure introductions were ever made. I underwent a beer initiation in lieu of a handshake.

Anyway, about this Meatyard thing: In the years since Ort made that startling declaration to me in Frijoleros, I have read a number of books about R.E.M. Not one of them mentions Ralph Eugene Meatyard, zen photographer from Kentucky. So I started looking into Meatyard for myself. When I searched for his name online and clicked "images," the first photo that popped up was an untitled 1960 print that features a blurry figure draped in white, arms outstretched, apparently suspended in midair. This image reminded me strongly of a moment in R.E.M.'s "Losing My Religion" video when Stipe, also clad in white, falls to his knees, with angel's wings superimposed on his outstretched arms. Coincidence? Possibly. But there is a skewed sensibility to Meatyard's work that is entirely in line with the visual aesthetic Stipe displayed during his early years with R.E.M. Virtually any of Meatyard's photographs would have slotted perfectly into Stipe's collage-based album artwork. The two artists share a number of overlapping preoccupations: an interest in discarded junk, overgrown landscapes, blurred and/or obscured figures and objects, and a fondness for juxtaposing the vaguely grotesque with the mundane. Meatyard typically asked his subjects (usually his own children) to don ghoulish Halloween masks before posing them in Norman

---

* Things got a bit chillier in September 2015, when Ort was arrested and spent the better part of two days in jail for a probation violation stemming from the dilapidated condition of his home. Given that his home has been in much the same condition for some time, we could call this the end of an era.

Front cover of Ralph Eugene Meatyard's *The Family Album of Lucybelle Crater* (Jargon Society, 1974); front and back covers of *Ralph Eugene Meatyard* (Aperture, 1974).

Rockwell–style tableaux. (He broke from this approach in his portraits of the celebrated Catholic mystic Thomas Merton, preferring to photograph the monk unmasked, though often blurred.)

Viewing photo after photo, I get a very strong sense that Ralph Eugene Meatyard must have exerted an influence on the young Michael Stipe—on his art and personality at the very least, if not also on his band's name.

In 2012 I reconnect with Ort with the intention of following up on the Meatyard angle. Ort agrees to an interview on one condition: I am to seek out a craft beer local to my new home state (Arizona) and bring him a supply ("cans preferred"). I initially propose that we meet at our old stomping ground, the Globe, but it turns out that Ort and some of his cohorts have, for unspecified reasons, been banned from that establishment for life. So instead we convene at Copper Creek Brewing Company, just a few blocks down.

Seeing Ort again, it's shocking to realize that twenty years have passed since our last discussion of this subject. The man has changed little; he has always looked simultaneously boyish and wizened, and his long, scraggly beard gives him the look of a Civil War draft resister, or perhaps a jolly, not entirely human character from the Tolkien universe. There is much white in that beard now, and his pace has slowed, but he still has the same full-bore enthusiasm for all manner of arcana.

After placing a six-pack of Kiltlifter on the table, I begin our conversation by reminding Ort of our previous talk at Frijoleros, when he had told me matter-of-factly about the Ralph Eugene Meatyard connection. "Why do you believe that R.E.M. was named after him?" I ask.

"Well, it's just a hunch, really. But I have gotten some feedback along the lines of: Yes, that was a deciding factor. Meatyard maintained a large correspondence, and when he sent out prints of his pictures, he would write, 'Thanks for asking, r.e.m.' On R.E.M.'s first few posters, when they were just starting to play out, they wrote the name exactly that way—in lowercase letters with the periods.

"I remember going to Louisville, Kentucky, in, let's say, 1986, when I was following Government Cheese, which was a Bowling Green band. And I opened a phone book and there was *Meatyard, Ralph Eugene, Mrs.* living in a house on Glenwood that he had bought. It was the same house. I came back to Athens and I ran into Stipe and said, 'Michael, Ralph Eugene Meatyard's widow is still alive, and she's living in the house on Glenwood.' He knew what I was talking about, because there's a marvelous book put out by the Jargon Society of North Carolina of Meatyard's photographs. You can find it occasionally in the library; a lot of them are falling apart and you'd be hard-pressed to check them out. But when Ralph Meatyard died at the age of 45 in 1972, he willed all of his photographs to the University of Kentucky, rights-free, in fact, and you can obtain copies—" Ort breaks off and begins trembling. A panicked thought briefly enters my mind that he may be having some sort of seizure, and I reach out and hold his arm. He chokes back a sob and continues: "—from them for free, because he didn't feel that he was doing anything special. I'm almost positive I'm correct on this. He never did photography for money; he did it to assuage his demons."

Now, there are two ways to evaluate Ort's unexpected show of emotion. One is that the guy is cracking up. That's what you might think if you didn't know Ort or his history with this town. The other is to be moved by the level of empathy he has for his fixations: whether we're talking about Meatyard or Philip K. Dick or D. W. Griffith, he seems to conjure up their ghosts—and, for that matter, their demons—when he speaks of them. He's all in with this stuff. And any discomfort or surprise I initially feel is soon replaced by recognition of a trait we share: we both spend a lot of our time wandering through the lives and experiences of others.

Ort continues as if nothing has happened. "I get the feeling from what research I've done about Meatyard that he must have been an incredibly intense person who worked on one thing or another day and night, day and night, day and night, slept very little, and ate when he got hungry, because these things simply didn't occur to him. He was a true original, and it's hard to find someone who is totally original, whose work is not like anything else.

"Michael Stipe asked me once—he asked obliquely the question—where had Meatyard's imagination come from? And I felt like asking him, where did *your* imagination come from? I've always thought Michael Stipe was a genius."

Our conversation carries on in much the same vein for the next few hours as the bar gets louder and we get deeper into our cups. Finally, our evening reaches its natural close when a beautiful blonde who can't be a day over 18 asks me if I will take a picture of her and Ort. Is she seeking a memento of the night she met one of the great legends of Athens, Georgia—a figure as inextricably linked with the town's history and lore as the black iron arch that marks the entrance to North Campus? No, it's not that. She thinks he looks like Santa Claus and this would make a fun photo for her Facebook page. Ort doesn't mind one bit. He gamely poses with her and asks that she e-mail him a copy.

Here's one of the many things I love about Ort: he may think that Stipe is a genius on a par with Ralph Eugene Meatyard, and he may even think R.E.M. is a band whose stature equals that of the Beatles, but I suspect that, in Ort's beautiful, whimsical way of looking at the universe, neither Stipe nor his great band will ever match the achievements of Government Cheese. And who is to say that his is not the correct ranking of things? R.E.M., after all, never wrote a song called "Fish Stick Day."

Continuing my Meatyard investigation, I burrow deeper into the Internet and come across two leads—thin ones, admittedly, but intriguing nonetheless. On a blog called *Unusual Kentucky*, artist and author Jeffrey Scott Holland writes, "In an early interview, Michael Stipe said that R.E.M. actually stood for Ralph Eugene Meatyard, a Kentuckian best known for his epic photographic work *The Family Album of Lucybelle Crater*."* Then, on the *Online Photographer* website, I find the following comment from James Rhem: "For years I've heard the rumor that the name of the band derived from the enthusiasm of one of its members for the photography of Ralph Eugene Meatyard. I tried to track this down and got close but never confirmed it."

Surely, I think, Kurt Wood will know something about this. Not only is he as near to a best friend as Ort has in the world, but he was also an acquaintance of the band at the very time they were choosing a name for themselves. I put the question to him.

"I don't know that story about the photographer," Wood answers. "I'm not familiar with him. That's the first time I've ever heard that, actually."

I was there at one of the naming sessions, I remember that. It was some time after the party. I think there were some people hanging

---

* Attempts to source this Stipe interview have proved unsuccessful.

out, and it was like, "Let's come up with a name." Mine was Fort Pain or something like that. I think Pete had Negro Wives. There was just all this . . . Cans of Piss* and all this ridiculous stuff, not taking it too seriously. It seems to me that maybe Michael Stipe came up with the name R.E.M.—not right then, but shortly after that.

So far, then, nothing directly contradicts Ort's theory. But leave it to Billy Holmes to further deepen the mystery:

I know there have been several theories about where the name R.E.M. came from, and I know Pete said he just opened the dictionary and pointed to the first thing he came to. But I do find it interesting that when you used to drive up Prince Avenue, into Normal Town, there were two big signs there. One said *AZ Rock* . . . it was like a painting or tiling company. Well, the big local cover band was AZ Rock. They named their band after the tiling company, and it was obvious why: they played rock from A to Z. . . The other big sign there said *REM Studios*. I think it was a photography studio.

For me this just about settles it. The evidence is only circumstantial, and it's very possible that Peter Buck and the rest of the band took the initials to stand for "rapid eye movement," but I believe Stipe was thinking of photography in general and Ralph Eugene Meatyard specifically when he lobbied for the name. The fact that the initials also refer to a deep, dream-filled phase of the sleep cycle would probably have been seen as icing on the cake. The world of photography and art was arguably more deeply embedded in Stipe's psyche than music was,† and it makes sense that he would draw on that background for inspiration.

It's tempting to oversell the similarities between Stipe and Meatyard, and I have possibly done so here. But I'd be willing to bet that anyone reading this who takes the time to delve into Meatyard's work will come away with similar impressions. As Ort says, "It's just a hunch," but in the murky world of R.E.M. that's as solid a foundation as any.

---

* According to Paul Butchart, this was actually Can O' Peas: "a pun on canopies suggested by Peter Buck's father. Bill Berry in an early interview mentions they could have also been called Can of Piss, mistaking the pun."

Other contenders not mentioned by Wood: The Third Wave and Slut Bank.

† During a 2016 appearance on Alec Baldwin's *Here's the Thing* podcast, Stipe referred to photography as "my first love."

At any rate, the members of R.E.M. have always deflected questions about the band's name, saying that it could mean anything. I suppose I ought to take advantage of the friendly, informal line of communication I have with the R.E.M. office and push for an official answer to this one question. But you know what? I can't bring myself to do it. What if Michael suddenly decided to give a frank answer? I wouldn't be able to bear it. Such an outcome would run counter to the sense of mystery that drew so many of us to this band in the first place. Let it stand.

Before we move on, though, a few words regarding those runner-up names. I may be wrong about this, but I'm guessing that a band of ostensibly Southern white guys calling themselves Negro Wives would not have gotten much traction. Then again, had the guys gone with that name instead of R.E.M., they would almost certainly have avoided the ignominy of being called "one of the nation's most liberal and politically correct rock groups" by the *Los Angeles Times* in 1996.

As for the other favorites: Can you imagine "And here's Slut Bank with 'Radio Free Europe'" slipping off of any announcer's tongue? Similarly, reviewers would probably have a tough time discussing "*Fables of the Reconstruction*, the new album from Cans of Piss" with any semblance of dignity. Sometimes a rose by any other name really doesn't smell as sweet.

T. Patton Biddle was not part of the art school crowd. Nor was he a new waver. In fact, like David Pierce, he was several years older than most of the people in the nascent scene. Already fairly accomplished in the music business, with a decade of playing and sound engineering behind him, he arrived in Athens in July 1980 to assist his friends in the band Turtle Bay with their various sound needs. They worked out an arrangement whereby Pat would lug the PA he and the band co-owned to whichever of the small clubs around town they were playing that night, do their sound to make some extra money, then take everything back down the street to the band's practice space in the so-called Triangle Building that also housed Farmer's Hardware. He cut quite a figure with his long hair, wild beard, and hulking frame swathed in an old West Point parade dress uniform, hauling that massive PA piece by piece up a steep hill with a handcart. And his expertise on the board made an equally strong impression. Before long, his pre-Athens nickname—Pat the Wiz— had spread throughout the scene, and more than a few people referred to him simply as "Wiz."

Pat had recently become a vegetarian—not an easy lifestyle to maintain

Pat the Wiz's business card. Courtesy of Paul Butchart.

in the deep South in 1980. But Athens boasted one vegetarian restaurant, the Bluebird Café, which was also heavily frequented by aspiring veggie Michael Stipe. One morning, Pat was standing outside the restaurant talking with Bob Hay of the band the Corks (soon to be renamed the Squalls) when he noticed "this kid with orange hair." Stipe introduced himself and invited Pat over to R.E.M.'s new practice space on Jackson Street to hear them play. Somehow, it seems, he never mentioned the name of his band. The two walked the several blocks over to the space and fell into an easy rapport. Despite their differences in age and personality, they'd had similar upbringings: Pat had also been a military brat and had lived in Germany, France, Texas, Montana, and Alabama, while his family on his mother's side had roots in Georgia going back several generations. This common background did not emerge completely during that first conversation, but it no doubt informed a shared language and worldview that enabled Pat to hit it off more easily with Stipe than most people would manage to do.

The two arrived at the practice space to find a note from Peter taped to the door. Bill and Mike had to go back to work, so there would be no practice today. However, a couple of girls were hanging around, waiting for Michael to show up; one of them also sported orange hair. They went inside and Michael promptly sat down at a Farfisa organ set up in the corner and started banging away like some eccentric composer played by Vincent Price in a Hammer horror film. The girls watched, entranced.

Pat took his leave, perplexed but also a little impressed: he knew from their conversation that Stipe's band had only been around for a couple of months, yet they already seemed to have fans.

A few months later the two met again when Pat was working the door at Tyrone's O.C. nightclub. R.E.M. were scheduled to play that night. Pat had heard of them. He knew they were a new but already very popular band. When Stipe walked up to the door, Pat began to ask for his ID but was cut off by his fellow door-person Libby. "He's in the band," she said.

Pat looked at Stipe. "Michael, you're in R.E.M.?"

Pat would go on to run sound for R.E.M. at a number of local and regional performances—most notably a string of headlining gigs at Tyrone's in the summer and fall of 1981. And he accompanied the band on their first foray to New York City, working the board for them when they played the Ritz.

That was in July 1981, just a year and a few months after the band's formation. They had packed a lot into that first year: 74 documented performances all over the Southeast and beyond, plus multiple recording sessions. They had also secured both a manager and a lawyer—albeit one who was still in law school. That would be Bertis Downs IV, who forged his relationship with the band at their second-ever performance (and first under the R.E.M.—or, more accurately, r.e.m.—name) at a little venue called the 11.11 Koffee Klub. Downs was an earnest young man, a missionary's son who had surely inherited some of his father's intensity. A huge music fan, he already knew Peter Buck from Wuxtry; the two shared a love of Neil Young and liked to trade records. Downs also knew Bill Berry via their mutual friend John Huie, who had worked with Berry and Ian Copeland at Paragon.

The Koffee Klub gig ended up getting cut short by the cops—the venue had neglected to secure a liquor license—but Downs had heard all he needed to hear. Echoing what Ort had told Kurt Wood, Bertis openly predicted that R.E.M. would become bigger than the Beatles.

It would nevertheless be overstating the case to say that Bertis Downs pledged his life to R.E.M. there and then. Like most law students nearing graduation, he had plans to go out into the wide world and ply his trade. His personal goal was to land a position with a legal aid firm. But when the Reagan administration took office in January 1981, it immediately began cutting budgets for such services. "There were absolutely no legal aid jobs anywhere in the country," Downs later told reporter Julie Phillips. "I got all these letters back saying, 'Thank you for your resume . . . but we're not hiring, because there's a freeze and we don't even have a budget.' So that's why I ended up staying here and teaching." So what started as an occasional bit of informal legal advice regarding fees and contracts ultimately blossomed into something much more significant. Like many of the fortuitous events in the R.E.M. story, Bertis's long-term involvement was an accident that gave the impression of having been carefully planned.

But back to 1980. R.E.M. began their live career with an advantage few bands are granted: their first performance at the church had been so well attended, and had gone over so well, that practically overnight they became one of the most popular bands in Athens. Granted, the moment they set foot outside town they were back to square one. Their popularity in Athens did not enable them to sidestep playing to audiences of five in shitty run-down clubs across small-town America. They had to pay their dues like anyone else. But in Athens they were essentially guaranteed a packed house from the very beginning. Just as Kathleen's party had been gate-crashed by a bunch

Packed house agrees that R.E.M. was the real headliner

Why Memorial Hall?

UGA UNION
PRESENTS A FREAK WEEK CONCERT WITH

the BRAINS

THURS., MAY 15, 7PM
LEGION FIELD
AND SPECIAL GUESTS
R.E.M.

NO ADMISSION
RAIN LOC.: MEM. HALL

Above: review from the *Red and Black* of R.E.M. opening for the Brains in Memorial Hall, and advertisement for the show; left: early zine review of R.E.M. from *Useless Knowledge* (Summer 1980).

```
6 JUNE*WARHOUSE*SPACE HEATERS
RED MEAT AND SPROUTS*R.E.M.

WHAT A GREAT IDEA, USING THE
WAREHOUSE FOR PARTIES. BANDS
AND BEER AND LOTS OF FUN. SPACE
HEATERS DIDN'T IMPRESS ME MUCH
ANOTHER POP BAND THAT SEEMS TO
BE NEW WAVE BECAUSE IT'S FASHION-
ABLE. RED MEAT AND SPROUTS, I'M
SORRY TO SAY FELL FLAT ON THEIR
FACE, APPARENTLY TOM WAS TOO DRUNK
TO PERFORM, BUT FORTUNATELY MOST
OF THE AUDIENCE WAS TOO DRUNK
TOO NOTICE. R.E.M. (RAPID EYE
MOVEMENT) IS ANOTHER ATHENS BAND
ONCE AGAIN WITH THAT GREAT 60'S
SOUND. THIS BAND DOES LOTS OF
COVERS, BUT DOES THEM WELL. GREAT
FOR DANCING AND FUN.
```

35

of fraternity and sorority types, so too their subsequent club gigs pulled a crowd drawn from across the student body. So R.E.M. never belonged to the art scene, even if their immediate circle of friends hailed from that group. They didn't go through an incubation period of playing the kind of intimate Athens house parties where men walked around in dresses and women wore outrageous wigs. Quite the contrary: they were, in the words of Rodger Lyle Brown, "dude rock."

This may be difficult to fathom now, on the other side of the band's 1991 "Losing My Religion" video, in which Michael Stipe and director Tarsem Singh introduced the world to a disorienting mishmash of highbrow lit (nods to Gabriel García Márquez's story "A Very Old Man with Enormous Wings"), surreal homoeroticism, religious imagery, and some highly idiosyncratic dancing from Stipe, but back in 1980 R.E.M. were a go-to band for frat boys who had little on their minds other than getting drunk and getting laid.

A recording made at Wuxtry Records in June 1980 captures the band just two months into their public existence, and it is an R.E.M. quite different from both the delicate yearnings of "Losing My Religion" and the overcast jangle of their just-over-the-horizon *Chronic Town* EP. Stipe may have telegraphed his high-art pretensions in his selection of a band name, but they did not carry over into the material itself. Not that these early songs aren't filled with hooks: Peter Buck's love of the Monkees had clearly served the band well, and on this first recording they are exceptionally tight—remarkably so given the brief amount of time they had been playing together. A lot of people talk about what a poor guitarist Buck was in the beginning, but to my ears his playing on this tape sounds sharp and inventive. At this early stage he had already developed his trademark style of alternated staccato strikes followed by torrents of fast-picked arpeggios. This gave an effect of continual tension and release throughout each song. It's solid stuff they're playing, and, most crucially for the Athens dance crowd, it has a strong backbeat.

The recording displays some weaknesses, of course. For one thing, as noted earlier, Stipe's lyrics are still undeveloped and largely uninspired at this early stage. What's more, the songs are repetitive in both tempo and structure. The style is very much 1950s first-wave rock 'n' roll—the verses of "Narrator" bear more than a passing melodic resemblance to Eddie Cochran's "Summertime Blues," for instance—but twangy and sped-up, kind of like a rockabilly Ramones. What's interesting is that this throwback style doesn't really reflect what any of the guys were listening to at the time. Based on their tastes alone, one would have expected a Patti Smith-Monkees-Motown hybrid (I'm still waiting to hear that band). But it's likely they went for the 1950s sound because the chord progressions were simple enough that they could all lock in and excel with the material. Which meant they sounded polished right out of the gate.

There is one notable exception here: a song called "All the Right Friends" surpasses these limitations and is by any standard a fairly accomplished piece of pop songwriting. Musically, it represents the first foray into what would become the classic R.E.M. sound: it has multiple clearly defined sections punctuated by dramatic stops and starts, ebullient guitar jangling during the verses, rhythmic variation on the bridge, and a tantalizing buildup to a soaring, hummable chorus. Then there's the contrast between the joyous music and the downbeat lyrics. "I don't wanna be with you anymore," Stipe sang. "I just don't want you anymore."

Stipe's early relationship songs were almost all preoccupied—on a superficial level at least—with a fear of commitment. On a deeper level he seemed to be fighting against any outside attempts to define him or hem him in. "All the Right Friends" marked his first successful attempt at getting these ideas across without sounding juvenile. It is not a lyrical masterpiece by any stretch of the imagination, but it gets the job done. "I've been walking alone now / For a long, long time," Stipe sings. "I don't wanna hang out now / With the friends who just aren't mine." It's simplistic, but there's a hint of a Dylan-style put-down in there. Had Stipe pursued this thread, he might have moved into the realm of confessional songwriting. As it turned out, "All the Right Friends" marked an end rather than a beginning. From this point forward, his lyrics would become increasingly oblique. And while he wouldn't abandon the subject of romantic relationships entirely, future treatments of that subject would be carefully veiled.

No one was paying much attention to his words at this point, though. Michael Stipe's most notable contribution to R.E.M.'s early success was visual.

How to describe the 1980–1982 Stipe stage persona? Let's try it from several angles. Imagine a malfunctioning robot trained as a whirling dervish. Or Elvis attempting to do his swivel-hipped dance while being assaulted by a gang of poltergeists. Or . . . James Brown having an epileptic fit? Stipe would careen around the stage wildly, with apparently no self-awareness, narrowly avoiding collisions with his bandmates. What matters is that he was in a constant state of frenetic motion, and, no matter how strange his movements, he was locked into the beat. Again, this might be hard to fathom for people who only know the "Losing My Religion" video, but the guy was a hell of a dancer. And when you saw him onstage going crazy to that music, you couldn't help but start moving yourself. Dancing was absolutely intrinsic to the vibe and the success of early R.E.M. The mystique and the thoughtfulness would come later. R.E.M. were, first and foremost, the premier party band in town.

That type of success brought with it unique challenges, particularly in a town as cliquish and insular as Athens. It wasn't too long before the band came to be resented by certain segments of the very community that had birthed it. A "Beatles vs. Stones"–style argument coalesced around R.E.M. and Pylon: Pylon were regarded as the artistically pure choice, whereas R.E.M. were somewhat questionable due to their overtly poppy sound and their fondness for crowd-pleasing covers. The two bands got along pretty well, though Curtis Crowe acknowledged that there was a schism. "I remember liking R.E.M. a lot," he told journalist Denise Sullivan in 1994, "except they were doing a lot of cover songs and at the time the whole art school/party crowd had this thing about cover songs. We were on the 'leading edge of a musical revolution' and we thought playing cover songs was taking two steps back and everyone kind of put their nose in the air about that."

Mike Green, a member of Atlanta-based band the Fans (one of Peter Buck's favorites), was blunter in his assessment: "I recognized early that they were like the 'digestible-by-frat-boys' version of the Athens sound."

Did such criticisms catalyze Stipe into writing stranger lyrics? It's quite possible. Certainly, by the time R.E.M. cut their first EP in 1981 they had moved well beyond the frat/party band sound. But it's also likely that Stipe's art school interests began to insinuate themselves naturally into his lyrics. Of the four band members, Stipe was the only one who enjoyed his studies, and, not coincidentally, he was the last to drop out of UGA when R.E.M. began to be successful. His two areas of focus at the school were painting and photography, and through his teacher Scott Belville he came into contact with the work of a local folk artist named Howard Finster. Finster had a childlike quality. He listened closely to his dreams, and his dreams told him to make five thousand paintings in service of the Lord and erect an elaborate Paradise Garden full of sculptures and knick-knacks. The former Baptist minister lived for his art. And his art, in turn, was meant to spread the Gospel of Jesus Christ.

Though Stipe had distanced himself from his Methodist upbringing as he became an adult, he quickly fell under the spell of Finster's work and personality. Paradise Garden—located in Summerville, Georgia—became one of his favorite spots to while away an afternoon. He may not have connected—at least consciously—with the religiosity of Finster's work, but the older man's quirkiness, originality, and lack of guile surely appealed to him. It's also possible that the Reverend Finster's evangelism triggered memories of the singer's preacher grandfather.

Stipe kept one foot in this art world for a couple of semesters after the band began, but once he went all in with R.E.M. he channeled his visual art aspirations into his management of the band's image. At first this consisted of flyers for shows, but it grew to encompass album artwork and other promotional materials.

The most ambitious member of R.E.M. in its first year was unquestionably Bill Berry. He had resisted the idea of playing music as a career path for many years, never believing it to be a viable option for him. Now that he found himself, suddenly, in a popular band, he seized the reins and determined to pursue it with the same level of seriousness he would have brought to an entrepreneurial dream. What else could he do? Things were not looking too good for his career as a student after all. Between gigging, practicing, and his part-time job at the local Holiday Inn, not to mention partying with his new friends, there remained little time for his studies. His grades and attendance dropped precipitously. Unlike Mills, who never really figured out what he was going to study at UGA, Berry had come in with a plan. To kiss that goodbye meant that he'd have to transfer his ambitions to his new venture.

"The thing that I really respected about him," Kathleen O'Brien says,

was that once they made the commitment of, okay, we're going to name the band and we are going to play in public and make money, from that moment Bill was adamant that the only way he was going to be part of it was if they treated it like a business. It was not just going to be them going out getting drunk playing. His whole approach to it was just very pragmatic and very realistic and very much an investment to secure their future. He was practical, he was grounded.

As a result of this decision, and given her closeness to the band as Bill's girlfriend, Kathleen became R.E.M.'s de facto co-manager, roadie, and chauffeur. Initially the band members didn't have any means of transportation, so her car became the first band "van." Sometimes she would drive them to gigs, sometimes she would just hand over the keys. Additionally, she helped get many of the early shows scheduled. "I was helping [Bill] do a good bit of the early bookings," she says,

> using what little contact I had through the club scene and through my days as a DJ. Though I couldn't be the manager, you know? Nope, nope, nope, I was his girlfriend. Couldn't be the manager even though I was doing managerial stuff. So that's when they went seeking a fifth party that could manage them.

That fifth party turned out to be Jefferson Holt, though it would be a while before the record store manager from Chapel Hill, North Carolina, would ascend to the official role of manager and "fifth member of R.E.M." Holt first booked, and then attended, the band's shows at the Station in Carrboro on July 18 and 19, 1980. He went back for more in Raleigh on July 21.

Jefferson Holt is one of the most problematic figures in R.E.M.'s history—problematic because the band members and their remaining management did their best to erase him from the R.E.M. story following their acrimonious split with him in 1996. They have been surprisingly successful in scrubbing his association with the band from the Internet, though there's nothing to be

done about the various pre-1996 R.E.M. books and articles in which Holt features prominently. As of this writing, he appears directly in just one clip on YouTube, as a participant in a 1988 video feed that went out to employees of Warner Bros. Records—the band's then-new label. In that clip, Holt comes across as a combination of Michael Stipe and the actor James Spader. Like Stipe, he is thin and somewhat gangly and conveys a sort of quirky charm mixed with an air of slumming Southern aristocracy. With Spader he shares an owlish face that seems to be constantly suppressing a smirk, along with a sharp dress sense and an ever-present pair of spectacles. His Southern accent is of the lilting, genteel type.

There is considerably more to be found online concerning Jefferson's mother, Bertha Merrill ("B.") Holt, a former member of the North Carolina House of Representatives. Her nearly twenty-year tenure in the House was distinguished by a commitment to the rights of minorities and women, culminating in the 1993 passage of legislation that removed a husband's exemption from the North Carolina rape laws. Bertha and her husband, Clay Holt, had three children, of whom Jefferson was the youngest.

At the time of R.E.M.'s shows in Carrboro, Jefferson was parlaying the many connections he'd developed in his record-store day job into a side business booking bands at local clubs. "I made use of what I had and I talked the clubs into booking bands," he later recounted. "But it was all in play . . . Everybody was just having a blast partying and wanted to make something happen so you could keep having fun and not have to get a real job."

It was in this capacity that Jefferson booked three North Carolina shows for Pylon. But Pylon pulled out and recommended their friends the Method Actors in their stead. The Method Actors bailed too, leaving Jefferson with three open slots he needed to fill quickly. A friend recommended R.E.M., which led to a phone call with Bill Berry and the securing of R.E.M.'s first string of out-of-state gigs. They had only recently graduated from using Kathleen's car to a beat-up van purchased with their show earnings.

Jefferson, like just about everyone in Chapel Hill, had never heard of R.E.M. and had no idea what to expect. But he dutifully showed up at the Station on July 18 and began working the door (another of his side gigs). Two factors conspired to make this a memorable evening for him. The first was the band's incendiary performance, which he likened to the Who. The other was the surprise arrival of the R.E.M. "wives"—Kathleen O'Brien, Linda Hopper, and Leslie Michel—in Kathleen's Plymouth Satellite. The girls began dancing on the bar, which kicked the show into a higher gear.

Shortly after his long weekend with the band—working the shows, partying with the Athens crowd, and getting swept up in the excitement of R.E.M.'s blitzkrieg performances, Holt made his way down to Athens, presumably to ascertain if there was more where this lot had come from. By October, he had taken up permanent residence in "the Classic City."

"Jefferson came to town, didn't have a job, and decided he wanted to be a band manager," Billy Holmes says.

> This is what Jefferson told me out of his own mouth. So, he asked if he could be [R.E.M.'s] manager.
>
> Well, you know, I would go to the post office to send out promo packages and stuff for my bands. And I swear to you I never went to the post office when I did not see Jefferson Holt in line, mailing some R.E.M. stuff out to somebody. He worked really, really hard for them, and is kind of like the Brian Epstein of R.E.M.

The band at that point had nothing to its name other than a van and some musical equipment. But, in collaboration with Bertis Downs, they registered themselves as a corporation. Several months elapsed between Jefferson's arrival in town and his appointment as band manager, but the rules of their legal arrangement would subsequently be amended to name Jefferson Holt as the official fifth member of the organization—to share equally in all of R.E.M.'s future successes.

This unusual arrangement seems to have motivated Holt to work his ass off, even though he didn't know the first thing about managing a band. But he did possess four crucial traits: he was good at talking to people, he had a strong work ethic, he knew how to book gigs, and he could drive.

Velena Vego, a musician (and later a booking agent and manager) who dated Holt in the mid-'80s, sums up his management style:

> One thing that was great about Jefferson, that no other manager did, was he toured with the band. He met every single college radio person. Nobody was not important to him. Before that, managers were in Los Angeles and New York. They're sitting behind the big desk with the cigar. They certainly didn't shake hands and kiss babies. Jefferson knew the routes and he was in the van with them. He knew every single one of their personalities, and every one of their personalities is quite different. It was funny because I would say, "If you're with Peter you're acting one way and if you're with Stipe you're acting another way." I was in my early twenties observing how different he was with each band member. He had to be. He really took care of all of them.

This would remain the band's template for touring through the end of the decade, the sole change being that the van was eventually replaced.

R.E.M. played just two additional out-of-state shows in 1980: at Phrank 'N' Steins in Nashville on July 26, and at a club called, appropriately enough, the Last Lap, in Knoxville, Tennessee, sometime near the end of the year. Their other 17 performances were split between Athens and Atlanta. Almost all of these were headlining slots, with one notable exception: on December 6 the band played for an audience of 4,000 at the Fox Theatre in Atlanta, supporting the Police. This plum gig was the direct result of Bill Berry's ongoing friendship with Ian Copeland. The band made the most of this opportunity, delivering a typically barnstorming performance, although Stipe's overexuberance, coupled with the band's lack of experience with big shows, caused some issues. Woody Nuss, who ran sound at a good number of R.E.M.'s earliest local shows, was in attendance that night and later told journalist Denise Sullivan:

> R.E.M. had no idea how to behave at a big rock show and they were kind of messing up. Michael invited the audience up on stage at the Fox, which you can't do because of the orchestra pit, and the audience rushed the stage. The band got in huge amounts of trouble. They had no crew, but they brought this guy from Athens down to tune guitars and do stuff. Someone at the Fox described him as a shave-headed speed freak. He was loading out drums through dressing rooms full of people and doing stuff you shouldn't do. They got in trouble from everybody and things were flying around like, "You'll never play in this town again."

Within a couple of years R.E.M. would be headlining the Fox on a regular basis.

Most of the band's Athens shows were at either Tyrone's O.C. or a new club called the 40 Watt. The former served as R.E.M.'s home base for about the first two years of their existence. The latter, which had been founded by Curtis Crowe of Pylon and his friend Paul Scales, went through a number of locations and eventually became Athens's signature club. (Velena Vego was later the 40 Watt's booker.) The Side Effects played the Watt's inaugural show, Pylon was a mainstay, and R.E.M. became regulars as well. They would do spur-of-the-moment surprise gigs there to test-run new material long after they hit the big time—a practice that continued into the early 1990s.

As for Tyrone's O.C. (which stood for "Old Chameleon"—a nod to the club's former name), it had begun hosting a New Wave Night right around the time R.E.M. made their debut at the church. R.E.M. came to quickly dominate

Stipe and R.E.M. will be at the 40 Watt Club Friday

this slot and were the club's most popular weekend draw. Tyrone's could legally hold only 600 people, but it was not unusual for R.E.M., once they really hit their stride, to draw a thousand. In an attempt to accommodate everyone, the club's owners would remove any piece of furniture that was not nailed to the floor. "The way we figured out that R.E.M. was the biggest band in town," says Billy Holmes, "was that the rest of us were charging $1 and $1.50 cover at Tyrone's."

They were charging $2 and the place would be packed. It was like, "Wow…R.E.M. charges fifty cents more a head than we do. They must be very big."

I did see the very first R.E.M. show at the 40 Watt, and there were three things that stuck in my mind. One was: Boy, these guys are really bad! Number two, the chemistry between them was just amazing. It was a powerful thing—you could feel it. And three, the place was packed wall-to-wall.

I went up to Pete Buck afterward and I said, "Hey, you guys don't need to add a keyboard player, do you?" And Peter said, "Are you kidding? We can't get it together with bass, drums, and guitar. How are we going to get it together with a keyboard player?"

Paul Butchart was also at that first 40 Watt show. "This is hard to describe," he says, "but I remember the crowd was dancing so much that the floor was moving up and down and the windows were pumping in and out like an accordion. It was just too crowded up there for me. The windows were sweating and all that stuff. If one of those windows had popped or somebody had opened the door downstairs, the floor would have collapsed—because it was like a big air chamber."

Things were definitely moving for R.E.M., and it's likely these blowout gigs in their hometown fortified the band for more sparsely attended performances in places like Augusta, Georgia; Charlotte, North Carolina; and Murfreesboro, Tennessee. Bill Berry remained a motivating force in terms of road strategy. He continued to work off of Ian Copeland's club circuit playbook. Having seen how successful that method had been in building an audience base for the Police and Squeeze, he strongly favored it over the Athens-and-New-York-City-only approach taken by Pylon and the B-52's. Indeed, there appeared to have been a conscious decision among the four members of R.E.M. to avoid playing New York City for as long as possible. It's unclear whether they simply felt intimidated or if they had some carefully thought-out plan to hone their skills away from the spotlight (and Augusta was most definitely out of the spotlight, even if the club they played there was called, oddly enough, New York, New York). The result of this delay—deliberate or otherwise—was that when they finally did hit the Big Apple, they looked and sounded like a band that knew what it was doing.

By the middle of 1980, the nucleus of the Athens music scene had migrated from the church on Oconee Street to a number of houses on Barber Street, just outside the downtown area. Michael Stipe, Linda Hopper, and their friends Mike Huff, Mark Phredd, and Leslie Michel took up residence at 169 Barber, a large dilapidated house at the top of a hill. Peter Buck and Mike Mills, along with their respective girlfriends, Ann and Lauren, moved into houses nearby. Bill and Kathleen had a place together in a different neighborhood, but eventually Bill too felt the pull and moved in with Mike Mills at 285 Barber, while Jefferson Holt duly moved into 169. Members of Pylon, the Side Effects, the $windle$, and a new band called Love Tractor all lived on the street, too.

On Barber, the nonstop party that had begun in the church continued at full velocity. Bill Berry's decision one night to tee up a bunch of empty beer bottles and smash them with his golf clubs was no anomaly. But Barber Street also became the new focal point for the DIY activities that had initially been incubated by the art school. Ingrid Schorr, a UGA English major (and onetime resident of Reed Hall) who fell in with the scene in early 1980 and joined the exodus to Barber, explains the mind-set:

> We all influenced each other and encouraged each other. Yeah, pick up a movie camera. Make a movie. Write a play. Put it on in an alley. We had nothing. It was so exciting to use a color Xerox machine. I'd go to the library and dump out everything in my bag and use all my money to make a color Xerox, 'cause that was the most exciting thing ever.

Schorr's many roles within the scene are illustrative of the low-budget, anything-goes creativity she describes. She played briefly in bands with

Carol Levy, Linda Hopper, and Lynda Stipe. She participated in neighborhood-wide "games," the most memorable being called the Loud Family—named, Schorr later wrote,

partly after the PBS documentary we all remembered only for the fabulously campy figure of Lance Loud, the son who came out of the closet during the series. Mostly it was called the Loud Family because we pretended to be New Yorkers who all lived within shouting distance of each other's tenement apartment windows (a setting based on the opening credits of *Welcome Back, Kotter*). In reality we all lived in airy, unheated Victorian houses with gigantic porches and for the most part had not a clue about New York or New Yorkers. I played a "neighbor" of the Louds called Minnie Minnola, an aspiring fashion model. Michael Stipe was called Shep; he might have been a plumber or something. That was the Loud Family: We just had these fake names and fake jobs and yelled at each other in fake New York accents.

But while her whimsical and creatively restless nature informed much of the spirit of the scene and has served Schorr well in her subsequent careers as a multidisciplinary artist, academic, and administrator, her greatest contribution to the R.E.M. story came about entirely by accident. By being summoned back to her family's home in Rockville, Maryland, right in the middle of the nonstop Barber Street party, she became the unwitting muse of one of R.E.M.'s best-loved early songs.

The trip to Rockville was "just for the summer," she says. "I'd forgotten about this, but my cousin reminded me: I have family in Sweden, and my cousin was coming to stay with us for the summer. He was like 14 or 15. So my mom told me I had to come home to Rockville because my cousin was gonna be there. My cousin now takes credit for the song."

The song was "Don't Go Back to Rockville," penned entirely by Mike Mills. A straightforward lament for an absent love buoyed by a disconcertingly joyful chorus, it took Ingrid by surprise. "[Mike is] really sweet. He's

Don't Go Back to Rockville

Looking at your watch a third time waiting in the station for the bus
Going to a place that's far too far away and if that's
not enough
Going where nobody says hello, they don't talk to
anybody they don't know

You'll wind up in some factory where it's full time
filth with nowhere else to go
And you'll walk home to an empty house and sit around
at night all by yourself
I know it might sound strange but I believe
you'll be coming back before too long

Don't go back to Rockville
Don't go back to Rockville
Don't go back to Rockville
And waste another year

At night I drink myself to sleep and pretend that I don't
care that you're not here with me
'Cause it's so much easier to deal with all my problems if I'm
too far gone to see.
But something better happen soon or it's gonna be too
late to bring me back...

Don't go back to Rockville
Don't go back to Rockville
Don't go back to Rockville
And waste another year

Above and on next page: **Mike Mills's handwritten lyrics to "Don't Go Back to Rockville." Courtesy of Ingrid Schorr.**

really extroverted. He can talk to anybody. He's really smart. So we just hit it off, and I thought this was someone who I really liked to be with. It was a long time before I realized he *liked* me and wanted to date me. I think I might've caught on to that when he wrote the song."

The story of how Ingrid first heard R.E.M. perform "Don't Go Back to Rockville" seems tailor-made for a Cameron Crowe movie:

I came back in July . . . like, moved back and just picked up where we left off. The night that I got back to Athens, I went straight to Tyrone's

[97]

It's not as though I really need you
If you were here I'd only bleed you
But everybody else in town
Only wants to put me down
And that's not how it ought to be
And I know it might sound strange but I believe you'll
    be coming back before to long...

Don't go back to Rockville
Don't go back to Rockville
Don't go back to Rockville
And waste another year.

Don't go back to Rockville
Don't go back to Rockville
Don't go back to Rockville
And waste another year.

For Ingrid.
    Love,
        Mike

17 Aug. 1980

where R.E.M. was playing and, literally, I walked in and they were playing "Rockville," and that was the first time I'd ever heard it. Mike had told me about it. He sent me the lyrics. I think he played it on an acoustic guitar, but I'd never heard the band play it.

So I walked in and made my way to the front and they pulled me up onstage and yeah . . . it was amazing. They were already midway through the song and I remember Joe Thomas who was our friend and, I think, was roadying or running sound or something, pushed me up front.

I remember thinking it was different from their other songs even though that was during the time when they played everything really fast. It was just sweeter somehow. Mike always had this kind of writerly purpose about the song. He would write songs and he would say, "I wanted to write a Ramones song, so I wrote this one. I wanted to write a Beach Boys song, so I wrote this one." I think with "Rockville," he wanted to write something countryish. It was really fictional, like it was inspired by me but he took on the narrative mind-set of someone with a different point of view. Of course, I wasn't going home to a factory.

It would take four years for "Rockville" to finally make its way onto record. In the meantime, the immediate concern on Barber Street was "picking up where we left off." Whether it was Ingrid returning from her summer trip, or R.E.M. coming back from a run of gigs, this close-knit community of artists and like-minded friends churned on and on in a cocoon of intoxicated, creative fervor.

History is written by the winners, and it is tempting to portray this group in the kind of rapturous tones we're familiar with from depictions of the American expatriate writers in 1920s Europe, the Beat Generation of the 1950s, or the Laurel Canyon music scene in the 1970s. But that's not how the Barber Street crowd was perceived by the larger community at the time. They were regarded with much the same suspicion and ridicule as hipsters in Brooklyn and Portland are regarded today. Rodger Lyle Brown sums up the prevalent view at the time: They were "asshole henna-heads who thought a ragged linen slip, oversized woolen pants, and a pack-a-day Camel habit made them better than anyone else."

And what of the world outside the cocoon? After a couple of moderate-to-liberal US presidents (Ford, Carter), the unabashedly conservative Ronald Reagan carried 44 states in the 1980 election, apparently signaling a shift in the American temperament. In retrospect (and as is usually the case), American voters were probably less interested in Reagan's ideology than they were desperate for change after a decade of crises: Vietnam, the Watergate scandal, oil shortages, and, finally, the Iran hostage situation that dominated the tail end of Carter's presidency. Nevertheless, a newly resurgent right wing was viewed as a threat by many of those with an artistic or outsider bent. This held true for the Athens scene, even though most of its participants were, at that time, largely apolitical. Partying, not voting, was their preeminent concern. At most, the oncoming tide of Reagan Republicanism was seen as one more reason to double down on the debauchery and the artmaking in a vague attempt to create a bohemian utopia in the midst of a wider world that seemed to be going mad.

The Athens music scene was peaking. Pylon continued to wow audiences, and exciting new bands continued to pop up on a seemingly weekly basis. The best of these was Love Tractor, an initially instrumental outfit headed by guitarists Mike Richmond and Mark Cline and augmented by a rotating cast of musicians that would come to include Kit Swartz, Armistead Wellford, Bill Berry, and, much later, Billy Holmes (who played in a Cline-less iteration in the 2000s). The Tractor specialized in clean, textured, guitar-based pieces that ticked along like a Swiss clock. They would later introduce vocals, but those early instrumentals, filled with wide-open spaces, made an ideal soundtrack to the Southern boho life.

In terms of popularity, though, R.E.M. were the undisputed rulers of the club scene at the close of 1980, quite a feat for a band that had debuted barely half a year earlier. They were admired by many and resented by some, but all acknowledged their position at the top of the pecking order. This was a role previously occupied, if briefly, by the B-52's. But that band had flown the coop for New York at the first opportunity, and by the time R.E.M. came to prominence in Athens, the B-52's had released two major-label albums and were beginning to flounder. It seemed that these sweet local heroes had gotten chewed up and spit out by the big time.* Perhaps as a reaction to this, or possibly for less conscious reasons, R.E.M. made the momentous decision to stay put.

Just two days after R.E.M.'s performance at Atlanta's Fox Theatre with the Police, John Lennon was murdered outside his New York City apartment. Lennon's ghost ruled the airwaves for the better part of December 1980. The single "Just Like Starting Over," from his *Double Fantasy* album, usurped Kenny Rogers's "Lady" at the top of the *Billboard* Hot 100 chart the week of December 27. Other artists in the top ten at that time included Neil Diamond, Air Supply, Pat Benatar, Heart, and Bruce Springsteen. Things got a little more interesting further down the chart: Devo's "Whip It" punched in at #27, David Bowie's "Fashion" jittered away at #72, and, peaking at #69, a collective billed as the Star Wars Intergalactic Droid Choir and Chorale made their first and only *Billboard* appearance with "What Can You Get a Wookie for Christmas (When He Already Owns a Comb?)."† In Athens, like everywhere else in the country, these songs issued forth from car radios and

---

* An unexpected comeback for the B-52's was still some years away.

† Yes, you read that correctly. The Droid Choir edged past Bowie. This song's parent record, the clunkily titled *Christmas in the Stars: Star Wars Christmas Album* also featured vocal work by a young Jon Bon Jovi, billed as John Boniva (his real name). But let's get back to R.E.M.

1980

That was the year Delbert shone and . . .

Critics select REM as best local band

The *Red and Black* votes R.E.M. "best local band" of 1980, January 8, 1981.

living room stereos. They served as the daily soundtrack for the vast majority of UGA students—the same kids who packed the clubs to see R.E.M. But on Barber Street, their volume was faint at best; by this point the artists on the "Street of Stars," as Linda Hopper had dubbed the neighborhood, were listening mostly to each other.

PYLON
R.E.M.
THE Side Effects
LOVE:.... TRACTOR
METWOD ACTORS
AT TYRONES
THURSDAY. MARCH 19
-- $WINDLES

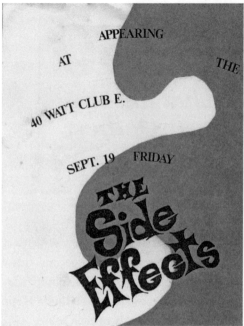

APPEARING
AT
THE
40 WATT CLUB E.
SEPT. 19   FRIDAY
THE Side Effects

Thursday, June 4
R.E.M.

Friday, June 5
Little Tigers

Saturday, June 6
Love Tractor

Monday, June 8
One Eye Open
**Ladies' Night: Happy Hour
Bar Drinks and Draft**

Tuesday, June 9
The Side Effects

Happy Hour Draft All Night

TYRONE'S O.C.

Wednesday, June 10
The $windle$
Ralph's Video Night
Famous Band Films

Thursday, June 11
Limbo District

Friday and Saturday
June 12 and 13
Eddie Hinton
and
The Rocking Horses
along with
Convalescent Egyptians
$2.00 Cover

Coming Wednesday, June 24
Gang of Four

Happy Hour 4-7 p.m. Monday-Saturday
110 Foundry Street • 543-1136

Three 1981 gig posters/ads. Courtesy of Paul Butchart.

Chapter Six

Patton Biddle and his wife, Jeannie, live in a ranch house just a few miles outside of Athens. From a front-room office overlooking a panorama of gently sloping hills populated by copses of Georgia pine, Pat spends much of his free time digitizing and mastering the thousands of hours of board recordings he made while running sound at Tyrone's, the 40 Watt, and other regional clubs. Some of this material gets teased out on the website Jeannie created for him—PatTheWiz.com—and much more of it is given away to interested music fans who write Pat from all over the world. When he's not working on the archive he enjoys dipping into military history; anything related to the American Civil War gets special attention.

Pat is a big, imposing guy. Diane Loring Aiken recalls being terrified of him in the '80s due to his mountain-man look and intense manner, but the years, along with a work injury, have softened him considerably. The once fiercely dark beard that would have been appropriate on an Old Testament king is flecked with white now. His brow is deeply lined and crow's feet stretch out from his eyes, conspiring to give him a look of gentle melancholy when he smiles. Some of that old intensity lingers, though. I can tell that he had a very exacting approach to his work, and even now he is not one to mince words about musicians he feels behaved unprofessionally. (Matthew Sweet draws particularly withering criticism, but Pat is far from being the only Athenian to hold a negative view of him.) On the whole, though, he is warm, affable, and generous with his time and memories.

Pat sits me down in front of his computer and opens up the index page for his archive. "Just let me know which ones you want," he says.

I am overwhelmed. Alex Chilton, John Cale, 10,000 Maniacs, Love Tractor, Pylon, Warren Zevon—the names go on and on. And there is a run of shows by R.E.M. stretching from 1981 through 1988. Initially, Pat was recording these shows not for posterity but as a means to get even better at what he did. He would take the reels home each night and listen to them intently, jotting down notes on what worked and what he should change in his mixing approach. As a result, some of his live recordings of bands have a better sound balance and fidelity than those artists' studio recordings. Much of this is subjective, but I'd take the Wiz's tapes of Pylon and 10,000 Maniacs over their albums.

As we've seen, Pat had known the members of R.E.M. since mid-1980, but his first professional work for the band wasn't until April 1981, when he was asked to work the board for them at the New York, New York nightclub in Augusta. This gig came about because 40 Watt co-owner Paul Scales had worked with a guy in an Athens sandwich shop a few years previously who had graduated, gone back to his hometown of Augusta, and opened a club. There wasn't a lot going on musically in Augusta, so he got back in touch with Paul and they arranged for some of the Athens bands to start traveling down there to play. And Pat, being a rock-solid sound guy, got recruited to run the board.

The existing recording of this show ("not a soundboard recording," Pat is quick to point out) captures R.E.M. at a crucial point of transition. They still sound like they're making it up as they go along, but there is a speed and ferocity to the performance that blasts through the lo-fi muck of the source tape. Jefferson's comparison of R.E.M. to the early Who may not have been far off; R.E.M. didn't aspire to be virtuosos like the Who, but they certainly had some of that band's combustible magic—that sense that the whole thing could run off the rails at any moment.

From the beginning there had been a musical tension at the heart of R.E.M.—a push and pull between the classically trained Mike Mills and the willfully ignorant (in terms of musical theory, at least) Peter Buck.

"Mike Mills at that point was a tremendous musician," Pat says.

A lot of people didn't realize, but he did a lot of the arrangement bread-and-butter stuff for the band. He knew so much. Peter was the new kid on the block. He felt that his age justified him having a little bit of influence in the band that he really didn't have. You could feel that tension back and forth. For example, if you listen real close—I think it was one of the September '81 shows—at the beginning of "Windout," you can hear Mike saying, "Are you okay?" And you can hear Peter saying, "Don't give me shit, will you?"—just real venomous. It would just roll off of Mike's back. He's just doing what had to be done. He was really the lead. If they had a baton, he'd be the one wagging them down.

If Mike Mills represented the structured, theoretical approach to composition and performance, Peter Buck represented raw intuition. "When I was going into Wuxtry in those early years, Pete would ask me to show him some chords," Billy Holmes says,

> and I would go, "Well, this is a B minor, and this is a D diminished," and Pete would go, "No, don't tell me the names, just show me the finger positions." His attitude for a long time was, "The less I know about formal music, the more creative I'm going to be, because this is rock 'n' roll. I won't know which rules I'm breaking; I will just be doing what I do." Mike's attitude, on the other hand, was, you learn music theory, you learn music harmony. You learn the rules, and then you break them.

At the time of the April 1981 Augusta show, Buck's and Mills's approaches hadn't gelled completely, but they crashed up against each other in exciting ways. In the recording you can hear Mills's melodic bass lines punching through Buck's insistent riffing. They were developing a style in which both guitar and drums anchored the rhythm, while Mills—out of frustration or a desire to innovate—took on some of the attributes of a lead guitarist. The approach was not dissimilar to what John Entwistle did in the Who, but sparer, more restrained. A lack of extraneous notes distinguished R.E.M.'s music from the very beginning.

Another transition captured on the recording of the Augusta show pertains to the group's songwriting approach. Because there was no opening band that night, R.E.M. were required to perform three sets, which meant they ended up playing just about every original song in their repertoire along with most of their covers. Rudimentary early songs such as "Baby I," "Different Girl," and "Hey Hey Nadine" rubbed shoulders with newer pieces such as "Radio Free Europe," "9-9," "Pretty Persuasion," and "Gardening at Night." The backbeat remained much the same, but the stylistic and thematic contrast between the newer and older songs couldn't have been starker. I get a firsthand glimpse of this during my interview with Patton Biddle. He breaks off from our conversation to say, "I've got something I'd like to show you." He disappears into a back room and re-emerges with a carefully folded piece of notebook paper bearing Michael Stipe's handwriting. "I asked him to write up these lyrics for me because I loved the song. This came out of my little spiral notebook. He wrote these out in the van on the way to New York."

At the top of the page are the words *Gardening at Night* in loose but

I see your money on the floor
i felt the pocket change the wall
feelings that broke thru that door
just didnt seem to be too real

your yard is nothing but a fence
the sun just hurts my eye somewhere
it must be time for penitence
gardening at nite is everywhere.

ch   gardening @ nite

your neighbors go to bed @ 10
call the prayer line for a change
change is changing every month
they said it couldnt be arranged.

you ankled up the garbage sound
but we were busy in the rows
i fell up not to see the sun
gardening @ nite just didnt grow

repeat 1

ch   gardening...

your sister says that your too young
she should know has been there twice
the call was 2 and 51
they said it couldnt be arranged.

Michael Stipe's handwritten lyrics to "Gardening at Night." Courtesy of T. Patton Biddle.

spirited handwriting, followed by the original lyrics of the song. "That's some really tremendous lyrical effort in there if you ask me," Pat says.

You ankled up the garbage sound
But we were busy in the rows
I fell up not to see the sun
Gardening at night

There's something evocative in these words even if they don't seem to make much sense. A cynic might take the view that they're complete gibberish. But I get the feeling that they're tapping into something deeper than linear thought.

With the exception of "Don't Go Back to Rockville," all of R.E.M.'s new material was in this vein. Since the strong beat and catchy hooks remained in place, audiences at first hardly noticed the change. But gradually, imperceptibly, R.E.M. performances began to accumulate more weight, to go beyond merely providing a good time.

Stipe's new writing style was hardly without precedent, even within the limited world of pop music. As we have seen, Patti Smith had been juxtaposing images in unusual ways from her debut album onward, though she had not typically scrambled her words at the sentence level to the degree that Stipe did. Colin Newman, primary lyricist of the British band Wire—a group Stipe listened to frequently—provided a more direct antecedent. Indeed, Wire's song "Map Ref. 41°N 93°W" provided a template for R.E.M.'s lyrical approach, if not their sound. Some lines—"Common and peaceful, duck flat, lowland / Landscape, canal, canard, water coloured"—would not have been out of place in one of Stipe's notebooks. "Interrupting my train of thought / Lines of longitude and latitude," Newman sings over a catchy, danceable rhythm. What does it mean? That we feel compelled to map and chart away all of the mystery and beauty of life? That's one interpretation, anyway. Similarly, each R.E.M. song conjures an impression in the listener's mind informed by both the words—alternately enunciated and mumbled—and the music.

But where did this all come from? It seems clear that Stipe was not simply aping Newman. He had specific reasons for doing what he was doing. "He took away that veil of comprehension everyone assumes they have when they hear a song with lyrics," David Pierce notes.

He took that away and forced people to listen to the style of the voice and how it went with the sound of the guitar. He'd always say that he wanted the vocals to be another instrument, like a saxophone. The words didn't necessarily go together into a cohesive sentence with an idea behind it, but they were words that sounded good together. It was up to you to interpret it. It was mostly emotion behind it.

"Radio Free Europe" represented the apex of this style. "Gardening at Night," for all of its obliqueness, still conjures up the image of someone . . . well, gardening at night. My wife thinks specifically of her late grandmother, Dolly Pearson, who used to do much of her gardening at midnight while the rest of the residents of her Wilmington, North Carolina, neighborhood— save, perhaps, the criminals—slept soundly. That conjures up some very specific emotions—peace and solitude, but also darkness—literal, or, if you like, metaphorical.*

But what the hell is "Radio Free Europe"? In one sense, that phrase does refer to a specific entity. Radio Free Europe is a still-extant organization that broadcasts news and information (some would say propaganda) into parts of the world deemed by it to be closed off to the free flow of ideas. Currently, that means primarily the Middle East, but at the time the song was written the target audience of Radio Free Europe was Eastern European countries under Communist rule, while its sister station, Radio Liberty, broadcast into the Soviet Union. And, as the name also suggests, there was an activist purpose to the enterprise, a "free" Europe being the desired endgame.

Such a subject is certainly ripe for poetic exploration, but R.E.M.'s "Radio Free Europe" isn't out to do that. Stipe either didn't know or didn't care much about what the real Radio Free Europe might be; true to what he told David Pierce, he liked the way the words sounded. And beyond the title, there is very little a listener can latch onto. Some have tried to transcribe the lyrics; one online attempt includes the lines "Keep me out of country in the word / Deal the porch is leading us absurd . . ."

To add to the confusion, different live recordings of the song feature what sound like completely different lyrics in some sections (or at least

---

* Lest we get too precious about this particular song, it's useful to consider Bill Berry's description of the title's origins, from the liner notes of the R.E.M. compilation album *And I Feel Fine... The Best of the I.R.S. Years 1982–1987*: "We were driving at night after a show (I don't remember where), and I was at the wheel of our old car, with a rental trailer in tow. One of my three passengers aimed a directive at me. Rather than inform me of his desire to evacuate his bladder, he instead suggested that I pull over so that he might engage in the task of roadside 'night gardening.' To four guys in their early twenties this was a glaring catalyst for a new song."

different sets of consonants; they are almost always indecipherable). Stipe himself subsequently described the song as "complete babbling."

I believe David Pierce provides me with the key I need when he describes Stipe as a trickster. What is "Radio Free Europe" if not a mischievous experiment—not a prank in the normal sense, but an attempt to send out a bunch of nonsense into the world wrapped in a catchy tune and portentous title and see what comes back.*

Some writers have commented on the similarity between Stipe's disjointed writing style and the "cut-up" method of William S. Burroughs. This technique, whose invention Burroughs credited to his friend and collaborator Brion Gysin, involved cutting up pages of linear text and rearranging the fragments at random. In an essay titled simply "The Cut-Up Method," Burroughs described the impetus for the technique while cleverly working cut-ups into that description: "Cutting and rearranging a page of written words introduces a new dimension into writing enabling the writer to turn images in cinematic variation. Images shift sense under the scissors smell images to sound sight to sound kinesthetic."

While that last sentence could pass for an R.E.M. lyric, there were two key differences between Burroughs's approach and Stipe's. Most importantly, Stipe's cut-ups occurred entirely in his head. He needed no scissors and tape—the words tumbled out already scrambled.

The other primary difference was one of subject matter. Burroughs gravitated toward the shocking and disquieting; his prose reveled in death, excrement, sexual violence. As I mentioned earlier, any sexual content in Stipe's early work was diluted by many layers of random word collage to the point of being almost invisible. Burroughs was going for a kind of horror. Stipe was going for an impressionism born of everyday words and objects, with the occasional colloquialism ("Katy bar the door") thrown in.

Marcus Gray notes that Stipe initially denied a Burroughs influence but eventually conceded parallels in their views on language—particularly the idea that words could be a virus. "I don't agree with a lot of what that man says, but I think he's kinda correct there," Stipe is quoted as saying. "I appreciate language, and I appreciate the different ways that we can abuse it or use it or twist it around to make beautiful shapes at the end of our fingers. And, y'know, in terms of communicating, sometimes it works and sometimes it doesn't. So it's a big mystery." (The fact that this quote only

---

*What came back was some unexpected attention from the *New York Times*, the kind of attention that careers are made on. But we're not quite there yet.

tangentially addresses Burroughs's "word virus" idea—the subject he was ostensibly being queried on—is illustrative of Stipe's tendency to drift, in both writing and conversation, from impression to impression.)*

It is intriguing that Stipe identified Burroughs's "word virus" idea as a point of convergence. Burroughs often stated that language and its underlying structure was a system of control, and that in his cut-up experiments he sought to "dynamite" or "short circuit" those calcified patterns. He had an ulterior motive, both in using the cut-ups and in his gravitation toward unpleasant subject matter, and that was to write his way out of the personal hell he had made for himself. (Burroughs had many demons, narcotics addiction being but one.) His ultimate aim was to reach a state of wordless thought—an interesting goal for a writer.

With a few notable exceptions, Stipe's lyrics never gave the impression that he was trying to exorcise demons. But the idea of chopping up language in order to break free of linear thought patterns seems very much to have been what he was aiming for. What remained, as David Pierce pointed out, was "mostly emotion," which is the essence of music.

Mike Mills and Bill Berry may not have fully grasped what Stipe was on about in his lyrics, but they gamely sang along. Carefully structured harmonies were another element that distinguished R.E.M. from most of the other Athens bands. Indeed, in this regard R.E.M. seemed to hark back to the dreaded hippie era of Crosby, Stills, and Nash, and the (more respectable) Byrds. Given Peter Buck's taste, it's likely that the Monkees were in the mix as well.

A crucial element of these harmonies—their anchor, in fact—was Berry's forceful baritone. Mills always took the high end, which left Stipe to wander the middle. "Pretty Persuasion," one of the newer songs performed during the Augusta set, essentially took the form of a duet between Mills and Stipe, with Berry joining in for the chorus. This song in particular showcased Stipe's fondness for unusual melodies. I doubt that any other songwriter, if presented with the chords for "Pretty Persuasion," would have come up with the careening melody that Stipe did. It's off-kilter and difficult to hum, but somehow it works. Perhaps with this song in mind, Peter Buck told *Spin*'s Barry Walters in 1986,

---

* Stipe eventually got to know Burroughs quite well in the 1990s, though it's unclear whether he sought the writer out due to a genuine interest in his work or because many of his friends—Kurt Cobain, Patti Smith, and the members of Sonic Youth among them—were unabashed Burroughs hangers-on.

Michael is so unpredictable . . . He never takes the easy way, which can be pretty frustrating. But quite often his left-field suggestions make you question things you took for granted, like how songs are arranged and the distinction between lead and background vocals. When we finally have a pretty good handle on the song, he tears and twists it apart so his lyrics and melody can fit in.

The Augusta recording is also notable in that it captures R.E.M.'s desire to control all aspects of the performance. Stipe routinely breaks from his front-man act to call out sound instructions to Biddle: "A little more in the monitors, Pat," "Could you bring up the guitar, Pat?" None of this comes across as bossy. One gets the sense of a careful collaboration and mutual respect: a dedicated effort from both parties to ensure the best sound possible. Even if this was just a small club in Augusta, the band treated the gig as an event of great importance—as it was. As was every gig during those first two years. In the incubator of these small clubs, "r.e.m." were turning into R.E.M.

The band were advancing on several fronts, in fact. In February 1981, they had traveled to Bombay Recording Studios in Smyrna, Georgia, for a whirlwind taping session. Over the course of one day, they recorded live in-studio versions of "Sitting Still," "Gardening at Night," "Radio Free Europe," "Shaking Through," "Mystery to Me," "Don't Go Back to Rockville," "Narrator," and "White Tornado." This marked the band's first time in a proper studio.

Virtually every other early R.E.M. recording has been leaked over the years, so it might seem surprising that these have never surfaced in public. This is entirely down to the discretion and professionalism of Bombay's owner, Joe Perry, who later told the *Athens Banner-Herald*, "Even if I could have sold [the recordings] for $25,000 or $50,000, it wouldn't have been worth it. I've always been in the music business, and I didn't think that was the way to go."

The band hoped that the Bombay session recordings would yield a demo tape that could be shopped to clubs and promotional outlets. The need for such a tape was reinforced by a radio spot that aired in Augusta prior to R.E.M.'s first show there. Against a backdrop of music by Devo, the B-52's, and the Police, a pro-wrestler-style voice breathlessly declared, "R.E.M. opened for the Police in Atlanta's Fox Theatre and brought the house down! R.E.M. plus New York will be playing lots of punk rock music and there will be a punk rock dance contest with $25 going to the winner! Tonight, most drinks at New York will be selling for a dollar. R.E.M.'s gonna be cookin' and the dance floor packed. Tonight, R.E.M. at New York, New York. Don't you be the one who missed it!" The ad conveyed the impression that R.E.M. were either the composers of "Whip It," "Rock Lobster," and "De Do Do Do, De Da Da Da," or a covers band that played those and other new wave "punk rock" tunes. Nowhere during those thirty seconds of airtime was any indication given as to what R.E.M. actually sounded like.

So the Bombay session was an essential and overdue step. The problem was that afterwards no one in the band seemed satisfied with the results— and that surely explains why the tracks remain unreleased. Which is a shame. Joe Perry later told Marcus Gray that the recordings "have a tremendous amount of raw energy. To this day, I do not think they [R.E.M.] know how hot those tracks really are."

The change of heart seems to have occurred when R.E.M. and Jefferson Holt listened to the recordings again after a couple more months of gigging. Peter Buck later stated that the tracks sounded "flat and dull" and repaid Joe Perry's hard work and professionalism with the comment, "I didn't know what I was doing. The guy who was running it was a nice guy, but he didn't know what he was doing either. We mixed it in about two minutes." (This assessment didn't stop Buck, Mills, and Stipe from going back to work with Perry on various side projects over the next couple of years.)

Jefferson Holt took charge of selecting the next producer and record-ing studio for the band to try out. Through his connections in the North Carolina music scene he was given the name of Mitch Easter, a talented songwriter and performer who ran his Drive-In Studio out of his parents' home in Winston-Salem.

In many ways, Mitch Easter was the perfect person to record R.E.M. He was the same age as Peter Buck, and the two shared an affection for jangly guitar sounds and catchy melodies. Easter had joined his first band as far back as 1970, and released his first album (with his band the Sneakers) in 1978. Easter also shared with Buck and the rest of R.E.M. a small-town sensibility: after graduating from the University of North Carolina in the late '70s, Easter followed his friends Chris Stamey and Peter Holsapple up to New York City, but soon realized that he preferred the perks of being a big fish in a small pond and returned to North Carolina. (Stamey and Hol-sapple stayed on and formed the influential band the dBs—whom Easter later produced.)

Easter started up Drive-In Studios in 1980, around the time he formed the band Let's Active with Sara Romweber and Faye Hunter. The group played a form of hypermelodic power pop that was not too far from what R.E.M. were aiming for. Both the band and the studio would become integral parts of R.E.M.'s story.

Easter's friendly demeanor and boyish appearance—his round cheeks, bashful smile, and shaggy mop-top gave him the look of a fair-haired Paul McCartney—belied an intensely perfectionist streak. He impressed upon R.E.M. the importance of using the studio itself as an instrument. In Easter's view, studio recordings should not simply be documents of a band's live sound (as the Bombay session had been); they should be works of art in their own right. Multitrack recording gave bands the ability to add additional textures to their songs. Two of Easter's favorite techniques were to echo bass lines with the low keys of a piano, and to bolster electric-guitar riffs with delicately plucked acoustic-guitar parts. In many instances, the result was a polished, baroque feel, though by their very nature such embellishments could sometimes dilute the raw power of a hard-rocking song.

R.E.M. made their first trip up to Winston-Salem on April 15, 1981, just 13 days after their Augusta performance. (It says something about R.E.M.'s busy schedule at the time that they played five gigs across three states during those intervening days.)

This first visit to the Drive-In was productive, though not in the same way that the band's session at Bombay Studios had been. At Bombay, R.E.M. had been prolific, recording eight songs. With Mitch Easter, they focused on two songs: "Sitting Still" and "Radio Free Europe." They also made a pass at the instrumental "White Tornado," but that may have been more to let off steam than anything else.

The results of the session were quickly pressed into service via a run of 400 cassettes sent to clubs and journalists. This immediately enhanced the band's ability to book shows farther afield than their little pocket of the Southeast, where word of mouth had managed to carry them up to this point. Prior to the advent of YouTube, *The Cassette Set*, as this tape became known, went largely unheard beyond its original 400 recipients, but in 2012 a YouTube user called CollapseN2murmur posted a pristine digital transfer. It's still not possible for us to compare these recordings to those done by Joe Perry at Bombay, but it's easy to see that Mitch Easter was an inspired choice to helm the band's first publicly released material. Both "Sitting Still" and "Radio Free Europe" represent a happy meeting of energized, tight performances with crisp, tasteful sound engineering. The overdubs are minimal but strikingly effective: a whispered backing vocal during a section of "Radio Free Europe," double-tracked guitars on "Sitting Still," and nearly subliminal sounds scattered throughout both tracks.

Easter's most noticeable contribution to the band's sound at this point is in the realm of vocal effects. Patton Biddle had told me of R.E.M. and Jefferson Holt's fondness for heavily reverbed vocals during live performances (Holt once approached Wiz after sound check and asked him to "use a lot of echo"); Easter managed to satisfy this desire for vocal otherworldliness while at the same time tempering it. On Biddle's live recordings from fall 1981, Stipe can sound like he's singing in a canyon,* while on the Drive-in tracks, Stipe sometimes sounds like he's singing inside a metal-lined phone booth; Easter had a shrewd understanding of just how much of this he could get away with. He'd keep that close echo going during a verse but would then open things up during the chorus, or vice versa. This augmented the tension-release effect inherent in the songs themselves.

Approximately 100 copies of *The Cassette Set* came with an added surprise: a three-and-a-half-minute "Radio Dub" version of "Radio Free Europe" that Mitch Easter had mixed sometime after the initial sessions. It's hard to gauge how seriously Easter intended this to be taken, and certainly it's not too successful. Jamaican dub style involves the deconstruction of an existing song and the isolation of certain elements to create something new. So, for example, a dub track by King Tubby might have begun its life as a finished track by Augustus Pablo, which the dub producer would then

slice and dice—isolating the drums and bass, for instance, and applying targeted reverb, and then bringing other instruments in and out of the mix as if he were tuning in new stations on a radio dial. Easter's dub mix of "Radio Free Europe" does all of these things, but the song itself—with its fast pace and lack of open space—is rather ill-suited to the style. There's a reason why dub works so well with reggae: that genre's lazy rhythms lend themselves well to the various punch-ins and echo treatments favored in dub; the overall effect is a hypnotic, chilled-out vibe. The overall effect of introducing dub techniques into "Radio Free Europe," on the other hand, is one hot mess. At one point Easter's piled-on manipulations create the impression that the tape is being eaten by the deck—an experience with which any cassette-deck owner in the 1980s would have been all too familiar.

---

* This was not Pat's preference. "I always tried my best to do what the band wanted me to do," he says. "That's why there's so much of that damn analog echo on those September shows. I did the best I could with that piece of shit [echo unit] that I had to work with."

Date: Friday, April 24th

Promotion by:
Tyrone's & The 40 Watt Club

Location: The B&L Warehouse

Music and Pandemonium by:

XTC
and
R.E.M.

Ticket Locations: Tyrone's, 40 Watt Club,
B&L Warehouse, WUXTRY, The Pants Shop.
and Barnett's

$5.00 Advance
$6.00 at the door

Sound ~~and~~ by lights by Gary Sharp & Associates
the Wiz!

**B&L WAREHOUSE
FRIDAY APRIL 24
TICKETS·40 WATT CLUB
TYRONE'S, WUXTRY
$5 NOW· $6 THEN**

Two flyers for the XTC/R.E.M. show in Athens on April 24, 1981. Note Pat the Wiz's handwritten correction on the left.
Left: courtesy of T. Patton Biddle; right: courtesy of Paul Butchart.

Again, it's difficult to know if this was the intended effect.

Even if it is a failed experiment, though, the dub mix of "Radio Free Europe" holds considerable value: by isolating certain elements of the recording, it highlights both Easter's meticulous production and the tightness of the band. It's in this dub mix that we most clearly hear Mills pounding away at the bass, doing his typical up-the-neck runs. We hear Buck's fast-paced arpeggios, Berry's insistent beat, and Stipe's voice pushed in and out of the forefront—the words unintelligible throughout. We also hear Easter's embellishments: wood blocks to accentuate the percussion, and a triangle or chime of some kind. Overall, the "Radio Dub" is a fascinating bit of sonic archaeology.

The end of April found R.E.M. back in Athens, opening for the British band XTC at the B&L Warehouse. Although not as high-profile as the Police gig, this was definitely a cause for excitement and pride on R.E.M.'s part. XTC had just recently hit their early-career peak with the release of their *Black Sea* album. The band's fusion of jittery new-wave rhythms with '60s-style melodies was hugely popular among R.E.M.'s friends and fans. On paper, R.E.M. and XTC seemed like an excellent fit, perhaps better than R.E.M. and the Police had been. For one thing, Dave Gregory of XTC shared Peter Buck's love of the jangly guitar sound. The only problem was that Andy Partridge, XTC's talented but troubled singer and co–lead songwriter, hated touring and suffered from panic attacks. It didn't take much to disrupt his equilibrium.

Enter R.E.M.

Billy Holmes helped set up the equipment for the show and witnessed the ensuing events firsthand. "I was thrilled to no end to be hired to do this particular show," he says.

> I was a big fan of XTC. They were onstage doing a sound check, and I saw Bill Berry come walking in the back door with a floor tom. And, I mean, this is how small-style R.E.M. was in those days: Bill didn't even have cases for his drums, and they did not have a road crew. So Bill is lugging in his own drums, and I watched Andy Partridge go nuts and start screaming at everybody: "I said the opening act was not allowed to come in here until we finished our sound check!" And he just cussed everybody out. I do not even know if Bill knew what was going on, but the people working the show certainly did.

This was the first and only time that R.E.M. and XTC played together. The following year, Partridge suffered a complete mental breakdown on-stage in Paris and retired from live performance. Thereafter XTC chose to work exclusively as a studio-based band in the manner of the later-period Beatles (and early '90s R.E.M., for that matter).

By the time of this show, R.E.M. had already established themselves as a headlining band in their own right. Regardless of how they might be seen in relation to a major-label band like XTC, R.E.M. were enough of a draw in their hometown to guarantee Michael Stipe a packed house when he gave a one-off solo performance. On May 6, 1981, he headlined the 40 Watt under the name 1066 Gaggle O' Sound, pounding away on his Farfisa organ. Stipe has frequently characterized himself as a non-musician, but David Pierce insists he could actually play. "He knew chords and stuff," Pierce says.

> He'd also play guitar. He wasn't trying to make traditional music [at the Gaggle O' Sound show]. His guitar would be sitting on a table, and he might walk over and strum it or put a capo on the neck, strum it, put the reverb on and have it sustain for a minute or so while he'd do other effects over it. And he did a dub thing where he'd play a loop of himself and it would come back around and he'd play over that. He'd have a tape recorder which would rewind and play that back and then he'd play along with the recording he'd just

made. He also had a bunch of other tape recordings he'd made of instruments, of noise, of him saying things, of chatter. And he would sit there at his Farfisa, and he had a reverb box, and he'd bang on the reverb box and play some chords over it and then turn the tape on.

Pierce reckons that Stipe's Gaggle O' Sound gig "might have been the most experimental thing that ever happened in Athens," but if so, a strong argument could be made that another Stipe-connected project that immediately preceded it—a rotating collective that at various points went under the names Pre-Cave, Nest (adj), and Boat Of—was a close runner-up. This group created punishing sound collages that seemed to blend the essences of Glenn Branca, Yoko Ono, and Lee Scratch Perry. In truth, Stipe was never more than an auxiliary member; Boat Of (if we may go with the one name for simplicity's sake) was the brainchild of Mike Green, Carol Levy, and a multi-instrumentalist/provocateur with a serious dub fixation named Tom Smith. Still, it seems probable that Stipe's solo performance drew inspiration from what he'd observed of Smith and Green's boundary-pushing tape manipulations and Levy's keyboard-and-voice wall of noise.

Pierce was on the bill himself that evening, playing drums in the opening act Oh-OK, a trio that also featured Lynda Stipe on bass and Linda Hopper on vocals. While Oh-OK were very much a pop group, their bare-bones instrumentation, combined with Hopper's unaffected, childlike vocals, gave them an avant-garde edge. This was the primitive music equivalent of Howard Finster's primitive art. Oh-OK would go on to garner a fair amount

Michael Stipe's handwritten flyer for a Boat Of show at Tyrone's, 1981.
Courtesy of Paul Butchart.

Linda Hopper, ca. 1980, outside the practice studio at 142 N Jackson St. shared by REM and Side Effects and later used by other bands, including Oh-OK. Photo by Ingrid Schorr.

of critical praise and local success, but their popularity ceiling was built into their sound: the band's limitations, which were a huge part of their charm, ensured that Oh-OK would never succeed at the level of R.E.M. or the B-52's, or even Pylon. And when they later moved beyond those limitations by incorporating singer-guitarist Matthew Sweet into the lineup, they lost some of that charm and uniqueness.

R.E.M.'s hectic pace, meanwhile, ensured that Stipe would never be able to devote more than a bare minimum of time to his side projects—though he made use of what little he had.

Jonny Hibbert crossed paths with R.E.M. shortly after the release of *The Cassette Set*. A law student at Atlanta's Woodrow Wilson School and the dynamic front man of a well-known local band called the Incredible Throbs, Hibbert had recently been approached by two Georgia Tech students, Cliff and Doug Danielson, who were eager to make a record with him before he went off "into the sunset of law school." Their intention was to record the Incredible Throbs, as the Danielsons were big fans of Hibbert's band, but Hibbert felt that it made more business sense for them to find "a band that's on the way up and not on the way out, and record *them*." With the Danielson brothers providing seed money, Hibbert set up a record label—Hib-Tone— and a publishing company, and went on the lookout for his flagship band. A conversation with an Athens friend led him to R.E.M.

Since the members of R.E.M. were aware of Hibbert's music and re- spected him as something of a musical elder, the pairing initially worked well. Hibbert proposed a one-off contract: he would oversee the release of R.E.M.'s first single on his Hib-Tone label and retain sole publishing rights to the songs featured on it. It was a one-shot deal; R.E.M. would be free either to re-up or to go elsewhere for subsequent projects. The band readily agreed. Not yet aware of their worth as songwriters, they were not overly concerned by Hibbert's stipulation that he maintain control over publishing rights.

Hibbert accompanied the band when they went back to the Drive-In to record overdubs for "Radio Free Europe" and "Sitting Still," the designated A and B sides of the single. Drawing on his own musical experience, Jonny had very definite ideas on how the recording should go, which irked Easter—though at this point tensions remained below the surface. As Hibbert remembers it, "They had most of the basics cut."

At the time Pete Buck wasn't a very off-the-cuff sort of player [like] he is now. He played very consistently. He would play the same part exactly the same every time, every time. So hearing that, in particular "Sitting Still," I said, "Pete, that's close but let's cut your whole part again." And then I told Mitch, "Look, save that other one and save that new track and let's cut another one and see how they stack and let's stack them way wide like super stereo," and the result was what I had hoped because he was doing that open picking. And it came out all Roger McGuinn-y. It sounded like a 12-string.*

For the backing vocals on "Radio Free Europe," Hibbert suggested Stipe pinch his nose for a "Rudy Vallee megaphone" effect. He and Stipe sang the chorus together, which did for the vocals what the stereo stacking had done for Buck's guitar lines: it made the song sound bigger, more anthemic.

The only difficulty arose over the final mix of "Radio Free Europe." As the label owner and the person footing the bill for the sessions, Hibbert felt he should have final say on how the record sounded. Not only did Easter see this as encroachment into his territory, he also actively disagreed with Hibbert's production choices, claiming that Hibbert's mix sounded "murkier than the original mix" (i.e., the *Cassette Set* version). Peter Buck agreed. It's

---

* Hibbert's recollection notwithstanding, this was not too different from what Easter had already been doing; the pre-Hibbert *Cassette Set* version of "Sitting Still" already featured a double-tracked guitar, though Hibbert may have beefed up the sound by stacking additional tracks and mixing them wider. In any case, the addition of a second guitar is clearly audible in the Hibbert version of "Radio Free Europe."

unclear if the others cared one way or the other, but Hibbert was to discover that having Peter Buck as a thorn in his side was problem enough.

In June, the band went to the neutral ground of Bombay Studios to do a comparison test between Hibbert's mix and an alternate mix that Easter had done on his own. R.E.M. came down in favor of the Easter mix, but it made no difference: Hibbert sent his own mix to be mastered. "I put my foot down," he says. "I was probably the last person to ever do that to them."

Meanwhile, in mid-June 1981, the band, along with Patton Biddle and Jefferson Holt, piled into the van for their first extended run of gigs outside of the South. The occasion was a plum opening slot for the British band Gang of Four, who had already toured with Pylon and would go on to play with a number of other Athens bands as a result of that association.

It would be difficult to overstate the effect of Gang of Four on R.E.M., yet it's an influence that is often overlooked: apart from the R.E.M. song "Feeling Gravitys Pull" and some guitar textures on *Document*, there are few sonic similarities between the bands. But something of the *spirit* of Gang of Four, whose explosive early singles and *Entertainment!* album came out in 1978–79, would inform R.E.M.'s work and aesthetic throughout the '80s. In terms of visual presentation, there were definite parallels. Both bands performed onstage at a level of sustained intensity, and both featured highly animated, almost spastic, front men. If Stipe's dance moves were unusual, Gang of Four singer Jon King came off as an outright alien. Hardly moving his hips at all, he jerked his limbs violently in time with the beat and bent forward and back from the waist as if he were hinged. Every now and then he would pause to carefully brush his hair back, then return to his simulated epileptic fit. This seems to have had an effect on Stipe; in subsequent years the singer would accentuate a more awkward and angular dance style very much in the King vein.

Similar to R.E.M., Gang of Four featured prominent, accomplished bass playing (courtesy of then-bassist Sara Lee*) that underpinned unorthodox guitar lines (courtesy of Andy Gill), though the Gang's songs were both more firmly in the postpunk mold and funkier than anything R.E.M. were doing. Gang of Four were also explicitly political, as their name—a reference to the four Chinese Communist Party officials who ended up getting blamed for the most extreme aspects of the Cultural Revolution—made clear. King could sometimes come across in interviews as self-serious and

---

*Lee had joined in 1981 after Dave Allen left (and following the brief tenure of Buster Jones). Allen can be credited with creating the signature sound that Jones and Lee further developed.

overanalytical. He once told Greil Marcus, "Pop songs as false emotional advertising and ideology as everydayness are themselves grounds for inquiry. Unless you have an awareness of your views as political manifestations, you won't believe you can change them." He looked askance at what he called "the published agenda of music which limits itself to a very small set of subjects . . . about missing or making up with your girl, driving the car, in some sort of all-white, Midwestern high school." In other words, he had little time for the sort of music R.E.M. had been writing and celebrating not too many months prior to meeting Gang of Four.

From my (admittedly limited, very much American) perspective, Gang of Four on paper read almost like a caricature of an issue-obsessed punk band as dreamt up by the staff of satirical publication *The Onion*. But introduce a backbeat and Gill's slashing guitar and you instantly go from the ultimate buzzkill to a great rock experience. This, too, cannot be overstated: Gang of Four could blow the roof off a club. They rocked, and they were *funky*. No one walked away from their shows unaffected. I think of R.E.M. and Gang of Four on the road together in 1981, partying together, sharing the stage night after night, partaking in the creative osmosis that can occur between a more established band and a hungry upstart, and I can almost see the wheels turning in Michael Stipe's head.*

This tour marked a rare instance of Pat the Wiz joining R.E.M. on the road. The first show with Gang of Four was to be in New York City—a location the band had deliberately avoided while they built up their chops away from the spotlight. Now that they were finally playing the Big Apple, they wanted to maximize their control over as many variables as possible—chief among them their live sound. Pat had proved his ability to nail down a good mix under difficult circumstances, so despite their very tight budget the band brought him on board for the tour. An illustration of just how tight a budget we're talking about: the band stopped in North Carolina the first night to play another gig at Fridays, a pizza parlor owned by a friend of Jefferson, in order to make enough gas money for the ride to New York.

They spent all the next day in the van, and made it to the city shortly after midnight. Patton then hopped on a train up to New Haven to visit "a lady friend from Athens who was there visiting her sister." If this departure

---

* King's withering take on the subjects of love and relationships—in "Anthrax" he sang, "Love'll get you like a case of anthrax / And that's something I don't want to catch," and in "Contract," "Is this really the way it is / Or a contract in our mutual interest?"—articulated the sentiments Stipe had been trying to express in "All the Right Friends" and, quite possibly, provided a template for "The One I Love."

Yes   Maybe or not

1 Radio Free   Nod...
2 Stumble   Nightto...
3 Laughing   S...
4 Romance   S...
5 Gardening   Action
   Without   Baby I
6,7 9→9   Perm Ver
8 Mystery   Dangerous
9 Rockville   Generic
10 Sitting Still   ~~That Beat~~
11 Burning Down   Rate Friends
12 Body Count   Wait
13 Just Q Touch   Get to the Air
14 Shaking Tru
15 That Beat
   Pretty Persuasion

Setlist for the Ritz, New York, show on June 17, 1981. Courtesy of T. Patton Biddle.

caused any trepidation on the part of the band, those worries were alleviated when Pat strode through the doors of the Ritz in the East Village the following afternoon, right on time for sound check. This entrance, seemingly on cue, prompted Bill Berry to yell out, "What a guy!"—a memory Biddle cherishes to this day.

The band did a two-night stint at the Ritz, then played a smaller headlining gig at the Left Bank in Mount Vernon, New York, on July 19. "Following that one we were driving back into the city at about 4 a.m. and trying to figure out which way to go," Biddle says, "when we caught up with a van."

> Jefferson was driving and I was in the jump seat, and he pulled up next to the van at a red light and asked me to ask the guy for directions to the high-rise we were staying at, and I did. When we started forward after the light changed, Jefferson handed me one of those [*Cassette Set* tapes] and told me to give it to the guy, and I leaned out the window of our van and reached over to hand it to him as we rolled along on a Manhattan expressway. I often wonder if he ever figured out who was on the tape and if he kept it, because it would be quite a collector's item today if he did.

Biddle describes a number of the venues they played on that tour as "Mafia hangouts." Of Emerald City, a club in Cherry Hill, New Jersey, he says, "They had emerald velvet upholstery on all of the seats, right out of *The Sopranos*."

Needless to say, the venues boasted quality sound systems.

Then it was down to the Bayou in Washington, DC ("I liked that room a lot," Biddle says), the Agora Ballroom in Atlanta, and, fittingly, a closing show at Tyrone's O.C. in Athens on June 24. In all, R.E.M. had logged seven shows in eight days.

Shortly thereafter, R.E.M. began a run of shows that in my view represents their performing peak. I have heard good-quality live recordings from all phases of the band's history, but none of those touches the mad energy of the shows they played at Tyrone's between July and September 1981, which were captured for posterity on Patton Biddle's soundboard tapes. This was not R.E.M.'s best period as songwriters or musicians, but to my ears they never *sounded* better as a live unit, and I'm guessing that few of the attendees of those shows would disagree. Patton says that the September 22 and 23 shows were "two of the most exciting nights I ever worked in my career. The crowds were electric and so was the band. Their performance left an indelible mark on my memory."

And what made the crowds so electric? R.E.M. were not riding the wave of an album release (though the "Radio Free Europe" single had just been released; more on this later). Nor were they the beneficiaries of any coordinated PR campaign. The specific energy of the audience on those two nights derived from a confluence of two factors: the strong word of mouth that had developed around R.E.M.'s live shows and the sudden surge in Athens' population of 18-to-22-year-olds due to the start of a new academic year. "It's fall quarter!" Stipe declared at the September 22 gig. "A show of hands for first-quarter freshmen!"

Freshmen—apparently a not-insignificant portion of the audience—brought with them the exhilaration of being away from home for the first time, plus finding themselves surrounded by hundreds of similarly unsupervised peers. At the same time, these young students may have been feeling some of the trepidation that usually accompanies newfound freedom. The returning students, on the other hand, were likely feeling a mix of excitement at seeing their friends again after the summer break and just a bit of sadness at the passing of summer itself. New classes meant new routines, new ideas, a new start, but also long hours spent hunched over books.

All of these factors contributed to an irresistible urge on the part of many to get blotto and dance the night away. And with alcohol serving as the fuel, R.E.M. were the vehicle that would get them to that destination.

To listen to these recordings is to catch a sonic glimpse of that energy. It's not a patch on being there, but Biddle's carefully preserved tapes have ensured that I can hear R.E.M. at least as clearly as the audience did that night, if not more so. The band's playing is not perfect—Buck, in particular, fumbles his way through certain passages—but the synergy of the four musicians working toward a shared goal makes this perhaps their finest hour (onstage, at least). Rarely have I heard Stipe so locked-in vocally, and never before or since have I heard Bill Berry play so enthusiastically.

There is also a living quality to the performance: a feeling that the show could go in any of several directions. One gets the sense that the set list had not been entirely predetermined, and so, as the performance unfolds, each moment holds the possibility of surprise, impulse, even improvisation. The latter is not a quality that R.E.M. have ever been celebrated for, and Buck tends to give the impression of looking askance at it—at least in a live context (the composition process would prove to be a different matter). But during fall 1981 R.E.M. came as close as they ever would to jamming. This came in the form of a song—and I mean that in the loosest sense—called

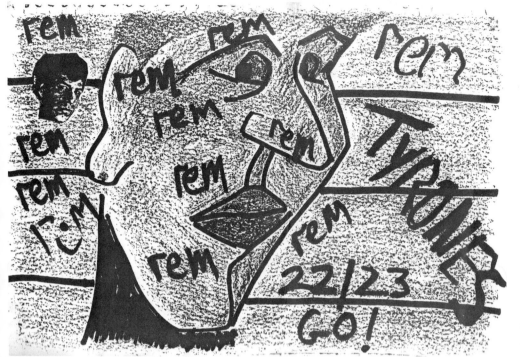

Flyer for two shows at Tyrone's, September 22/23, 1981. Courtesy of Paul Butchart.

"Skank" that the band would insert into a different part of the set every evening. They always tacked "Skank" on to the end of another song, giving the impression that they were stretching that song out and going into a free-form bit, and they never played it the same way twice. Sometimes Stipe would sing an actual verse, but more often he spewed unintelligible phrases or simply barked and yelped his way along with the music. At the July 23 performance he took one of his tape machines onstage and created vocal loops on the fly, thus edging R.E.M. closer, if only for a moment, to his Gaggle O' Sound experiments.

The antecedent for Stipe's vocal improvisations was an obvious one: Patti Smith's free-form work on "Gloria" and "Land" on *Horses*. But tacked on top of the band's half-assed reggae riffing, it sounded unique; I can only describe it as a mix between *Ummagumma*-era Pink Floyd (surely an accidental influence) and the Police (more likely a deliberate one).

In all, these recordings of a small-town band playing to a "perfect circle of acquaintances and friends" capture R.E.M. at the tail end of their apprenticeship phase. As a live unit they had fully arrived; as a songwriting entity, they were just getting started.

Legion Field, Athens, April 22, 1985. Photo © Joanna Schwartz.

Chapter Seven

R.E.M.'s achievements as an unsigned band were impressive. In short order they had gone from opening for the $windle$ to opening for major-label recording artists such as the Police, XTC, and Gang of Four. On their own, they had steadily won hearts and minds across the Southeast, dive bar by dive bar. As we have seen, this approach owed a lot to the innovative booking strategies Ian Copeland had developed while at Paragon to break new wave acts in the US. Given his continuing friendship with Bill Berry, it was perhaps inevitable that Copeland would deploy those strategies on behalf of Bill's new musical endeavor. And so, in 1981, Copeland's recently established booking agency, F.B.I. (Frontier Booking International), took on R.E.M. as a client. From that point forward all their gigs would be booked through F.B.I.'s New York office, an arrangement that created some minor headaches for Athens club owners. (Chris Edwards, the co-owner of Tyrone's, recalls the absurdity of having to call New York to book his friends who lived a few houses down on Barber Street.) This development, along with the $2-per-pitcher beer charge, signaled to many Athenians that their favorite cover band might have a future that stretched beyond the limits of Clarke County.

Copeland knew that he was taking a risk in bringing an unsigned band onto his roster, but, like Jonny Hibbert, he could sense R.E.M.'s potential. He had enjoyed their show with the Police the previous December, but it was their New York debut with Gang of Four that really clinched the deal for him. "This time I was paying attention and noticed how good Mike and Bill really were," he recalled in *Wild Thing*.

> The singer, Michael Stipe, had an unusual voice but endearing charisma. The guitar player, Peter Buck, played intricate riffs while flailing around the stage like a drunken Pete Townshend. Together, the four of them were terrific. What's more, the show received rave reviews in all the music press, confirming to me that they really were a great band, not just a band I liked for personal reasons. I decided to take them on.

After July 8, 1981—the release date of R.E.M.'s "Radio Free Europe"/"Sitting Still" single—Copeland would no longer feel the need to justify his involvement with R.E.M. The record didn't earn the band much money, but it generated more buzz than anyone could have anticipated. College stations all over the country put the track in heavy rotation, and critics fawned. Tom Carson of the *Village Voice* declared "Radio Free Europe" "one of the few great American punk singles" and Robert Palmer of the *New York Times* included it in his annual Top Ten Singles list. Hibbert had a difficult time keeping copies in stock.

So why was Peter Buck so down on this record? In subsequent years he has claimed that the single was mastered incorrectly, and he has perpetuated the story that he broke a copy of the record in frustration and nailed it to his wall. This tale has been accepted as fact by most R.E.M. biographers, but it sounds to me like another instance of Buckian hyperbole. The guitarist had been in a recording studio only a handful of times at that point; his knowledge of what constitutes correct mastering would have been limited to nonexistent. Whatever reservations he and the rest of the band may have had about the sound of the released record, they were not strong enough to prevent Berry, Buck, Mills, Stipe, and Holt from mailing almost a thousand copies to radio stations, club owners, and critics all over the country. Furthermore, almost everyone else loved the record and seemed to have no problem with the sound. It is more likely that the personality conflicts between Buck and Hibbert, along with Buck's siding with Easter in the "my mix vs. your mix" dispute, colored the guitarist's subsequent depiction of events.

Hibbert, for his part, concedes that compromises were made during the mastering process out of necessity. "Mike Mills's bass parts always reminded me of the happier-sounding Who stuff," he says.

> And so I went for that. I wanted Mills's bass to be "Meaty, Beaty, Big and Bouncy." We went back to Nashville twice on the mastering, and I'd say the first time through, the metal masters had been bruised too much . . . One of the reasons they were was because the bass was so big. But we wanted that big bass . . . There was always a trade-off and the band didn't seem to get that.

I got the chance to do my own comparison test to see what all the fuss was about. First, I gave a careful listen to the original Easter-produced *Cassette Set* version—recall that this was recorded and mixed prior to Hibbert's involvement, and thus lacks the additional guitar and vocal overdubs. I then moved on to a ripped copy of the Hib-Tone version, courtesy of my friend Vaughn Sterling—possibly one of the biggest R.E.M. fans on the planet— who bought a copy on eBay for this purpose. I finished up with Mitch Easter's mix, which was ultimately released on the R.E.M. compilation *Eponymous*. Here are my notes from the listening session:

> *Cassette Set* version: Punchy sound, whispered backing vocals. Prominent bass, but trebly. Single guitar. Less Byrds-y, but cutting, jagged riffing—more punk rock, MC5ish. Chorus is spare with maybe one additional vocal.
>
> Hibbert/Hib-Tone: Whispered vocals further back in the mix. Second guitar adds a chorus-y, 12-string effect. Nasal backing vocals in chorus clearly audible. Triangle more prominent. Definitely bassy, accentuating Mills. Cool, rich tom sound.
>
> Easter mix/*Eponymous*: Bass is way down. Second guitar *more* prominent. Whispered vocals prominent again, like in *Cassette Set* version. Jonny's voice mixed further down in chorus? Triangle super loud.

I actually like the *Cassette Set* version the best, before they started adding stuff. It has an immediacy and clarity that the subsequent tinkering obscured slightly. After that, I give the Hib-Tone single the edge because of the bass sound—which would have sounded killer coming out of cheap turntables in 1981. On the other hand, Easter's mix makes better use of the dual guitars that Hibbert himself instigated, so the choice between the Hibbert and Easter mixes, for me, comes down to a preference for big bass over big guitars. Of course, it's all subjective. I can't imagine anyone being heartbroken over the way the record sounded. Was it "murky" and "muffled," the two adjectives most commonly used to describe it? Maybe, but in my view those shortcomings add to the charm. When you consider that the *Billboard* Hot 100 at the end of that July was topped by Air Supply's "The One That You Love," all that murk and mud on the R.E.M. single sounds pretty refreshing. The Air Supply song is not a bad tune by any means, but it's so slick it almost doesn't sound like it was performed by humans. No one could level that charge at "Radio Free Europe." Ultimately, this dispute over arcane details in a mix seems hardly the sort of thing to have ended a friendship (between Buck and Hibbert), but it did. Oh, to be young and passionate!

Given the clashes with Hibbert, it's not surprising that R.E.M. chose to look elsewhere for a partner for their next release. They were egged on by Jefferson Holt, who, according to Hibbert, suggested to the band that the label owner had not done enough to secure the success of "Radio Free Europe." "Nothing could have been further from the truth," Hibbert says.

There was still a possibility, if a remote one, that R.E.M. might re-up with Jonny Hibbert at some point down the road for another project, but for now they settled on David Huber Healey—a recent Princeton graduate who had fallen hard for the band during their May 9 performance at the school's Beaux Arts Ball—as backer for their next venture, a proposed EP. Like Holt, Healey had been smitten enough to pick up stakes and move to Athens after graduation. If you're at all inclined toward superstition, then you may feel, as I do, that Dasht Hopes was not the best choice of name for Healey's fledgling record label. But at the time the informal deal seemed like a win for everyone. The guys and Healey got along socially, and Healey was willing to foot the bill for further recording sessions at the Drive-In.

Recording for the new EP commenced on October 5, 1981. The band wanted to take more gear to the session than would fit in their single van, so they asked Kurt Wood to drive two members of the band in his Volvo station wagon. It was during these sessions that Kurt truly grasped R.E.M.'s potential. "On Saturday morning, when they were getting going," he says, "I spent the morning hitting thrift stores and yard sales and whatnot with Faye [Hunter, Easter's girlfriend and bandmate in Let's Active]."

> When we came back, I guess it was early afternoon. The band had already done some recording. I think they were finishing up on "Box Cars." I was like, "Wow, that's a great song." And then they were working on "Gardening at Night," and I was like, "Wow, that's even better." They had written songs before, but most of them were just OK, or kind of derivative of other stuff, which was fine. But I thought [the new material] was some really great music. It was very impressive.

From a commercial standpoint, this new material represented a step sideways. None of the songs had the immediacy of either "Radio Free Europe" or "Sitting Still," and while the resulting EP, titled *Chronic Town*, would go on to far outsell the debut single, it did not generate an equivalent level of excitement or hyperbole. Still, the songs were arguably a leap forward artistically—a confident move away from obvious melodies and hooks into more complex, quiet, subtle terrain. This was R.E.M. abandoning the unspoken mandate that every Athens band must be a dance band. It should be noted,

Michael Stipe, 1982. Photo © Paul Cooper. Courtesy of Fred Mills.

though, that not every member of the group greeted this change of direction with enthusiasm. Bill Berry's reported reaction upon first hearing the music for "Carnival of Sorts (Box Cars)" was, "This song sucks!" Nevertheless, he rose to the occasion, and his drumming on this song ranks as some of his most unorthodox and exciting. Berry features prominently throughout *Chronic Town*, in fact. His backing vocals are strong and clear, and on tracks like "1,000,000" and "Wolves, Lower," one gets the sense he and Mills are attempting to one-up each other on their respective instruments.

In a lyrical sense it would have been difficult for Stipe to get any more obscure than he already had on "Radio Free Europe," but the *Chronic Town* material amped up the atmosphere. Taken side by side, "Wolves, Lower" and "Carnival of Sorts" function as a call-and-response of furtiveness and dread. The former contains the line "Suspicion yourself, suspicion yourself / Don't get caught," the latter, "Gentlemen don't get caught / Cages under cage." Attempts to extract further meaning from these songs will only end in tears. However, the feelings the songs evoke are specific and identifiable, which was a step beyond "Radio Free Europe," which sounded great but meant and evoked nothing.

Much of R.E.M.'s best material—and *Chronic Town* arguably belongs in that category—is distinguished by a fascinating tension. Even at its most inventive, their music remains conservative relative to that of most of their peers and influences: there are no bold fusions of punk and funk à la Gang of Four, and very few excursions into Patti Smith–style free-form improvisation, "Skank" notwithstanding. The similarity between R.E.M. and Wire has often been noted, but that really only pertains to Wire's first two records. R.E.M. would never venture anywhere near the bold art-rock of Wire's third LP *154*. Even the Velvet Underground, the band R.E.M. would come to mimic most directly, represented a bridge too far on songs like "Black Angel's Death Song" and "Heroin."

What were the reasons for these constraints? It's easy to argue that the band members were hemmed in by their musical limitations. But so were Wire. Peter Buck, the guy whose rudimentary guitar technique supposedly held R.E.M. back, had the most eclectic musical tastes of anyone in the group and, as we will see, was chomping at the bit to play in the more experimental Love Tractor. Bill Berry, the "good ol' boy" with the Southern/classic rock background, actually did play with Love Tractor for a time. Mike Mills yearned to take R.E.M.'s music in a more sophisticated direction, and Michael Stipe leapt at every extracurricular opportunity that came his way. Everyone in R.E.M. apparently wanted R.E.M. to be more than what R.E.M. actually was. And, to be fair, the band would move into increasingly more sophisticated terrain over time. But after that first giant leap from the early material into the shadowy terrain of *Chronic Town*, it would seem that each successive step was taken with great deliberation. There was definitely an R.E.M. formula; subtle changes could be made around the edges so long as the core remained intact. As Bill Berry explained in a 1987 interview with *Rolling Stone*:

> We're not so versatile that there's not going to be something in common in all our records. I think we've developed a little more now, to where we can get away with doing a "King of Birds" on a record and break it up a little bit. But that's still not going to stop "Heron House" from sounding a little bit like "Gardening at Night" slowed down. We try to diversify as much as possible, but a lot of our stuff does tend to sound the same. That's one of our weak points, I'll admit it.

Berry's implication here—that the stylistic uniformity of R.E.M.'s music is due to a lack of versatility—is directly contradicted by something Billy

Holmes tells me. "I was lucky enough to hear a lot of R.E.M. stuff that never made the cut," he says.

> Quite frankly, I think some of their better material never got put out. I heard stuff that just rocked. I mean totally, totally *rocked* like the Stones' *Exile on Main Street*. I heard electronic music, synthesizer stuff that never came out. What they would do is they would all go home and make demos, and then they would all present them to each other, and then it would be four-person democracy, and they would decide, thumbs up or thumbs down.

It's also contradicted by a track that has surfaced called "Jazz Lips," a "Revolution #9"–style mindfuck that was recorded during the *Chronic Town* sessions. Mitch Easter described this track to David Buckley as a "fun mess-around in the studio," but it sounds to my ears like there may have been more intent behind it, especially when compared to some of the other "mess-around" tracks R.E.M. has let out over the years (such as "King of the Road," from the rarities compilation *Dead Letter Office*). It has a punishing, almost industrial sound, like something from PiL's *Metal Box* album, overlaid with Stipe reading "cut-ups" from a 1950s men's magazine. Definitely a fascinating glimpse at a road not taken.

It's likely that the real reason for the band's strict adherence to formula is revealed in Berry's statement, "We can get away with doing a 'King of Birds'..." *Get away with* is the key phrase here. R.E.M. were always acutely aware of just how far they could push things while still retaining their core audience. From the moment they began playing club shows and realized they were drawing people from outside the Athens art school scene, they took care to preserve the aspects of their music that appealed to such a wide cross-section—tight song structures, strong melodies, and prominent harmonies. There was never any obvious musical flamboyance, and the songs almost never exceeded the four-minute mark. Furthermore, almost all their songs had defined verses, choruses, and often bridges. This still gave Stipe plenty of room to maneuver in, and he made use of every opportunity to art things up. This was R.E.M.'s real genius: your average listener could enjoy the catchiness of the songs, while more arty and literary types could swoon over the clever ambiguities in the lyrics and the album covers. It was a winning formula in every sense, and I don't think it's a coincidence that R.E.M. began to falter only when they abandoned it in the mid-1990s.

It was also a formula built on compromise, which flies in the face of the frequently trumpeted idea of early R.E.M. as an uncompromising artistic force. But there it is: R.E.M. compromised from the very beginning. Of course, simply being in a band involves compromise of a sort, but when the members of R.E.M. decided they wanted to pursue their musical ambitions professionally, which was pretty much from the moment they stepped up to that altar in front of hundreds of people on Kathleen O'Brien's birthday, they embarked on a path of constant compromise, making the sorts of daily creative and business choices that never would have occurred to Pylon or the Method Actors. On an artistic level, this involved a constant calculation of just how much they could "get away with."

The band member who had the most difficult time with all this was Michael Stipe. It's not that he wasn't all in along with the rest of them, but he made a concerted effort for a while to keep his various other artistic pursuits going. Of the four, he seems to have been the only one to have enjoyed being a student; as noted earlier, he was the last to drop out of school, toward the end of 1980. After that, he embarked on a number of side projects concurrent with his work in R.E.M. First came 1066 Gaggle O' Sound. Then came Tanzplagen, a collaboration with David Pierce, bassist Neil McArthur, and Krautrock-obsessed guitarist William Lee Self. Although the German band name translates to "Dance Plague," Tanzplagen was quite possibly the least-dancey Athens

40 Watt Club announcement board, November 1981. Courtesy of Paul Butchart.

band during those early years. They were, in fact, full-bore art rock bordering on prog, more reminiscent of Can, King Crimson, and even Pink Floyd than anything out of the UK or New York post-1977. Self, a professed fan of King Crimson's Adrian Belew, wrote much of the material, but Stipe's Farfisa organ became a defining element of the band's sound. The few recordings that have surfaced settle the argument once and for all as to whether Stipe could play an instrument. Like Peter Buck, he may not have had great technique or range, but his organ parts for Tanzplagen are always exactly what each song needs; his chords and single notes float into the spaces between the other instruments and vibrate hypnotically, leaving, for this listener anyway, a more lasting impression than Self's more accomplished guitar work.

When playing live, the group steered in the opposite direction of R.E.M., improvising constantly and expanding the songs well beyond the ten-minute mark. This too seemed uncharacteristic for Athens. While experimentation was always a prerequisite in the scene, and it was not unheard of to stretch songs out in a live setting, this was almost always with the aim of creating an extended dance groove. Tanzplagen were going for a more immersive sort of experience. They always booked their local shows on nights where there would be a full moon, which, according to Self, took the band and audience to higher levels of intensity and communion.

David Pierce concurs. "We had huge shows," he says. "Of course, Michael was in a band that everybody had heard."

Some of the best Tanzplagen shows were when we opened for R.E.M., like at the 40 Watt. The night of the show, they would announce that they were going to play, and then 5,000 people would show up.

But Michael was a pretty humble guy. He would sit in the back behind the keyboard. He wouldn't take center stage. Sometimes he would go in and take duct tape and would tape down the keys on his Farfisa that he wanted to play before the song had even started. He would tape down one note at a time until he had a chord going or he had some kind of interesting sound going. He'd leave the stage! Then we'd play the whole song over that and then Michael would come back and take the tape off the keyboard and leave. Sometimes he would take the mic behind the curtain with him—behind the stage. He would do sing-songy vocals but you couldn't see him. He always liked to be a little bit aloof and unapproachable. I don't know if that comes from being shy or being shrewd. He's a little bit of both.

Tanzplagen was very much a serious enterprise. They toured the Southeast and, like R.E.M., inked a deal with David Healey's Dasht Hopes label. They recorded tracks for a planned single with Joe Perry at Bombay Studios, and brought in Lynda Stipe to duet with her brother on the song "Treason." Certainly, both William Lee Self and David Pierce invested a lot of energy in the band.

I ask Pierce if there was ever the intention of going for the big time with Tanzplagen. "Well," he says, "Michael was just so busy it was never really an option. When he was in town we'd put together a show and play and then he'd go off for six months. He had obligations to R.E.M. at the time and you couldn't stand to leave something like that. They were all over the US at that time and they were hardly ever home."

To hear Tanzplagen now prompts a host of intriguing what-ifs. For instance, what if Tanzplagen, not R.E.M., had been the group to make a name for itself internationally? How would Stipe be regarded now? The "Dasht Hopes Single," as it is now known, is rough around the edges, but moody and powerful—"Treason" is not too dissimilar in its foreboding atmosphere to what UK band the Cure were doing on their *Faith* album, released around the same time that the Bombay recordings were taking place, while the Farfisa organ, so reminiscent of a mellotron, adds a hint of 1969-era King Crimson. Had Tanzplagen become Stipe's main preoccupation and continued, it's likely that he would have become a cult figure but not a mainstream celebrity—someone akin to Japan's David Sylvian or perhaps even Brian Eno: a quiet innovator haunting the edges of various projects, shaping images and sounds from behind a curtain.

As we know, it was not to be. It seems odd in retrospect that Stipe's Farfisa did not make its way into R.E.M.'s music—especially in light of Patton Biddle's recollection that the instrument held a prominent place in the band's original practice space. But then again, when you've got a proficient keyboardist like Mike Mills in the band, with Bill Berry running a strong second, Stipe and his instrument were bound to be fairly low in the pecking order. Perhaps, too, expanding Stipe's role beyond singing would have upset that crucial balance in the band's music. At any rate, Tanzplagen provided an outlet for such impulses well into 1982, at which point it became impossible for Stipe to sustain his involvement in such an elaborate side project and he let it go. William Lee Self made his way to Germany and embarked on just the sort of eclectic journeyman career that might have awaited Stipe in the absence of R.E.M.—one that was creatively fulfilling and conceptually interesting, but financially precarious.

I no longer remember how I first met Mike Richmond, co-founder of the band Love Tractor, though I can piece together a vague outline based on our known connections. We were in a statistics class together (which I'm fairly certain I failed) in the mid-'90s. I clearly remember sitting with Mike toward the back of a sparsely populated lecture hall and talking about music on a couple of occasions. I believe it was in the context of these conversations that his association with Love Tractor—a band with whom I was passingly familiar—emerged. Lean, shaggy-haired, always sporting an expression somewhere between brooding and bemused, Richmond had a youthful energy that belied his age. Until I learned who he was, I would never have suspected he had been a key participant in the community that produced the great bands of Athens' first wave. It's funny to think about this now that I'm in my forties, but back then I viewed the R.E.M. guys and their peer group, all barely into their thirties, as untouchable grown-ups, as far removed from me and my experiences as my parents were. More so, in fact, given R.E.M.'s international fame. But there was Mike, smack in the middle of his undergraduate career just like me (he had gone back to school after a long hiatus in the 1980s). He looked about the same age as me, and had a girlfriend, and was footloose and fancy-free (albeit quietly so), just like any other college student.

The second connection is that Richmond and his girlfriend frequently house-sat for my art history professor, who was the neighbor of my good friend Lee Johnson. I have an image in my mind of standing next to Lee's fig tree and talking to Mike across a backyard fence. But in all honesty I don't know if this is a legitimate memory or a conflation of my experiences with a recurring motif from the then-popular sitcom *Home Improvement*. At any rate, our association was significant enough for me that I went to see Love Tractor at the 40 Watt, but fleeting enough for Mike that he doesn't remember any of it; I suspect the only reason I remember him is because he was in a famous Athens band.

Not that Mike's lack of memory of our brief acquaintanceship prevents him from being warm and gracious when I call him up on a Saturday afternoon. Like many of the people I've interviewed for this book, he treats me like I'm an old friend. It's a Southern thing.

"I'm sitting here watching a marathon of *Star Trek: The Next Generation*," he says in his slow drawl. "Which I'm obsessed with. I love it. I don't know why. I just think it's some of the best television ever made."

And with that, we're off to the races. I've called Mike to ask him about Bill Berry's brief dual-citizenship phase, when he was a member of both R.E.M. and Love Tractor. No one can remember exactly when this took place, but everyone agrees it was over by the time R.E.M. started courting record labels. "We had already done some shows with R.E.M., and I'm just going to be honest and say that R.E.M. were big fans of Love Tractor," Mike says.

> In fact, the first time we ever played, after the show, Pete came up and said, "I want to join your band." We didn't necessarily take it seriously . . . Anyway, he didn't join the band—obviously. But at one point, Kit, who was in school, was playing in the Side Effects—he was a singer in that band and he had a girlfriend—decided that he couldn't do Love Tractor anymore, and so he bowed out. Bill just jumped on it; he's like, "I want to be your drummer." So he became our drummer for several months. There was never really this rivalry, like "Who's going to get Bill Berry as the drummer?" R.E.M. and Love Tractor, we were always like sort of pals. At the time neither band was anything, really.

Although the members of R.E.M. thought little of Bill's involvement with the other band, Bill's time in Love Tractor initiated a minor personal crisis that nearly changed the entire trajectory of this story.

"Bill was on the verge of quitting R.E.M. and going with Love Tractor," Mike says, laughing. "As bizarre as that may seem. There was a night when Bill was like, 'I don't know how I'm going to tell those guys. I'm going to quit R.E.M.!' And we were all like, 'We don't know either.'"

Why did Bill Berry come so close to jumping ship? There seem to have been two factors at play. He really liked Love Tractor's music and the easy camaraderie within the band, for one thing. As with Stipe and his Tanzplagen project, Bill enjoyed the outlet "the Tractor" gave him to do things he couldn't necessarily do in R.E.M. When it came right down to it, their songs were fun to drum on. All those interlocking parts made for an enjoyable challenge. But also, Berry was not sure at first if the other members of R.E.M. shared his commitment to making a career out of their little project. He and Mills had quit school fairly early, but Stipe kept one foot in academe right up to the last possible moment. In drumming for both bands, Bill may have been playing them against each other in an effort to determine which one had the right stuff. In the end, there was no contest. "It was really meant to be that Bill went back to R.E.M. and Kit came back to us," Mike says.

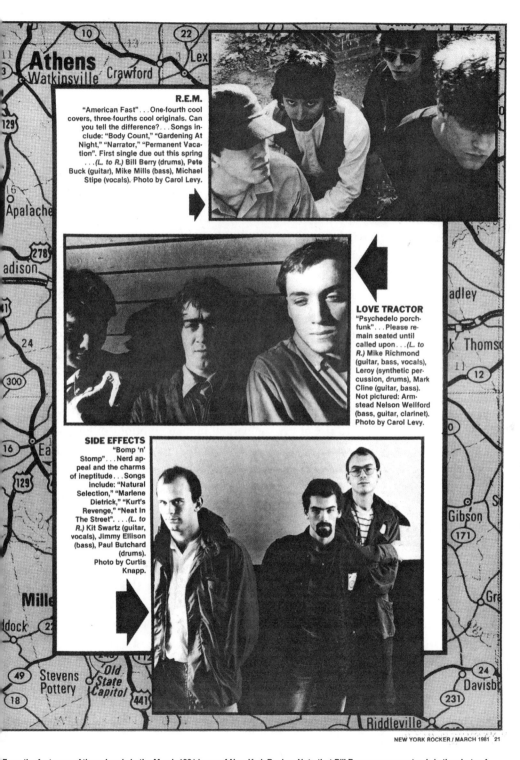

R.E.M.
"American Fast"...One-fourth cool covers, three-fourths cool originals. Can you tell the difference?...Songs include: "Body Count," "Gardening At Night," "Narrator," "Permanent Vacation". First single due out this spring ...*(L. to R.)* Bill Berry (drums), Pete Buck (guitar), Mike Mills (bass), Michael Stipe (vocals). Photo by Carol Levy.

LOVE TRACTOR
"Psychedelo porchfunk"...Please remain seated until called upon...*(L. to R.)* Mike Richmond (guitar, bass, vocals), Leroy (synthetic percussion, drums), Mark Cline (guitar, bass). Not pictured: Armstead Nelson Wellford (bass, guitar, clarinet). Photo by Carol Levy.

SIDE EFFECTS
"Bomp 'n' Stomp"...Nerd appeal and the charms of ineptitude...Songs include: "Natural Selection," "Marlene Dietrick," "Kurt's Revenge," "Neat In The Street"....*(L. to R.)* Kit Swartz (guitar, vocals), Jimmy Ellison (bass), Paul Butchard (drums). Photo by Curtis Knapp.

From the feature on Athens bands in the March 1981 issue of *New York Rocker*. Note that Bill Berry appears not only in the photo of R.E.M. but also—credited as "Leroy"— in the photo of Love Tractor. Also, the Side Effects are incorrectly listed: left to right, it's Paul Butchart, Kit Swartz, Jimmy Ellison. Courtesy of Paul Butchart.

Bill went back to R.E.M. because, really, we . . . were not prepared to hit the road and tour. We didn't really believe on the whole that we were the right musicians. Bill was going to quit R.E.M. and go with us, but we weren't prepared to do anything, and I think they were.

It's interesting, when I think back on it. I don't think that Bill Berry, Pete Buck, or Mike Mills knew the star power that Michael Stipe would go on to have, and I don't think anybody else did. I certainly didn't. I don't know that *he* knew. And I think they all liked Love Tractor better in some sense. I know that Pete and Bill and Mills all loved Love Tractor. They loved it, you know. The difference between the bands was that Michael Stipe went on to have this star power.

I find Mike's honesty refreshing. One of the questions I keep putting to the musicians from the Athens old guard is how they felt about R.E.M.'s rapid escalation in popularity. Even the other bands that had some success, such as Pylon and Love Tractor, tended to move at a slower and steadier pace relative to R.E.M.'s ascent. The response I usually get is along the lines of: "We were all friends; we all supported each other." I'm sure on one level that's true, but the reaction has to be more complicated. Very few of us are mature—or detached—enough to rise above the natural human emotions of envy and resentment when a peer starts getting a lot of attention while we remain in the shadows. Mike, to his credit, is secure enough in his friendship with the members of R.E.M. to be able to acknowledge those feelings.

None of the other bands will ever get credit for this, but I really think that R.E.M. benefited from being on the scene when all the other bands were doing more bizarre, original stuff—Pylon, Method Actors, Love Tractor, or whatever. And there was this pressure, maybe, on them—that they didn't feel cool. What happened was that they came up with this perfect marriage of traditional and weird which might still fit into the *Rolling Stone* magazine idea of what a band should be.

I'll be honest with you and say that it was hard for Love Tractor, because we felt we were an original band and R.E.M. was just this cover band, and all of a sudden that wasn't true. They had already been on the road. When we went on the road, what happened was . . . we got considered as kind of an R.E.M. clone, and it was kind of devastating to us. We talked to R.E.M. about that and they know what happened. I can't speak for the other bands—the other bands may not feel that way—but R.E.M. and Love Tractor were almost like two brothers. They both had their talents and they were both going out into the world and one of them just skyrockets to the top and the other one goes the other way. So it was tough, obviously. There's a lot of misconceptions from people and critics about how the whole thing developed. It would piss anybody off to be labeled a band that just follows R.E.M.'s example because, for one thing, it's not true—but that's just how it worked out.

Make no mistake: Mike Richmond is enormously proud of R.E.M.'s achievements and he feels honored to have been part of their story. But when he was building his own dream in the early 1980s, he didn't see himself as anybody's footnote; he was the star of his own story—which is the necessary mind-set for an artist with any degree of ambition. I've interviewed a fair number of musicians and they don't get more laid-back and self-effacing than Mike. So if he felt as he did about R.E.M.'s rise to fame, you get some sense of how the scene as a whole might have felt about that paradigm shift.

The members of R.E.M. were quickly realizing that it was going to be tricky to navigate their existing friendships in the wake of mounting success, particularly when those friendships intersected with the business opportunities that were opening up for them. Perhaps the most wrenching compromise R.E.M. had to make in their early years pertained to their business arrangement with David Healey. The Princeton transplant had funded both the *Chronic Town* sessions with Easter and the Tanzplagen sessions with Joe Perry and, as we have seen, had dreams of launching a homegrown label with R.E.M. as its centerpiece. R.E.M., meanwhile, had been drawing a lot of interest from much bigger fish ever since "Radio Free Europe" had made a splash with the music critics. New York club promoter Jim Fouratt and *Village Voice* writer Tom Carson had tried mightily to broker a major-label deal between their new favorite band and RCA Records. This involved the band dashing up to New York in February 1982, fresh off a weekend of additional *Chronic Town* recording at the Drive-In, to track seven songs at RCA's studio. These demo recordings are tight, crisp, and energetic; they give a tantalizing glimpse of what R.E.M.'s first album might have sounded like had they gone with this mega-label. But the group's collective heart was not in it.

"I do remember early on that R.E.M. turned down a major-label deal," Billy Holmes says.

It was with RCA. And my exact words to Peter were, "Dude, that's David Bowie's label! You turned down David Bowie's label!" And their attitude, or what they said in those early days, was: We are a do-it-yourself, punk rock–style band. And, you know, we have street cred in that department, and we want to keep it, and we like being our own boss. We don't want to give that away.

In truth, an official offer from RCA was never forthcoming, but neither was a rejection. It's quite possible RCA would have offered to sign R.E.M. had the band waited around long enough, but concurrent with the Fouratt/Carson courtship, R.E.M. were actively attempting to gain the attention of I.R.S. Records, the independent label owned by Ian Copeland's brother Miles. I.R.S. seemed like the dream label for the band: it enjoyed the benefit of major–label distribution (via A&M), while at the same time nurturing upstart groups like the Cramps and the Go-Go's and marketing UK groups like the Buzzcocks and Magazine to a US audience. There was little danger of R.E.M. getting lost or ignored at such a label.

Ultimately, I.R.S. did sign R.E.M. It is often assumed that this came about as a direct result of Bill Berry's long-standing friendship with Ian Copeland, but while Ian did indeed go to bat for them and was the first to provide his brother with a recording of the band, Miles Copeland initially refused to consider R.E.M. precisely because of that prior association. He wasn't particularly interested in signing a bunch of his brother's friends. Independently of Ian's efforts, however, an A&M college radio rep named Mark Williams sent a rough copy of *Chronic Town* to I.R.S. vice president Jay Boberg. Boberg fell in love with the songs, caught an R.E.M. gig in New Orleans, and offered the band a deal even though he hadn't secured Miles's permission. Miles gave his assent, though brother Ian claims in *Wild Thing* that this was only secured as the result of some horse-trading:

Miles said he needed me to help him with his new band the Bangs [later renamed the Bangles]. The problem was that they didn't impress me all that much when I saw their show . . . But Miles wouldn't take no for an answer. He needed them to work on the road to improve their performance, and to keep them from costing him retainers while they sat around in LA. In the end, we struck an informal deal. I would sign the Bangs to F.B.I. if Miles would sign R.E.M. to I.R.S.

R.E.M. got the deal they wanted. There was only one problem: Boberg wanted the *Chronic Town* EP too—which meant Healey was out.

To say that David Healey was devastated by R.E.M.'s decision to go with I.R.S. may be an understatement. It didn't matter that I.R.S. paid him back for the cost of the *Chronic Town* sessions. To the young would-be entrepreneur this marked the abrupt end of the dream he had pursued diligently ever since he'd first laid eyes on the band. He immediately left Athens, never to return. Collateral damage in the swift collapse of his now appropriately named Dasht Hopes label was Tanzplagen, whose "Lost Single" would not see the light of day until 1993.*

Before the I.R.S. deal could be closed, there was one other loose end to tidy up: Jonny Hibbert's ownership of the publishing rights for "Radio Free Europe" and "Sitting Still." Given the negative comments that have subsequently been directed his way by Peter Buck, Hibbert's take on what transpired seems more than gracious. "R.E.M. had a great, great guy representing them on the law side," he says. "Bertis Downs. And Bert really gave them super-good advice." That advice was essentially that R.E.M. needed to have a stake in their own publishing. They could achieve that either by renegotiating their deal with Hibbert or by buying back the rights to the songs completely. They opted for the latter route and presented Hibbert with a figure to buy him out. Hibbert told them, "Give me a little while to see what I can do here."

"Basically," he says, "I wanted to find a deal where I could compete with I.R.S. and offer them more, and a better, sweeter deal. And I went to a lot of folks in the music business and I couldn't get anyone to stand up and salute or to believe."

At this point Hibbert felt he had no other choice but to capitulate. Although this was not the outcome he wanted, he continues to manifest a general feeling of goodwill toward his former partners, with one caveat.

> I could probably, in another lifetime, learn to love Pete [Buck], and I definitely tried to back then. And I respected him. I respected his work ethic and his sharp-edged approach. Mike Mills and I got along great. He was a hard-nosed bargainer and he'd fight you, but it was always a fair fight. He's one of those classic Southern gentleman

---

*On November 18, 1998, a memorial notice appeared in the *Princeton Alumni Weekly* for one David Huber Healey, who had died August 25 of that year of "head injuries sustained in a bicycle accident." The memorial noted that the 38-year-old artist had "lived with great energy and intensity" and had left behind a large number of completed oil paintings in his studio at his time of death. The notice did not mention his onetime association with R.E.M.

types, real good guy, good-hearted. Same with Bill Berry. I love both of those guys. And Michael was always kind of a deeply introspective poet and a lot of fun onstage. And except for being nervous about some of his artistic details, I mean, mostly the little paper sleeve, he was very good to work with, easy to work with.

Despite such magnanimous words, Hibbert does admit to some bruised feelings—though even these are tempered by an understanding of the bigger picture.

There were a lot of times there where it was just too painful, . . .[but] I'm proud of my part in it and I'm proud of them. And they did a thing, I mean, they did a big thing. There were thousands of bands attempting the same thing at the same time. They managed to take it to the limit. They took it all the way. So you've really got to admire them for that. And the very thing that really caused me pain was, for a band like them, a strength. And that's their capacity to close ranks. And rational or not, it's sort of like if you were not one of them, then you had to either be really pleasing them or die. And that was a strength for them, I think.

My take is that Jonny Hibbert is a good guy. The fact that he praises Bertis Downs in particular, even though Downs's advice to R.E.M. about their publishing rights ran counter to Hibbert's own interests, speaks to his character, as does the fact that he maintains friendships with and holds in high regard many of the other Athens/Atlanta figures I interviewed for this book. But he has strong opinions on certain matters and is not afraid to back them up. In this regard he and Peter Buck are actually quite similar. Had they been in agreement regarding the desired sound and vision of that first single, theirs could have become a very productive partnership. But it was not to be. Even though the differences between Jonny Hibbert's mix of "Radio Free Europe" and the Mitch Easter/R.E.M.–approved version may seem negligible to most outside parties, the fact remains that Hibbert overrode the band's wishes in order to get his mix released, and that action would have likely cast a cloud over any subsequent collaborations.

If Bill Berry and his bandmates had assumed that in Miles Copeland they were getting another Ian, they were mistaken. Which is not to say that Miles was not the correct person for them to be working with at that point in their career—but it would never be an easy relationship. Miles was headstrong in a way that made Jonny Hibbert look like a pushover. He also boasted a formidable ego, though it could be argued that his sense of self-worth was well justified; he was the manager of the Police, who were then well on their way to becoming one of the biggest rock bands in the world. That alone would have made him a major player in the industry, but in addition, in his brief time as the head of an independent label, he had presided over the meteoric rise of the Go-Go's and helped lesser-known groups such as the Fleshtones and Wall of Voodoo find a wider audience.

Michael Stipe, ca. 1982. Ingrid Schorr recalls, "I had this great striped knit cotton jersey from the Potter's House, the thrift store that we all frequented downtown. Michael borrowed it for a few years and quite a few tours . . . I believe this was when REM played a "new wave night" at a disco in Augusta, Georgia." Photo by Ingrid Schorr.

Copeland was as outspoken in the early 1980s as he is now, and his views did not always mesh with the prevailing mind-set of the music community. "Copeland is a sort of right-wing fascist," Don Dixon—one of R.E.M.'s producers during the I.R.S. years—told author David Buckley. "I think he's proud of the fact that he's a right-wing fascist and I don't think he'll mind me saying that about him. I had to spend one night at his house with him going on and on about NATO and how nuclear disarmament was bad. It was kind of a difficult time, with me being the grotesque peacenik that I am."

It's true that Copeland was a Reagan guy, which to certain people of an artistic bent in the 1980s would merit the "fascist" label. Given the hard right turn the Republican Party has taken since then, however, such an orientation would probably put him squarely in the middle of the road now. Copeland, like a number of "foreign policy realists" who supported—and, in some instances, worked for—Reagan in the 1980s, later came to support Barack Obama and has articulated how that shift does not constitute a particularly dramatic change in outlook. At any rate, to the then-apolitical R.E.M., Copeland's politics would barely have registered in 1982 and would not have been any kind of factor, pro or con, in their decision to work with him.

Brains and arrogance will get you far in the music industry; they are good qualities for a label chief to possess. And if you're a young band hungry for wider exposure, Miles Copeland is the sort of pit bull you want on your side. Furthermore, Copeland's extremes were balanced out by the more even-tempered Jay Boberg. If Copeland was the visionary at the top, Boberg was responsible for the nuts-and-bolts operations of I.R.S. And Jay got R.E.M. He understood what they were going for musically and was in thrall to their artistic vision, their mystery, their otherworldliness. Not everyone at the label, or in the wider world of college radio, quite grasped the nuances of *Chronic Town* when it was finally released in August 1982. But more than a few influential people—DJs, journalists, promoters—couldn't help but get caught up in Boberg's enthusiasm for, and commitment to, his new act. Had *Chronic Town* been released on another label—RCA, even—these tastemak-ers might not have given the record the considered listen it demanded. But I.R.S. had a reputation for quality, for mining beneath the surface.

Given its opaqueness, *Chronic Town* actually sold fairly well: 20,000 copies by the end of 1982. It ranked high in the *Village Voice's* Pazz & Jop Critics' Poll and secured the band its first *Rolling Stone* profile—penned by Andy Slater, a former college friend of Peter Buck. R.E.M. had cultivated its contacts well. But *Creem's* Robert A. Hull summed up the prevailing reac-tion of many listeners: "This EP is so arcane that I had to play it six times in a row to get a handle on it—and even now, I'm still not sure." Many could not decide if this effort represented a bold declaration of intent or simply a display of confusion. In the end, most gave it the benefit of the doubt; "Radio Free Europe" had been almost universally loved and now R.E.M. had I.R.S. Records behind them. If *Chronic Town* was a difficult work to love, it was at least an easy work to admire. It suggested hidden depths and telegraphed the possibility of future glories in nearly every measure.

At first, the new record deal and its accompanying infusion of cash did not translate to a more comfortable life for the band. It was time to get to work. While the touring circuit now included the entire country, the band's MO remained the same: a beat-up van, shared accommodations, lots of alcohol, and very little sleep. This was, after all, an Ian Copeland–helmed operation. They did pickup gigs in obscure venues in flyover states, and on one occasion, when getting ready to play an opening slot for a "Hot Legs" competition at a bar in Albuquerque, New Mexico, they were paid at the last minute *not* to perform.

Ian Copeland knew what he was doing, though. What had worked for Squeeze and the Police also worked for R.E.M. And R.E.M. *definitely* knew what they were doing by now. They could blaze through a performance with confidence and enthusiasm, and were experienced at tweaking a set list on the fly—or throwing it out entirely—based on how the audience responded. Each show had its memorable moments, but the show at First Avenue in Minneapolis on April 26, just a couple of weeks before the I.R.S. deal was formally signed, brought a ghost of the not-too-distant past rapping on the door of their van. The guys had just pulled up to the curb and were getting their stuff together for sound check when the knock came, followed by a shrill voice in an oddly indeterminate Midwestern accent: "Hey, you guys need help unloadin' or anything?"

Mike Mills cracked the door open, saying, "No, we're fine," peered around, and then did one of those double-takes you'd see in a silent comedy. "ORT!"

Sure enough, there was their dear friend, in his rumpled clothes, grinning from ear to ear. It was as if he had picked the precise moment between their carefree past and their regimented, label-bound future to appear out of thin air, a living reminder of the place and the people that had kicked this whole thing off. Sometimes, when you miss home enough, home comes to you. Dropping the put-on accent to speak in his regular baritone, Ort told them he was in town for the annual Beer Can Collectors of America* convention and had learned of R.E.M.'s upcoming show via the newspaper. Recalling the story for me many years later, over beers at Copper Creek Brewery, Ort laughs heartily at the memory of Mills's reaction. "Little did he know that I had acquired some of their 45s, and I had been selling them to record stores," Ort says. "I had given one to the University of Minnesota student radio station, and so on and so forth. So I had been a sort of Johnny Appleseed. But it was quite the reunion, and no, I didn't have to pay to get in." Ort pauses to gaze wistfully at some unfixed point beyond his beer glass. "And I think back to a lovely woman I met that day at the University of Minnesota student union, and I realize I could've gotten her in to the show with me; it wouldn't have been any problem in the world." He pauses, and then, as he often does, Ort says something that moves and surprises me. "And I wonder if she has ever thought of me as I have over and over thought of her."

R.E.M. closed out the year auditioning a potential new producer, Stephen Hague. Though he would go on to huge success producing Orchestral Manoeuvres in the Dark, New Order, Pet Shop Boys, Erasure, and more, Hague

---

* This is a real organization. They have since rebranded as BCCA: Brewery Collectibles Club of America, and publish a quarterly magazine called *Beer Cans & Brewery Collectibles*. Their "CANventions" are still going strong; the one in 2015 was held in a town that might be considered their mecca: Milwaukee.

was at that time a relative newcomer in the field. But his work with his own band, Jules and the Polar Bears, and another group called Gleaming Spires, demonstrated a direct and melodically airtight pop sensibility—a quality I.R.S. hoped R.E.M. would accentuate in their own work. It was there in the songs, they knew, but Stipe had a tendency to slur his words and pull back from overt emotion—as demonstrated by his rather tepid vocal on the *Chronic Town* version of "Gardening at Night." (Live, he sang that song rather more forcefully.) Perhaps a more pop-oriented producer would be able to overcome such obscurantist tendencies.

Recording with Hague at Synchro Sound in Boston, R.E.M. tracked a version of "Catapult" that stands out now as possibly a greater oddity than "Jazz Lips." It starts out strongly enough: a new, layered guitar arrangement at the beginning ramps up the drama, then Stipe's voice comes in clear and strong. Impressive harmonies add to the excitement. So far, so good! But then, during Stipe's "Did we miss anything?" refrain, a thin, noodly synth line—something more appropriate to a Thompson Twins song—crawls all over our beloved melody and dies there, taking down the entire song in the way a deadly virus takes down its host.

The Hague-produced version of "Catapult" is justifiably considered a train wreck. And yet it's important to understand that it is a train wreck primarily in the light of established history. Had R.E.M. gone in a different direction at this particular fork in the road and adopted the early '80s "new pop" synth sound, we might now be discussing Hague's recording as the place where R.E.M.'s sound really began to come together. And perhaps in that context the synth wouldn't sound so jarring. What's more, if you remove the synths entirely and turn down the reverb, you are left with a great version of "Catapult" that—in my opinion, however heretical—surpasses the one on R.E.M.'s debut album. So I'm going to extend some love to Stephen Hague here. He showed up and gave it his best shot. And, in those early days before R.E.M.'s sound was fully solidified, this session helped crystallize for the band members exactly what R.E.M. was—and what it was not. In the short run they found the experience demoralizing. But in the long run it proved defining.

Clearly, I.R.S. wanted R.E.M.'s debut album to be less murky than *Chronic Town*. Because of this, they were concerned about giving Mitch Easter a further shot at producing the band. But R.E.M. were on Easter's side. They had chafed at Hague's more regimented recording style; Berry, in particular, had found the process of playing to a click track constricting and demoralizing. With Easter they knew what they were getting: a relaxed but focused environment in which the music would be allowed to come forth organically.

Easter made a pitch of his own: He would record an audition track with the band, this time using upgraded facilities. And he would bring in his friend and mentor Don Dixon to help him navigate the expanded world of 24-track recording. Don had already worked with Mitch on an early version of "Wolves, Lower" and was therefore known and trusted by the band. It certainly helped that Don was an accomplished musician, having played in the popular South Carolina group Arrogance—a band that Peter Buck admired.

On January 6, 1983, the producers decamped with R.E.M. to Reflection Sound Studios in Charlotte, North Carolina. Over the course of that day they recorded and mixed the impressive "Pilgrimage," a song that made full use of the additional tracks at their disposal. The recording not only concentrated all of R.E.M.'s previously established strengths into a tight, four-minute mini-epic, it also pushed the band into new territory. Harmonies had always a been high point for them, but here the three vocalists really went for it in the chorus—Stipe singing "Take a turn," Mills repeating the line in clear, celebratory tones, Bill Berry answering his bandmates with hypnotic incantations of "Ah-ah," the three melodies weaving in and out of each other to powerful effect. Then, in the bridge, Bill went low while Stipe chanted "Pilgrimage! Pilgrimage!"

Other highlights of the demo were its creative arrangement—Easter's signature use of a bass line doubled on the low keys of a piano, along with a vibraphone—and Bill Berry's innovative drumming. "The pilgrimage has gained momentum," indeed. This was the sound of R.E.M. responding to the Stephen Hague challenge and demonstrating how they could deliver striking pop on their own terms. It was a pop song, yes, but one that managed to incorporate lyrics like "They called the clip a two-headed cow" and the fabulous "Speakin' in tongues, it's worth a broken lip."

When presented with the finished track, I.R.S. conceded its superiority to Hague's "Catapult." And with that, Easter and Dixon got the green light to produce R.E.M.'s first album, *Murmur*.

L.E.A.F. (Legal Environmental Assistance Foundation) benefit, Moonshadow Saloon, Atlanta, February 18, 1985. Photo © Joanna Schwartz.

Chapter Eight

My friend and fellow writer T. Kyle King attended the University of Georgia as an undergraduate in the 1980s and then returned as a law student in the 1990s. During those years, he recalls, he was surrounded by R.E.M. not only literally, in the sense that one couldn't walk down Broad Street in the '80s without passing someone from R.E.M. going in the other direction, but also figuratively: their music served as sonic wallpaper for anyone living in Athens in that decade, regardless of whether they were a fan or not. Kyle himself never paid much attention to R.E.M. during those years. They were just there, as much a part of the town as the Mayflower Restaurant or, for that matter, Ort.

In 2014, perhaps prompted by R.E.M.'s demise three years earlier, Kyle decided to take a closer look at the band he had more or less taken for granted his entire adult life. He started with *Murmur*, and after several days of immersion in its mysteries, he had this to say:

> It is noteworthy that, when listening to *Murmur*, one does not think, "Oh, yeah, right; this is from 1983" until the chorus of track seven ("Catapult"). 1983 was the year of the Police's "Every Breath You Take," Yes's "Owner of a Lonely Heart," Lionel Richie's "All Night Long," Michael Jackson's "Beat It," Irene Cara's "Flashdance," Michael Sembello's "Maniac," and Billy Joel's "Tell Her About It." This is the world into which *Murmur* was unleashed.
>
> Yet it is also noteworthy how much it sounds like what had become conventional music a decade later. I knew the work of mainstream artists circa 1993 was somewhat derivative of R.E.M., but I hadn't really been aware of how early and how overarching that influence was. Frankly, from this point forward, I probably will regard most of the singles that charted in the early to mid-1990s the way I regard every romantic comedy made after "When Harry Met Sally"; namely, as a cheap knock-off of the real thing.

Indeed. With *Murmur*, R.E.M. set out to make a record that made no concessions to current trends. There would be no synthesizers, no Phil Collins–style gated reverb drums. Instead, they filled the record with pianos and acoustic guitars. And though they were recording in a state-of-the-art 24-track facility, they did not seem to use a single instrument or guitar effect that the Beatles would not have had access to in 1966. Again, this seemed a deliberate reaction to Stephen Hague's efforts to bring the band in line with the British "new pop" sound. Mike Mills said as much, without referencing Hague specifically, in an interview with *Pitchfork* in 2011:

> Some musicians need to reject the past in order to do what they want to do, but we weren't trying to create something brand-new. We were trying to do something original, but not necessarily ground-breaking. We were making music that made us happy, whatever that happened to be. We just knew we didn't want to do the crap that was on the radio at the time.

And they pulled it off. Not only did their concerted effort at timelessness set them apart from most of their peers, but it also, as King notes, set the tone for much of what came after them.

Murmur was recorded during January and February 1983, often in two- to three-day bursts bookended by shows in Athens and Charlotte and one lone gig in Davison, North Carolina. R.E.M. played the shows with their usual full-bore power, then went into the studio to recast the same material in rather quieter tones. In this, they were surely influenced by Easter's view that albums should be self-sufficient works of art and not simply approximations on wax of a band's live sound. The addition of Don Dixon's expertise and discipline ensured that *Murmur* took a step forward sonically and melodically while maintaining the sense of experimentation and adventure that had distinguished *Chronic Town*. For the justifiably nervous Jay Boberg, whose reputation was on the line, the end result proved the best of all possible worlds: a seriously catchy album with fathomless depths.

Stipe's lyrics, pushing further into fragmentation, still yielded snatches of meaning. "West of the Fields,"* with its references to "Dreams of Elysian" and repeated chants of "Long gone, long gone" takes on the subjects of death and the afterlife. The dense and dissonant "9-9" ends each of its sections with the

---

* This song features a rare instance of lyric co-writing; Stipe's friend Neil Bogan is credited alongside the band.

refrain "conversation fear." It's impossible to know if this was a reference to Stipe's ongoing social anxiety, but he certainly sang the lines with conviction. "Laughing" obliquely references *The End of the Road*, a rather dark satirical novel by John Barth that deals with, among other things, ennui, identity confusion, casual sexual relationships, and its protagonist's paralyzing fear of emotional intimacy. All Stipean obsessions, to be sure, though we probably wouldn't know that this provided a model for the seemingly impenetrable "Laughing" if Stipe himself hadn't said so in interviews.*

Then there is "Perfect Circle," a ballad that featured Stipe's mournful lyrics spread across an elegant, circular piano pattern written by Bill Berry.

Pull your dress on and stay real close
Who might leave you where I left off?

What's it all about? *Who* is it all about? All Stipe would say was that it was about an old girlfriend. But Peter Buck had other ideas. As he told band biographer Tony Fletcher several years later:

> I was standing in the City Gardens in Trenton, New Jersey, at the back door and it was just getting dark. These kids were playing touch football, the last game before dark came, and for some reason I was so moved I cried for twenty minutes . . . I told Michael to try and capture that feeling. There's no football in there, no kids, no twilight. But it's all there.

Fletcher dates Buck's story to October 1982, at which point the band had been performing relentlessly for over a year. Some readers may wonder why a young man in his early twenties who was well on the way to seeing all of his dreams fulfilled would get so choked up watching a football game. Such a reaction, a sort of "Rosebud" moment, would seem more appropriate in someone twice Buck's age mourning his lost youth. But perhaps that was precisely what was happening. On a barely conscious level, the image of the kids playing at dusk may have brought Buck face-to-face with the realization that his own carefree days were already behind him. He could practically still smell the food Kathleen O'Brien had cooked for everyone on New Year's Eve, 1980—food

---

*I am intrigued by this anonymous Amazon reviewer's comment on the book: "Barth, himself, seems to be an author whose message is simple—the world is going straight to hell and we are going with it, so why not have a laugh on ourselves now and then?" Which sounds a lot like the premise of a very popular R.E.M. song that would come our way in 1987.

that he and Stipe had proceeded to hurl at each other, instigating—to O'Brien's horror—a massive food fight. And yet that was already ancient history: visions and scents of a former life. Not that Buck was necessarily more mature now, but most of his future drunken escapades would function primarily as moments of release from an increasingly stressful existence. When you decide you're in it to win, you never again have nothing to lose.

It's hard to find any of this in Stipe's lyrics for the song, but it's certainly there in Buck's playing, particularly the melancholy electric guitar notes that rain around Stipe's line "A perfect circle of acquaintances and friends / Drink another, coin a phrase." It was during the recording of this song that R.E.M. began to sense their own power, though they would never have put it in quite those words; the most they might have said is that it made them realize that something was happening, or that here they truly began to feel like a real band. "Perfect Circle" was, after all, a proper ballad. Furthermore, it was based around the piano, an instrument the musicians could not yet afford to bring with them on the road. This inconvenient detail would render "Perfect Circle" virtually unplayable in a live context for the next few years, but the trade-off seemed worth it. R.E.M. had freed themselves from the concern of "How is this going to sound live?" and were focusing on "What sound is best for this song?" instead. They were now composers first, performers second. And they had reached this crucial point in their artistic development just in time for their debut album.

As mentioned earlier, the music for "Perfect Circle" was written primarily by Bill Berry, offering an early example of his strong melodic instincts. And yet, memorable as the song is, Berry's best songwriting lay ahead of him. It could be argued that *Murmur* represented his peak as a drummer, though, if we are to judge his drumming contributions on their creativity rather than their forcefulness. (There would be plenty of loud pounding in a more traditional "rock" style later in the decade.) Consider the reggae-tinged skittering of his hi-hat and toms in the intro to "Laughing," the tribal-style rolls in the chorus of "Moral Kiosk," the sly disco beat surfacing on the second half of each verse in "West of the Fields," or the deliberately faltering rhythms in "9-9"; all these contributions pushed the songs into uncharted territory without drawing undue attention to themselves—indeed, the moment you pick up on what he's doing, he's back to a straight Ringo-style 4/4.

Murmur was released on April 12, 1983. It was a momentous occasion in the band's career, to be sure, but it is not the date from that April that a lot of the people who had helped R.E.M. get to this point will recollect. I doubt it is the date Michael Stipe thinks of, either. *That* date would be one day later, April 13. R.E.M. were in Rochester, New York, where they had just finished a set opening for the English Beat, but the event that transformed the Athens scene in general, and Stipe's life in particular, occurred several hundred miles to the south on a stretch of highway between Atlanta and Athens. A car full of people including Michael's longtime friend and collaborator (and sometime lover) Carol Levy, local musician Larry Marcus, and future *Party Out of Bounds* author Rodger Lyle Brown was run off the road on the way back from a concert by another driver who, according

Carol Levy. Photo courtesy of Paul Butchart.

to Paul Butchart, was "changing a cassette in her car." A number of passengers were injured; Levy and Marcus were killed. In a Facebook posting marking the thirtieth anniversary of the accident, Butchart noted that the crash signified the end of the innocence of "the crazy Athens music lifestyle we had all been leading up to this point." He remembered "going downtown and seeing friends wandering dazed and crying . . . We were all in shock and it would take a while for us to recover."

Carol Levy's spirit hangs palpably over the origins of the Athens music scene virtually everywhere you turn. It leaps from the few photographs of her that are in circulation; the one I've seen most often is a blurry black-and-white shot in which an impossibly young-looking Levy stares out from under a Beatles-style mop-top—young-looking, that is, apart from her eyes, which seem defiant and a little sad. Then there are the pictures of her band Boat Of, in which the young artist's expression in each freeze-frame seems to encapsulate, in bandmate Tom Smith's words, her "disdain for the easy and the obvious." It's easy to see why she got on so well with Stipe; she seemed to embody that iconoclastic Patti Smith–style energy that had so captured him when he first heard *Horses*. "Carol was fearless," says Ingrid Schorr. "That's the word that comes to mind. She was outspoken and quick-witted and I don't think I ever heard her express a doubt or hesitation . . . She made gazpacho once out of a can of Campbell's tomato soup and a chopped-up onion . . . She used a paper lunch bag for a purse . . . I loved her a lot."

It was not until 2011 that Michael Stipe said anything much in public about his relationship with Levy, and even then he did not mention her name. But anyone from the Reed Hall days who read Christopher Bollen's piece on Stipe for *Interview* magazine knew exactly who the singer was talking about. The context for his comments was a question about past drug use. "I stopped taking drugs [in 1983]," Stipe told Bollen.

> There were a lot of things that led up to it. One thing was that a lover died. An ex of mine died in a car wreck and I was really trashed when I found out about it and I couldn't cry. I woke up the next morning and I said, "That's it," so I quit then. It was horrible. A bunch of people died around that time and she was one of them. I wrote a song about her—that was when I still did pull from autobiographical material. I didn't really have my voice until after that.

The song in question is "Camera," which would appear on the band's sophomore album, *Reckoning*. In the recorded version, Stipe sings, "When the party lulls, if we fall by the side," which is most likely a reference to those fevered couplings at the church just a few years previously—years that by then must have felt like lifetimes ago. Then, "I still like you, can you remember?" Denise Borschell, a friend of Paul Butchart's, commented in his Facebook thread about Levy that Stipe changed this line during a 1999 performance to "I still love you, can you remember?"

There is a lot to unpack in Stipe's comments from the *Interview* piece. Most surprising of these is the assertion that he didn't find his voice until after the accident. That means, by his own reckoning, Stipe didn't become a fully formed artist until after his acclaimed work on *Murmur*. We will be examining the post-*Murmur* lyrics in some depth in succeeding pages, so you can decide for yourself whether you agree with him on that point.

Then there is Stipe's claim that he gave up all drugs in 1983, a claim that anyone who has spent time watching 1980s-era R.E.M. footage would perhaps view with some skepticism. If you set this book down for a moment, go to YouTube, and take a stroll through the clips of R.E.M. from MTV's *The Cutting Edge* in 1984, or the band's appearance at Hamburg's Rockpalast in 1985, or the clip of "These Days" from 1987's Work tour, you would be hard-pressed to find an instance where Stipe does not appear to be bombed out of his gourd. And apart from his behavior, there's the matter of his physical appearance. Rarely the picture of robust health, the singer seemed at various points during the '80s and '90s to be aspiring to emulate the gaunt, hollow-eyed Confederate boy-soldiers you see staring out from crumbling sepia-toned Civil War photographs.

Yet one source of mine after another has confirmed the essential truth of Stipe's statement, many commenting on how conspicuously uninterested in drugs and alcohol Stipe seemed throughout R.E.M.'s virtually ceaseless run of tours in the 1980s. In fact, no one can seem to remember a time when Stipe *did* show an interest in such things. One source who worked closely with Stipe on a nearly daily basis for much of the decade can recall Stipe partaking of cocaine only once, and that was when the source offered it to him at a party back in 1981. "He just didn't seem to have the appetite for drugs and alcohol that the rest of us did," this person says.

I mention to Kathleen O'Brien the apparent incongruity of Stipe's crazed behavior in the live footage I've seen, given what I'm learning about his private life. What would cause someone to appear to be high on drugs if that wasn't the case?

"He wasn't much of a drinker, and he just wasn't into recreational drug use at all," she confirms.

> He didn't need it . . . It wasn't anything like, he got drunk and did this . . . Whatever his eccentricities were, whatever he did, he did it just because that's who he was. I think Michael also was very shy, and I don't think his eccentricity is at all affected. I think it was totally him. I think it was kind of a coping mechanism for him to deal with attention, because they were getting a lot of attention from the very get-go.

I believe O'Brien and my other sources. They have no reason to protect Stipe, particularly when the man himself has been very forthcoming on this subject in recent years. As for his unhealthy appearance, that may have been due to an on-off struggle with an eating disorder, something he revealed for the first time in the same *Interview* profile (more on this later).

R.E.M., to their great credit, have never glorified drugs—either in their music or in interviews. In fact, in 1988 the band enthusiastically endorsed the Basement, an Atlanta-area drink-and-drug-free teen club, and their stamp of approval helped boost that establishment's numbers. But there's no denying that illicit substances were firmly in the mix, at least for those individuals not named Stipe, during the road-heavy years of 1981 to 1987, just as they were at every party going back to the days of the Reed Hall subwastement gatherings. As might be expected, the type and quality of drugs evolved over time as bank accounts swelled. R.E.M. biographer Johnny Black notes that Bill Berry has admitted to having used cocaine, but given his surroundings that's a bit like admitting you got wet in a swimming pool.

Both Denise Sullivan's *R.E.M.: Talk About the Passion* and Rodger Lyle Brown's *Party Out of Bounds* expend a fair amount of ink on the history of intravenous speed use in Athens. While neither associates R.E.M. directly with such practices, there is a reason both authors featured these stories. Powder drugs were everywhere—in the clubs, in the bathrooms, in the van. Roadies used them. Club owners used and dispensed them. Wannabes flaunted their abuse of them.

"Well, you can imagine, the Velvet Underground and Warhol were big influences on a lot of those Athens kids," Billy Holmes says.

> You know, that was all gritty and nasty . . . And I think there was that whole thing—Athens wanted to be New York. I always said when people asked me, "What was Athens like?" I would say, just imagine a town that is half Hooterville and half Greenwich Village. It is a college town, and college kids don't just drink, they do drugs. It was like . . . your crazy uncle would fall out of the closet. But he would not be your typical Billy Carter type, he'd be William Burroughs.
>
> A lot of kids were doing crystal meth and all of that. Those drugs were what you would snort. But there was a form of crank [low-purity crystallized methamphetamine] which was so chemically unstable you couldn't snort it. They called it "biker crank." And people would shoot it. I don't know that a whole lot of people were doing that . . .
>
> People consider me just an old fuddy-duddy, you know, but to my mind a lot of what ruined the Athens music scene was that people started shooting up crank. And then they went from snorting cocaine to smoking cocaine to shooting cocaine, and then, you know, it went from shooting cocaine to shooting a mixture of cocaine and heroin, and then shooting heroin. . . Yes, unfortunately, people were not just taking pills. And the whole college scene got out of hand up there, and it has been that way for a long time.

What does this have to do with the music? Quite a bit if we're talking about R.E.M.'s live performances. Stipe has admitted that the band used speed in the early days (pre-1983), though if "biker crank" ever came into the picture it was not as part of the regular diet. Given the band's punishing schedule, it's hard to blame them for relying on some extra fuel to keep going. There is no doubt that speed and other uppers contributed to the high energy of R.E.M.'s early shows. Add in nerves, adrenaline, and copious amounts of alcohol, and you have a powerful elixir that took the music to some surprising places. To deny the crucial role these drugs played in R.E.M.'s formidable early stage show would be disingenuous. But at the same time, the band made a conscious decision to remove that mad energy from the equation on *Murmur* in order to showcase the songwriting. *Murmur* was almost a reaction against the high-intensity live persona that had done so much to cement the band's reputation. The album was essentially saying, "Now that we've gotten your attention, let's draw a little closer and have a real conversation."

It was a gamble, for sure—one that, in the short term, may not have seemed to have paid off. If we strip away the album's subsequent reputation as one of the all-time great rock debuts and take a cold, hard look at the reality, we find that *Murmur* initially sold around 200,000 copies. Not bad by any stretch, but, according to Jay Boberg, not the sort of figure I.R.S. had hoped for. In terms of positive reviews and critical accolades, though, *Murmur* was a bigger hit than anyone could possibly have imagined. It seems that some of the appeal, oddly enough, derived from R.E.M.'s perceived provincialism. They were, after all, a band from *somewhere else*—not New York or LA or Chicago—a band that had steadfastly refused to leave home. And what was the story with Athens, Georgia, anyway?* The photograph on the front cover, by Sandra-Lee Phipps, showed a strange, lumpy, viney thing that appeared half animal, half vegetable, like a forest creature out of Tolkien. The back featured an image of some kind of rickety bridge stretching off into the distance. Factor in the evocative, present-era-shunning music and the whole package seemed to call out from some sort of ultrahip backwoods oasis where a bunch of successors to Flannery O'Connor and William Faulkner were strapping on guitars and forming bands.

In reality, though, these cover images were more a testament to the evocative power of photography than anything else. That "creature" on the front cover was the ubiquitous kudzu vine, a weed that, left unchecked, will overrun virtually anything in its path. It is widely considered a blight on the land. As someone who moved to the South at the age of 18, I can attest that kudzu, to my outsider's eyes, did indeed have a sort of alien beauty to it. But any self-respecting Southerner will laugh at such romanticized notions. And that "bridge" on the back cover was an abandoned train trestle,

---

* *Musician* magazine dispatched J. D. Considine to R.E.M.'s hometown in an attempt to find out what all the fuss was about, but the resulting piece was a mix of predictable condescension— he writes that the other guests at the Athens Holiday Inn where he stayed were all in town for a conference on, he speculates, "bovine prosthetics or some such"—and genuine bewilderment that R.E.M., or anyone else of merit, could have emerged from such a place. The inability of Considine and other critics to unravel this mystery may have inadvertently added to the mystique.

as unremarkable in the South as a shuttered factory in Detroit. Nowadays the trestle provokes heated arguments between music fans and local government, the former wishing to preserve a musical landmark, the latter at a loss for how to maintain this decrepit and potentially dangerous relic of the railroad days. Certainly, the place had no real significance for Phipps or the band. As Phipps told the *Wall Street Journal* in 2012, "Why do they need to preserve it? To be honest, today I don't even know where the trestle is . . . It was just done randomly. Somehow it ended up mattering to people."

Lyrically, there was nothing on *Murmur* to pin it to Athens, to Georgia, or even to the South. Musically the story was much the same, apart from some half-assed yodeling on "Shaking Through" and a vague Southern twang here and there. It would seem, then, that the band's celebrated sense of place, at least on this first album, was largely achieved via smoke and mirrors. Yet the intent was there. In a 2013 interview with *Salon*, Peter Buck explained the band's subtle approach: "Art isn't something that happens in New York or Paris, it happens everywhere. And if it's good, you can represent where you're from, to a certain degree. That's a little bit of what R.E.M. was trying to do. We didn't say we're super Southern, but I think we gave a sense of place."

Something of the place does come through on *Murmur*, even if it is somehow buried between the actual notes. Later R.E.M. albums would reference Athens and the South more explicitly, but it seems to me that the one-two punch of *Chronic Town* and *Murmur* captures the *spirit* of the town the best—perhaps because the band members were still spending most of their time there. The delicately picked guitar patterns, nasal vocals, and lyrics steeped in mystery seem to suggest a self-contained world willed into existence by its inhabitants. When I first heard *Murmur*, a good four years after its release, these qualities called out like a siren song; they played a larger role in my decision to attend the University of Georgia than I was willing to admit at the time. I had a vision of an eccentric small town somewhere off in the murky woods, a place where a community had fallen under the spell of art for art's sake and students and scenesters alike flocked to clubs in droves to pogo-dance to quirky, angular art rock. Astonishingly, the place I found largely matched the place I had imagined (probably the only time in my life that has happened). Now, it's quite possible that the Athens I envisioned—this mecca of free-spirited creative enterprise—didn't actually exist when *Murmur* appeared in 1983. The scene that has been described to me was certainly a vibrant one, but it was also more underground than what I found when I arrived in Athens a decade later. It follows, then, that what I found had, at least in part, been *created* by *Murmur*. "As above, so below," the Hermetic expression goes. Begin with the idea, the myth, then watch it manifest itself in reality.

Murmur received nearly unanimous critical praise both in the US and the UK, but by far the biggest boost came from *Rolling Stone*—first, in a review from Steve Pond that praised it as an "intelligent, enigmatic, deeply involving album . . . revealing a depth and cohesiveness to R.E.M. that the EP could only suggest," and then in the magazine's end-of-year poll, in which R.E.M. nabbed "Band of the Year" and "Best New Artist" accolades and *Murmur* bested Michael Jackson's *Thriller* in the "Album of the Year" category.

These plaudits must have come as a shock to the many Athens residents who still regarded R.E.M. as a thoroughly mainstream party band. Steve Pond had concluded his *Rolling Stone* review with the words "R.E.M. is clearly the important Athens band," which would have been perceived as a slap in the face by—well, just about every other musician in town. It would be easy enough to simply chalk this statement up to overexuberance on the part of Pond and *Rolling Stone*, except that Stipe himself had been uncharitable toward his peers in an earlier short profile in *Rolling Stone* (titled, tellingly enough, "R.E.M.: Not Just Another Athens, Georgia, Band") written by the band's friend Andy Slater. Stipe had told Slater, "We're not a party band from Athens, we don't play new wave music, and musically, we don't have shit to do with the B-52's or any other band from this town. We just happen to live here." While there is nothing factually untrue in the statement—R.E.M. had ceased being a party band with the release of *Chronic Town*—it does seem somewhat astonishing that Stipe would say something like this to a national publication when he and the other guys still lived on Barber Street among the other bands he "didn't have shit to do with." But on another level, can we blame him? Some of those friends and neighbors had been looking down their noses at his band for years. Tom Smith could hardly be bothered to acknowledge his friend's main gig. In 2002, Smith reminisced to *Wire* magazine about the time when, "out of a misbegotten display of group solidarity," he "ventured into frat-boy redoubts to witness R.E.M. in concert. I was utterly appalled by their set." Smith characterizes his view as a "minority opinion," but it was by no means unusual.

In years to come, R.E.M. would be extremely generous toward their friends in the Athens scene, often bending over backwards to produce and promote their efforts. They would give back more than anyone could reasonably have expected. But in this first flickering moment of national exposure, the temptation to do a little dancing in the end zone proved too strong to resist.

Even some of R.E.M.'s local supporters did not warm to the band's apparent change of direction on *Murmur*. Jeff Walls, a guitarist whose band Guadalcanal Diary would later tour with R.E.M., falls into this camp. "Those first few shows we played with them [in 1981], I thought they were great," he says.

> They were real energetic onstage. One thing that I liked about them and what made them unique, I thought, was that a lot of their songs were minor chord change songs that were kind of driving. "Pretty Persuasion" would be a good example. They would work their dynamics well, and it was impressive; the song's over and your heart's beating a little faster. It's like seeing the Who or something. That's what I was equating it with at the time. I remember being really disappointed with that first I.R.S. album. It was like, what have they been smoking? Everything was much more laid-back than I'd remembered.

Walls was hardly the only person who wished more of the R.E.M. he knew had made it onto *Murmur*. For the most part, though, the difference between R.E.M. on record and R.E.M. live worked very much in the band's favor. The pattern would usually unfold like this: a DJ or critic or casual listener would discover the band via *Murmur*. Sufficiently intrigued, that person would then go to see R.E.M. in concert and be floored by the intensity of the performance. He or she would then tell his or her friends, those friends would buy the album, see the shows, and tell *their* friends, and so on. It was a great way to build a grassroots fan base. The fact that the band was so different live than on record created a rite of passage for fans, similar to what Grateful Dead fans experienced when seeing that band live for the first time.

As could be expected, curious listeners got plenty of opportunities to see R.E.M. onstage in 1983. The band toured virtually nonstop, just as they had the previous year, pausing only for a few weeks in September—and even then they continued to work, rehearsing steadily, doing a couple of impromptu local gigs, and contributing music and "acting" to Laura Levine's experimental film *Just Like a Movie*. The year saw their circuit expanding, as they continued to play small venues in flyover states in the West, Midwest, and South, consolidated their reputation in the large cities, and made their first forays into Canada. This was still the era of living out of the van, but now there was much more publicity work to be done: the band was interviewed on college radio stations everywhere, but on occasion also on local late-night news segments.

Everything seemed to be on a natural upward slope; the pace was intense, but progress seemed gradual and sustainable. There was just one aberration—a moment when R.E.M. were suddenly, and somewhat uncomfortably, thrust into a higher realm of rock stardom. In August they played seven gigs opening for the Police, who were then at the height of their fame. The shows came about, naturally enough, because of R.E.M.'s association with the Copeland brothers, who no doubt felt they were doing the band a huge favor by getting them a plum gig that bands with far more experience would have resorted to physical violence to land. To hear the R.E.M. guys tell it, though, these shows amounted to a nightmarish version of the Cinderella experience: four nondescript small-town musicians who had never played anything larger than a midsize theater were suddenly thrown in front of thousands of screaming people in a stadium—but everyone was there to see another band. R.E.M. have subsequently trotted out a litany of reasons why the whole thing was, in retrospect, a bad idea: it was too fast, too soon; it seemed grandiose and excessive; they didn't feel they had any chance of making new converts in such a large, impersonal setting; and anyway, this was not really their crowd or their scene. The usually even-keeled Bill Berry was especially caustic, describing the tour as "the most wretched and abysmal experience of our lives . . . We shoulda stayed home and got drunk for all the fucking good it did us."

This all seems a bit perplexing coming from a band that two years earlier had made it their goal to build a career around their dream of playing music. The Copelands were attempting to help them realize that dream. One would think that anyone, handed this kind of once-in-a-lifetime opportunity, would set aside their reservations and try to make the most of it. Beneath all the grousing, R.E.M. may in fact have done precisely that. According to Ian Copeland, the band rose to the occasion during the Shea Stadium show, even in the face of a torrential downpour:

> In all the years of going to outdoor shows, I never saw it rain so hard. R.E.M. played on regardless, and the crowd loved it. This was the band's first time on such a big stage, in front of so many people, and though the elements were against them, I could sense from the crowd reaction that R.E.M. would one day be a huge act.

Even Peter Buck, the biggest naysayer regarding this tour, conceded that the Shea Stadium show was "kinda neat."

Marcus Gray notes in *It Crawled from the South* that a recording of the band's performance at the Capitol Centre in Largo, Maryland, showcases both the band's bad attitude and the fierceness of their playing:

> The songs have obviously been chosen for reasons of accessibility, and stand up well in the stadium setting. The crowd grows noticeably more enthusiastic as the set progresses but, save for a terse, "thank you," following "Sitting Still," the band makes no effort to acknowledge this. The overall impression given is that R.E.M. would not have had to eat overmuch crow to have made a lot of friends that day.

Buck later claimed that the band "didn't sell one record" as a result of their brief tour with the Police, but Jay Boberg has contested that; in his view, "those shows were probably a lot more successful in their career than they will ever acknowledge." This would seem to be borne out by the number of fans who posted on Facebook and elsewhere following R.E.M.'s retirement that they had first discovered R.E.M. at one of those 1983 Police concerts.

Time to speak some truth to power. Just about any non-fan reading the group's negative comments above would probably conclude that R.E.M. were a bunch of ungrateful jackasses. Apart from the rain and the challenge of playing to another band's audience, how wretched could this experience have possibly been? They played a total of six concerts with the Police, and their sets rarely exceeded twenty minutes in length. That's roughly two hours of onstage time spread over the whole run—one-fourth of a typical person's workday. Obviously, that doesn't include travel, load-in, and sound checks, but even if you factor in those things we're still not talking about a huge time commitment. What's more, a percentage of the Police's audience would have been—in theory anyway—sympathetic to R.E.M. If you remove Sting's faux Jamaican accent and just listen to the music of the two bands, they're not light-years apart. This wasn't a mismatch on the scale of, say, Jewel opening for Peter Murphy (which really did happen in the 1990s). Put it this way: if you're on a road trip and you queue up R.E.M.'s *Murmur* right after the Police's *Zenyatta Mondatta*, you're not going to get a lot of complaints or questioning looks from your passengers. Take a closer listen to the syncopated bass-and-drums intro to *Murmur*'s "Laughing." It wouldn't sound at all out of place if Sting's high-pitched voice came in over the top.

R.E.M.'s problem here was more an issue of tone-deafness than anything else. Their public comments on the situation were awkwardly expressed, but their reservations were well founded. The Copelands wanted to push the band into stadiums as quickly as possible, and it's difficult to fault them for that.

Music

Radio wakes up to R.E.M.

By Bill King
Staff Writer

When R.E.M. put out its first release for I.R.S Records last fall — the five-song EP "Chronic Town" — the promotion was low-key, the radio airplay confined pretty much to non-commercial college stations and the sales nothing spectacular.

The Athens-based band didn't consciously do anything different for "Murmur," its debut album on I.R.S. But sales of the album already had doubled those of the EP just two weeks after the LP's release. And with a big push from the label (known for hits by The Police and The Go-Go's) and surprisingly early action from now much more receptive commercial radio stations, R.E.M. just might be on the verge of real, take-it-to-the-bank stardom.

"We're real excited. The album is being added by a whole lot of commercial stations and I think that took (I.R.S.) a little by surprise," guitarist Peter Buck said last week from New York. The group — also including bassist Mike Mills, drummer Bill Berry and singer Michael Stipe — was there winding down from some dates opening for The English Beat before heading home to Athens to make a promotional video for "Radio Free Europe," which will be the first of the 12 tracks on "Murmur" to be released as a single by I.R.S.

Why is commercial radio — which is blasted in the lyrics of the single, a new version of the group's first independent release in 1981 — taking to a group that it largely shunned just a few months ago? "I think everyone's really scared right now because the radio stations and record companies don't know what's happening," Buck said, "and so a lot of stations are going to new music. We're sort of sneaking in the back door."

As for the I.R.S. marketing push, it helps, he said, "that this is a small label (distributed by the larger A&M Records) and there aren't any new records out on I.R.S. right now except for ours. But it's really nice that they're behind us."

The sound of "Murmur" is more commercial than was "Chronic Town," he granted, "but we didn't plan it that way. I think mainly it was that we were a little bit more knowledgeable about going into the studio and putting sounds down. On the EP (recorded a year before its release and before the band had signed a record contract) we didn't know what we were doing. We were learning how to work in the studio and we used anything that came into our heads. We threw it all on and overdubbed everything. Because of that, there are some things on that record I don't like."

But the album, he said, is "pretty much straightforward and simply done. It doesn't sound too busy."

R.E.M. did approach the recording of their first album a little differently from the way most groups do, Buck said. "We felt that rather than make a typical first album — which most often is basically the live show put on record — we would approach each song differently. That meant the band didn't have to be in the bass-drums-guitar configuration all the time and we could add some keyboards and things like that."

PETER BUCK: Guitarist.

Another slight departure from the norm in the making of "Murmur" was R.E.M.'s insistence on recording where the band — and not the record company — felt most comfortable. The LP was

GETTING NATIONAL ATTENTION: R.E.M.'s Michael Stipe.
LINDA SHERBERT/Staff

recorded in January at Reflection Studios in Charlotte, N.C. and produced by relatively unknown engineers Mitch Easter and Don Dixon. "I.R.S. was a little bit hesitant," Buck said. "They kind of wanted us to use another producer at first. I think they had this image of these guys down in the swamps of the South. And they would have rather had us in Los Angeles, but that would have harmed the record because we would have been so bored out there. They were worried, but they could see we were bright enough not to make a stupid record. They were very supportive."

After making the "Radio Free Europe" video at a folk artist's garden outside Athens, the band will be back on the road touring for the next two or three months. So far, Buck said, R.E.M. has been very well received outside its native South. "We get encores just about everywhere. The reception varies from area to area. In New York, they kind of stand around and watch you. In the South, everyone dances. In the Midwest, they're kind of slow to warm up but then get very enthusiastic. And California, I still haven't figured out. In San Francisco and Northern California we got tremendous crowds. But in Los Angeles the scene is really segmented and weird. No one knew who we were at all. It was really more of a non-response there."

The fact that R.E.M. is from Athens, the same town that produced The B-52's, is still a calling card for the group, but most audiences know enough now not to expect another B-52's, Buck said. The music press fascination with the Athens connection occasionally has rankled. But, he said, "we're proud to be an Athens band. We like playing there because we know just about everyone in the audience. Athens is probably the funnest place we play. It's just that every interview wants to know about the 'Athens Scene' and there really isn't one. It's just a bunch of bands and a real supportive club scene.

"It's ironic that Pylon, R.E.M., The B-52's and Love Tractor (all originally from Athens and all still based there except The B-52's) will all have albums out at the same time. You know they'll review them together.

"It's too bad we couldn't have been home when Pylon's album came out," he joked. "We had talked about having some sort of mud wrestling match with the winners becoming the champions of Athens."

Outside of having recorded an album and traveled a bit, not that much has changed for the band since it signed with I.R.S. last year, Buck said. "We're still touring constantly and playing the same places and the money hasn't really improved yet. We're making exactly the same as a year ago. But before we signed we were almost at the starvation level."

Still, he said, the members of R.E.M. aren't too concerned with getting rich. When the band first formed at an Athens party in March of 1980, nobody was thinking of it as a way of making money. It was for fun and, he said, "we're still doing this because we like to do it. We're not in it for the Cadillacs and cocaine."

■ **R.E.M.** Saturday, May 7, at the Agora Ballroom, 665 Peachtree St. 9 p.m. $7.50. Tickets at SEATS locations, except Omni. 872-4672.

Article in the weekend edition of the *Atlanta Journal-Constitution*, May 7, 1983, on R.E.M.'s expanding national profile

They were businessmen working in the fickle field of rock music; they wanted to maximize the success of their latest signing as quickly as possible, because the longevity of a band's career is always in doubt. And this would have been a good move for many bands. But at an instinctive level R.E.M. knew that such a rapid acceleration would *not* be good for them, and so they pushed back following these shows. And for this, every R.E.M. fan ought to be grateful. The band opted for a more gradual ascent, which gave us several more years of low-key magic. The mixed results of R.E.M.'s eventual (inevitable?) foray into stadium concerts of their own in the 1990s underscored the soundness of this original impulse. Most fans and critics would agree that R.E.M. were usually at their best when they resisted gigantism in favor of intimacy.

Supporters of R.E.M. often like to highlight the myriad ways they perceive their favorite band to be different from every rock band that preceded them. Some of these distinctions can be overstated—R.E.M. weren't really the first band to work the college circuit, or create a homegrown management infrastructure, or (as they did later in their career) call for political action, though they probably were more successful in all these endeavors than the small number of other artists who had tried earlier. At least in one regard, however, they truly were unusual: at key moments in their climb toward success, they tapped the brakes. They were not quite like those punk artists who loudly denounced mainstream success (yet in many cases accepted major-label deals with alacrity); for R.E.M., success was always very much an understood goal. But they knew when to say, "Not yet. Not now. Not this type of success." That takes a level of confidence, plus big-picture thinking, and plain old faith that is indeed remarkable for four young rock musicians who, in the not-too-distant past, had been living around the poverty line.

One great irony of the R.E.M./Police story is that the exact same situation had played itself out just a couple of months earlier—on a smaller scale—with R.E.M. in the Police's position. Minneapolis band the Replacements had opened for R.E.M. on six dates that summer. The experience was reportedly difficult for that always volatile band and almost led to their early implosion. The Replacements' singer and primary songwriter Paul Westerberg later commented, "We'd much rather play for fifty people who know us than a thousand who don't care." Scale up those numbers and this quote might as well have come from the lips of Peter Buck.

This did not stop the Replacements from forging a strong friendship with R.E.M. For a time, the members of the Twin Cities band made Athens their second home and insinuated themselves deeply into the Barber Street community. Shortly thereafter, Peter Buck would contribute a key guitar part to their song "I Will Dare"—the intro track on their acclaimed *Let It Be* album. The two bands were in a similar position: both had sprung from thriving local scenes and were attempting to carve out an alternative route to success. Both had opted to remain based in their hometown. Both were on independent labels and had the support of critics (in some cases the same critics: Robert Christgau, for example, championed both bands). Also, to put it delicately, both bands knew how to have a good time.

R.E.M. also played quite a few shows in 1983 with Mitch Easter's band Let's Active—another recent I.R.S. signing—as their opening act. I can find no record of Easter complaining about this arrangement, though it has become clear in subsequent years that he wishes he could have gotten more recognition as a songwriter and not just be known to most people as the guy who produced R.E.M. He has some justification; in this writer's view the Let's Active catalog is a treasure trove hiding in plain sight. If you're reading this and aren't aware of those albums, then put this book down for a moment, bring the band up on whatever legal streaming service you use, and get them playing in the background. Might as well queue up the Replacements while you're at it. There was considerable cross-pollination going on between all these groups, and you'll miss the full story if you listen to only one of them in isolation.

Which brings us to Matthew Sweet. He is remembered now for his breakthrough 1991 album *Girlfriend*, which provided a robust power-pop alternative to the then-ascendant grunge sound. In style he's closer to Let's Active than R.E.M., albeit with the addition (on *Girlfriend* and its follow-up, *Altered Beast*) of fiery lead guitar work from Television's Richard Lloyd. If Sweet is ever thought of as being from somewhere in particular, it is usually his native Nebraska. Few would associate him with R.E.M. or the Athens, Georgia, scene, but for a brief period he was inextricably linked with both.

Sweet had first crossed paths with R.E.M. in 1982, when he attended their performance at the Drumstick in Lincoln. Still a high school student at the time, Sweet in some ways mirrored the teenaged Stipe: shy, introverted, an avid reader of *New York Rocker* and other left-of-center publications covering the new "underground" music. And just as Stipe had discovered Patti Smith in the pages of the East Coast alternative magazines, so Sweet discovered R.E.M. via the very same channels. Of the couple thousand people who had purchased the Hib-Tone "Radio Free Europe"/"Sitting Still" single on its release in 1981, Sweet was probably one of the youngest.

In other aspects, Sweet was perhaps closer in background to Mike Mills. Precociously talented, Sweet knew his way around several instruments, had an intuitive knack for composition, and was obsessed with melody and harmony. Also like Mills, he favored the bass and had spent a fair amount of his early teens listening to Yes records, memorizing Chris Squire's bass lines. By the time he saw R.E.M., he had already done quite a bit of multitrack recording in his bedroom, the results of which—captured on cassette—he passed on to Michael Stipe when he got the chance to chat up the singer after the Drumstick gig. Stipe thought enough of the tape to pass it along to both his sister Lynda and to Linda Hopper, and before long all three of them were sending Sweet postcards cajoling him to come visit Athens.

Like many who have been lured by the siren's call of the town (including the author of this book), Sweet convinced his parents that the University of Georgia was the school most ideally suited to his needs; he duly arrived in Athens in the summer of 1983. "Of course I moved down there and promptly blew off school," he later told Jud Cost of *The Bob* magazine. So what did Sweet do in place of his studies? He joined Oh-OK, performed onstage with R.E.M., formed a duo with Michael Stipe called Community Trolls, and another band called Buzz of Delight with David Pierce.

Some of the other players in the Athens scene were perplexed and a little put out by the sudden entry of this shy kid from Nebraska into the inner circle of the most successful band in town. "Things really turned dark there when R.E.M. got famous," Sweet told Jud Cost. "Because everyone wanted that fame so bad. Maybe I wanted it too, but I had this musical goal all of my own and wasn't going to go along with the way it was done there."

This is not to say that Sweet was scorned in Athens. Far from it. Oh-OK was a very popular band and Sweet's contributions filled out their sound considerably, even if his influence moved the band in a more conventionally pop direction. Buzz of Delight, his duo with David Pierce, was based around an intriguing creation: the "bagbo"—a bass guitar strung half with bass strings, half with guitar strings. Sweet's ability to maneuver his way around this unwieldy instrument was genuinely impressive, though even now Pat the Wiz shudders when he remembers how quickly and drastically the bagbo went out of tune, and how difficult it was to get good sound at a Buzz of Delight gig.

Sweet's collaboration with Michael Stipe has yielded fewer recorded artifacts than his work in the other groups, yet the two apparently wrote a fair number of songs together. It took until 2002 for their duet "Tainted Obligation"—recorded in 1983 with local producer John Keane—to appear on a compilation of early Sweet recordings (it had appeared earlier on scattered bootlegs), but it was arguably worth the wait. The song is a beguiling country pastiche featuring Stipe and Sweet harmonizing over acoustic guitar and accordion. And, although Stipe's Southern accent comes off as forced, it's hard not to be charmed by the duo's very sincere homage to the Stanley Brothers and other country-gospel greats. The other recording that has surfaced is a low-key version of the Velvet Underground's "Pale Blue Eyes" featuring

Sweet on guitar and Stipe once again on vocals and accordion. This too has a certain understated beauty that just might give it the edge over R.E.M.'s better known plugged-in version of the song.

Both of these recordings seem to have been made in September 1983, when R.E.M. were supposedly taking a break. This turned out to be easier said than done. Laura Levine, a New York–based artist/photographer and friend of the band, came to town that month to work on her ultra-low-budget independent film *Just Like a Movie*, which starred not only the four members of R.E.M. but also Levine, Sweet, Linda Hopper, Cyndy and Lynda Stipe, Chris Slay, and Jerry Ayers. Shot entirely on Super 8, the film was an homage to D. A. Pennebaker's iconic Bob Dylan documentary *Don't Look Back*. In Levine's playful re-imagining of the early-'60s Dylan/Donovan rivalry, Hopper played the Donovan role while Stipe channeled Dylan. But in *this* version the two fall in love at the end. The Community Trolls' version of "Pale Blue Eyes" emerged from this project.

Levine needed to get footage of R.E.M. performing, so the band allowed her to film a rehearsal on the afternoon of September 30 at the old Stitch-craft sewing factory, located across the street from the church where they had made their debut. They then threw open the doors for a massive party and impromptu gig. Pat Biddle manned the board that night and recorded the entire debauched performance—which featured Sweet playing second guitar on a number of songs—for posterity.

Between R.E.M.'s second and third sets that night, Community Trolls played their first and perhaps only proper gig, not counting one or two sidewalk busking sessions. "There's a new band in town called Community Trolls," Stipe announced to the audience of friends and passers-by. "They've only played once before, outside the 40 Watt Club about four months ago, and got plummeted with not enough coins by this one fat guy from Atlanta. So in honor of that fat man from Atlanta who highly insulted a friend of mine, we're gonna do some Community Troll cover songs. Featuring Mr. Guitar Man." Stipe and Sweet then launched into a song called "Six Stock Answers," which featured one line—"Six stock answers for 74,000 questions"—repeated on and on, punctuated with a little bit of yodeling. From the sound of it, they just about cleared the room. The song finished to dead silence, which was broken finally by one lone whistle that seemed to emanate from somewhere in the back of the warehouse. The Trolls* followed this bold opening

---

* I'd like to tip my hat here to a very amusing post one Blake Guthrie made to Movoto.com in 2014. Titled "30 Things You'll Never See In Athens, GA Again," this blog entry, hosted by an online real-estate brokerage firm based in San Mateo, California, logged an impressive 49,000 views and 270

with a more conventional—and quite lovely—ballad titled "My Roof to Your Roof." "From my roof to your roof, there's a lovin' line / I can see your window shade at night," Stipe sang. "The alley is down there, it's deep and it's wide / But I'd jump the moon for you tonight." This tossed-off performance in the middle of the Stitchcraft show is the only known recording of this song, which is a shame; with a little polish it could have been a keeper. It was certainly a rarity in being perhaps the only unabashed love song Stipe penned during the first ten years of his professional music career (unless you count 1988's "You Are the Everything," whose lyrics are ambiguous enough that I'm not sure it fits into that category).

The coda to Matthew Sweet's brief association with Athens is not pretty. His ambition had always been to establish himself as a songwriter and studio musician in the Mitch Easter mold. Like XTC, he would have preferred simply to make records and send them out into the world. Consequently, his chief desire was to secure some kind of record deal and publishing contract for himself. Recognizing his talent, Jefferson Holt made inquiries on his behalf and secured a meeting with Columbia Records. They were impressed with his abilities, like everyone who heard his tapes, and quickly offered him a deal. And here's where things get a little messy: Sweet left town immediately after signing. "Unfortunately I got a deal," he told Jud Cost. "It happened so fast, and I was young and I didn't know what I was doing, and was hated for it."

Rodger Lyle Brown's portrait of Sweet in *Party Out of Bounds* is especially harsh. He characterizes Sweet's "machinations" as "the beginning of the next era: an era of admitted and explicit ambition, more intentional band-marketing, competition, and strategic styling. The folks would say, again and again, it was then that innocence was banished." It is true that when Sweet got his deal he abandoned not only Athens but also David Pierce, and this experience does seem to have affected Pierce's desire to play music. But this needs to be tempered by the fact that in my own interviews with Pierce, the former drummer had nothing but kind things to say about Sweet and seems to genuinely treasure his memories of that time.

As for R.E.M., they might arguably have felt the most aggrieved, since they helped Sweet make his connections. But they instinctively understood why he acted as he did. Peter Buck put it most succinctly: "The guy wanted to make records. I don't see anything wrong with that."

In his interview with Jud Cost, Sweet spoke of the moment that R.E.M.

Facebook comments. Number 8 on Guthrie's list of vanished Athens artifacts was Community Trolls. "The 'Trolls,' as no one refers to them ever," Guthrie wrote, "never released an album but played a couple of sidewalk shows."

"became famous" as both a major turning point for himself and for the scene. Fame is a relative term; a wider public did not become aware of R.E.M. until "Losing My Religion" took the airwaves by storm in 1991. But the moment Sweet referenced was most likely R.E.M.'s appearance on *Late Night with David Letterman* on October 6, 1983. Letterman's staff made a point of keeping up with the latest developments in the music press, and they had booked the band on the strength of the *Murmur* reviews. Everyone I interviewed for this book seems to have caught this performance on the night it was broadcast. Mike Doskocil (Stipe's casual acquaintance from the East St. Louis days) was working late shifts for the Teamsters at the time and always made sure to go into the break room at 11:30 CST to catch the Letterman show. On that particular night, he was only half paying attention when Dave introduced "a group of gentlemen from Athens, Georgia, called R.E.M." As the band kicked into a rousing version of "Radio Free Europe," Doskocil found he couldn't keep his eyes off the odd-looking singer who seemed to teeter back and forth at the microphone, holding on for dear life. *Who the fuck is that guy? I know that guy.*

Craig Franklin, the student from Collinsville High who had cajoled Stipe into singing at a talent show in the mid-'70s, also had an eerie feeling while watching the broadcast. *That looks like Michael*, he thought. He recalled how just a year or two previously, a mutual friend had reported that Michael had a new band. His reaction at the time had been something along the lines of, "Oh, that's nice—he was so shy and maybe this will pull him out of his shyness." Now, he scrutinized his television set. Could it be? Then, between songs, Letterman walked up to the band to conduct an impromptu interview and Michael sat down and looked away, ignoring the host. Then Franklin knew: *Man, that's him!*

In Athens, a number of the band's friends gathered at the 40 Watt and watched it on a TV someone had rolled in. To those in attendance who might have lost track of R.E.M. after the early Tyrone's days, it immediately became apparent that Michael's performing style had changed drastically. Instead of dancing around like a maniac, now he simply leaned hard on the microphone stand, wrapped his hands directly around the head of the mic (an action that no doubt made Pat the Wiz cringe), and sang out from behind his mass of brown curls, shuddering dramatically every now and then. Perhaps in an effort to pick up the slack, Buck and Mills twirled and jumped around with wild abandon, Buck launching the occasional karate kick at some invisible assailant. Behind them, Berry bashed away. This new approach was an exact inversion of the old one, with Stipe having abdicated his role as the dynamic focal point, opting instead to become the impassive eye of a hurricane. It was an interesting effect, compelling in its own right, though some of the earlier fans couldn't help but feel disappointed by this change of direction.

There were probably a number of factors at play here. First and foremost was Stipe's continuing effort to assert an integrity for his band that the more snobbish elements of the Athens music scene had initially denied them. So R.E.M. were the "frat party band"? Well, what would happen if the party band stopped being the life of the party? The first step in that direction had been to write increasingly obtuse lyrics. Before long, an equally obtuse stage presentation followed. There may have been personal issues involved as well. Don Dixon has noted that by the time R.E.M. began recording their second LP at the end of 1983, Stipe had "begun to withdraw." Seen another way, he may have been simply returning to his default state as a fundamentally shy person. Any introvert knows that the act of projecting oneself as an extrovert—or, as Stipe puts it, becoming "loud shy"—can be exhausting if such an outward presentation conflicts with one's inner nature. Yet this is exactly what Stipe had been doing since that first performance in the church. Indeed, his outsized stage antics had helped put the band over the top; sources cited by both Denise Sullivan and Rodger Lyle Brown mention that more than a few fans went to R.E.M. shows specifically to see Stipe dance. Possibly the singer became weary of those expectations. It is also worth remembering that he was only three years removed from being "Pigpen," the derided second-line cook at Steak and Ale. Going so quickly from that to *Letterman* is a fairly dramatic leap. At the local level alone, R.E.M.'s success was rapid enough that Stipe had observed University of Georgia frat guys who had once antagonized him turning up at R.E.M. gigs just a year or two later, singing along to his lyrics. That's bound to throw a person.

Stipe's move toward a quieter, more introverted stage persona had a performance aspect all its own, however. One need only compare footage of Stipe onstage from this period with early footage of his friend and sometime collaborator Matthew Sweet to see the difference between a performer playing up the more inward-looking aspects of his personality and one who truly suffers from crippling shyness. Sweet always had the look of cornered prey, but Stipe, even when he was standing still and staring at the floor, had a presence and a confidence about him that came from having stood in just such a spot hundreds of times before. The television and film actor Nick Searcy (best known for his key role on the TV series *Justified* but back then a struggling musician in New York) saw R.E.M. play a club date around the time of the *Letterman* taping and was struck by Stipe's almost theatrical shyness. "He came onstage wearing layers and layers of clothes, as if he were cocooning himself from the audience," Searcy recalls. "Then as the show progressed he peeled each layer off. It was really unique. I thought he was such an interesting performer."

When Stipe turned his back to the audience on occasion, the gesture seemed born less of self-consciousness than of Miles Davis–style defiance: a deliberate, somewhat ostentatious display of being "difficult." Stipe's apparent refusal to be interviewed by Letterman seemed very much in the same vein. Was he really too shy to talk to the *Late Night* host? He had already logged a considerable number of interviews on radio and in print media by that point. Many viewers, including nearly all of Stipe's friends, saw his action as a sort of passive punk-rock gesture: *Just because I'm coming on this show doesn't mean I'm going to jump through your hoops.*

But perhaps it was all a misunderstanding. In an interview with *Salon* in 2015, Mike Mills attempted to set the record straight regarding that famous "snub":

> Everybody thought Michael didn't want to talk, but it was only because it was originally planned that Peter and I were going to go sit by [Letterman]. Then Dave didn't do that. He walked over to us, and Michael had already sat down by the time Dave walked over. Peter and I were standing there. But there was nothing mysterious about it. He wasn't expected to sit next to Dave, so he just sat down.

Mills's account is bolstered by what happened when the band got ready to play their second song—a composition which, Letterman quipped, was "too new to be named." As the host thanked the band for coming on the show, Stipe stood up, smiling broadly at Letterman and nodding—hardly the actions of a defiant Johnny Rotten. Still, a certain impression of churlishness had been made, one that contributed to his growing reputation for being an artist not quite tethered to this world. Within a few months he added an additional performance tic that sealed the deal: a tendency, during the more intense moments of a song, to lower his eyelids to half-mast and rotate his eyeballs back so that only the whites showed. In those moments the rock singer became a sort of trance medium, serving as a conduit for a most inscrutable muse.

As for that second song, it too was something of a departure for late-night TV: a sign of both the band's and Letterman's propensity for pushing the envelope. It was unusual enough that a relatively unknown musical guest would be allocated time for two songs—doubly unusual that the artist would premiere an unnamed, unrecorded new song on national television. But that's exactly what happened. This song, which would come to be known—and loved—as "So. Central Rain," had clearly been carefully worked over and rehearsed prior to the broadcast. And although R.E.M. had not yet committed it to tape, they seized this opportunity to showcase one of the best songs they had ever written. Who knew when such a chance would come around again?

Lyrically, "So. Central Rain" was indeed a breakthrough, marrying Stipe's penchant for impressionistic phrasing with a relatively concrete portrait of a dissolving romantic relationship. The causes of the dissolution seem to be distance, time, and an inability to communicate:

The trees will bend, the conversation's dimmed
Go build yourself another home, this choice isn't mine
I'm sorry

Some believe the song to be about Carol Levy, though Stipe has never confirmed this. Since he has singled out "Camera" as being specifically about that relationship, it's possible that "So. Central Rain" is a more general commentary on love and loss. Peter Buck saw some of his own experience in the lyrics, just as he had with "Perfect Circle." He told an interviewer that the song drew its inspiration from a time he had been trying to reach his parents from the road while Georgia was experiencing a heavy storm. "The weather report was, 'South central rain, all the phone lines are down,'" he said. "It's a kind of being-away-from-home song without having the Holiday Inn and groupies in it."

The decision to play "So. Central Rain" on the Letterman show created quite a headache for I.R.S., as it generated demand for a record that did not yet exist. But R.E.M. quickly went to work on that, returning in December to Reflection Studios to begin recording their second album. This time around, the band had very little time to prepare consciously for the process. Indeed, when they arrived in the studio on December 8, they were just barely off the plane from a brief whirlwind tour of the UK and mainland Europe. On November 18, they had appeared on the influential British TV show *The Tube*, again performing "So. Central Rain," along with "Radio Free Europe" and "Talk About the Passion." They shared the stage that night with ZZ Top, Wham!, Imagination, and Dr. John—an eclectic lineup, to say the least. Their overseas trip included shows in London and Amsterdam, and two shows in France—in Paris and Rouen. The trip had been successful in the sense that the small club shows had been packed and the critics had been won over. The general population in those countries, however, were still largely oblivious to

R.E.M.'s existence, and would remain so for some time to come.

The album R.E.M. recorded in Charlotte, in a few jam-packed weeks before and after New Year's, functioned as a reflection of the band's current life on the run. The acoustic guitars and elaborately layered arrangements that had dominated *Murmur* were largely absent, replaced with a stripped-down approach that closely mirrored how the songs sounded when performed live. Still, this being an Easter/Dixon production, it was meticulously engineered. All the instrumentation came through clean and crisp—particularly Mills's Rickenbacker bass work, which pounded and drove the music in a sort of album-length homage to Chris Squire. In a 2011 interview with British radio host Pete Mitchell, Michael Stipe revealed that he had not truly understood the distinction between bass and six-string guitar until these recording sessions. While it's endearing that it took him so long to grasp what his bandmate Mike was up to, it makes sense that this would be the moment when it finally sank in; if *Murmur* had been Bill Berry's defining moment as a drummer, this new album—soon to be titled *Reckoning*—did the same for Mills's bass playing. Wherever one turns, one can hear the distinctive, grinding sound of a Rickenbacker getting put through its paces. In the cases of "Harborcoat," "7 Chinese Bros.," and "So. Central Rain," Mills contributes countermelodies with his instrument, then sings a completely different melody over the top. Juxtaposed against Stipe's vocals and Buck's spare but distinctive guitar work, the end results are surprisingly sophisticated given their elementary building blocks. On *Murmur*, this sort of polyphonic effect had been achieved by adding layers of additional instrumentation and harmonies. In the interval between the two albums, it seems R.E.M. had internalized that process and figured out how to achieve much the same effect without relying on the luxuries of multitrack tape.

Which is not to say that *Reckoning* was a completely bare-bones affair. There were still flourishes here and there: a jaunty barroom-style piano on the newly countrified "Don't Go Back to Rockville," bongos and assorted unusual percussion on "Time After Time (Annelise)," organ and Tibetan singing bowls on "Camera," and percussive piano strikes on "7 Chinese Bros." Buck's newfound facility with guitar effects further contributed to a varied sound. Nevertheless, *Reckoning* was a leaner and meaner beast when compared with its more baroque predecessor.

The album also served as a showcase for Michael Stipe's expanding range of vocal approaches. On songs such as "Second Guessing" and "Pretty Persuasion," he snarled aggressively, biting each word off in the manner of a young Mick Jagger. On a few other songs, most notably "Harborcoat," he continued in the melodic mumbling vein of *Murmur*. On some of the quieter songs, he sounded unsure of himself. "Camera," Stipe's eulogy for Carol Levy, would arguably have benefited from a more committed vocal delivery, yet Stipe was either unwilling or unable to go there. The resulting take was almost completely inflectionless—the polar opposite of his heartfelt vocal on "So. Central Rain." It's quite possible that this was a deliberate choice, an attempt to convey emotional numbness—if so, it's one he quickly came to reconsider. By the time the band played Boca Raton, Florida, the following September, Stipe had reworked his approach to the song. His singing during that performance, while still restrained, conveyed all the shock and grief appropriate to the subject matter.

Reckoning is largely a triumph for Stipe, yet according to Don Dixon and Mitch Easter, the singer required quite a bit of coaxing in order to deliver the goods. Easter spent a lot of time trying to get a good vocal for "Camera" and eventually gave up. "With that one we had to make him work a bit to make it a little more technically accurate," he told writer David Buckley. "He wasn't happy about that. He was thinking more about getting it across. At one point he refused to do it anymore. I remember thinking, well, that's pretty good. I'm not going to argue with you at this stage." Dixon, too, found himself fighting an uphill battle to get a usable take for "7 Chinese Bros."

"He didn't have to scream it," Dixon told Buckley. "But he did have to have noise coming out of his mouth so I could get something on tape." Exasperated, Dixon grabbed a gospel record that had been left in the studio—*The Joy of Knowing Jesus* by the Revelaires—and tossed it to Stipe, saying, "Maybe this will inspire you." Stipe immediately started singing the liner notes from the record over the "7 Chinese Bros." backing tracks. Luckily, Dixon got Stipe's loopy, effusive outpouring of gospel goodness and Southern twang on tape. This wry alternate version of the song was given the title "Voice of Harold" and was eventually released as the B-side to the "So. Central Rain" 12" single. Stipe, thus inspired, went on to track his actual "7 Chinese Bros." vocals with strength and clarity.

Stipe did almost all of his singing for the album in the studio's stairwell. The producers snaked a microphone out to him and, apart from the coaching, left him to his devices. It was perhaps just as well that he separated himself from the band, because the singer—already a committed vegetarian—was simultaneously becoming more enamored of garlic and less interested in personal hygiene. He seemed oblivious to or unconcerned about the odors he was bringing into such an enclosed space. Day after day he arrived with Tupperware containers full of garlic-soy concoctions, which he blithely dipped into throughout the sessions.

What, one wonders, was the reaction of Stipe's bandmates to his increasingly erratic behavior? It would seem that they generally viewed it as "Michael being Michael." This was, after all, someone who had exhibited unusual behavior as far back as anyone could remember. While there is a difference between the act of brushing one's teeth mid-conversation in a crowded room—as Stipe had been known to do at early Athens gatherings—and stinking up a studio while refusing to talk to anyone, it is essentially a difference of degree. Stipe's slide from quirky, possibly prankish behavior into full-on difficult mode had been gradual, and none of his actions at any point had seemed especially out of character. To someone like Dixon, who only saw the band at intervals, the change seemed more pronounced than it did to Stipe's bandmates, who interacted with him virtually every day.

What of Stipe's claim that he hadn't truly found his songwriting voice until the making of this album? There is some merit to it. Previously, Stipe's words—intelligible or not—had sounded pretty good emerging here and there amid Buck's arpeggiated guitar lines. But starting with *Reckoning* they began to look good on paper. We have already seen how "So. Central Rain" represented a leap forward. "7 Chinese Bros.," "Harborcoat," and "Time After Time" continued the trend. Of "Harborcoat," the song Ort's mother called "pure impressionism," Stipe had this to say during a performance at the Olympia Theatre in Dublin in 2009:

> So many of the early songs have absolutely zero meaning. So those that do, I'm really proud of now. So I'm going to tell you what they're about. This song was written about Lillian Hellman, who was an early hero of mine . . . I always loved the idea of her riding on the train from New York to Boston, and they have to stop, and she gets off to smoke, because she's a smoker probably from the cradle to the grave. You could tell from looking at her face. She was madly in love with Dashiell Hammett, and I somehow concocted this idea of her giving him a blow job with a mouthful of smoke. That's not in the song, though, that was years later. I just thought that was a very romantic image.

This may have all been clear as day to Stipe, but no listener or critic had discerned the Hellman connection until Stipe casually mentioned it to UK journalist Andy Richardson in the mid-1990s. Even after that, it did not become widely known until the Dublin gig. Not having the benefit of this knowledge, blogger Matthew Perpetua summed up the prevailing impression of the song in 2007: "Like much of the band's early-'80s material, 'Harborcoat' is not overly deterministic about its message, and seems as though it was specifically designed to arouse curiosity and stimulate creative extrapolation of its words."

They are, indeed, lovely, provocative words ("They shifted the statues for harboring ghosts / Reddened their necks, collared their clothes"). But discerning the link to Lillian Hellman, the trailblazing and often controversial left-wing screenwriter/playwright who was blacklisted in the 1950s, is not an easy task. Apart from references throughout the song to Communism ("Lenin," "reddened their necks"), which seem, if anything, to carry negative connotations, there is the line about the "books with the middles cut out," which could refer to McCarthy-era censorship and blacklisting. We now know that the "she" in the song is likely Hellman, and the additional vocals by Mills—which go something like "Please come with me my baby / Can't ever watch you go"—could have something to do with the tragic arc of the Hellman/Hammett relationship. (Hammett, the—also blacklisted—mystery writer, died a lingering death from cancer and tuberculosis.) Except that Mills never consulted Stipe when writing his vocal parts. And then there's . . . Oh, what's the use? I give up. What the hell is a harborcoat, anyway?

Less perplexing than the lyrics he wrote about her is the fact that Stipe considered Hellman a hero. It's not difficult to surmise that Hellman had some influence on Stipe's nascent politics—not so much in her pro-Communist leanings (even at his most strident, years later, Stipe as a political animal was usually more oppositional than pro-anything)—but rather in her outspoken defiance of those who sought to contain her, and her stirring public defense of her fellow blacklisted artists. She was also very much a freethinker when it came to sexuality and personal relationships. All of this is detailed in three volumes of memoirs she published between 1969 and 1976. It later emerged that she had probably fabricated portions of these memoirs, exaggerating the extent of her participation in the battle against fascism abroad and the fight against McCarthyite witch-hunts at home. Stipe remained oblivious to such controversies until the day of that 2009 Dublin performance, when Peter Buck apparently clued him in. "Peter dashed all of my romantic ideas of her as a writer earlier this afternoon," Stipe said during his intro for the song. Then, following a quick off-mic exchange with Buck, he added, "Okay—she's a great writer. She's dead; she can't defend herself."

The song "7 Chinese Bros." also had literary origins, albeit of a decidedly different nature. The title is possibly a garbled reference to a 1938 children's book called *Five Chinese Brothers*, which was itself an adaptation of an old Chinese folk tale called "Ten Brothers." In the book, one of the brothers possesses the ability to swallow the entire sea for a period of time. He agrees to do so while a young boy goes out to retrieve fish from the now-dry seabed. However, the brother eventually runs out of breath and is forced to release the water, resulting in the boy's death. He is put on trial, but his other brothers, who also possess supernatural powers, come to his defense. For many years, most listeners assumed that the song was a retelling of this popular story, albeit routed through the scrambler that is Stipe's brain. Never mind that in the book there were not "seven Chinese brothers swallowing the ocean" (as Stipe sang), but only one; the source material, at least, seemed clear. But in an interview with *Spin* in 2008, Stipe threw a curveball. "'7 Chinese Bros.' was about me breaking up a couple," he said, "and then dating both of them, a man and a woman, which is a terrible thing to do, but I was young and stupid." Perhaps the ensuing fallout from that impulsive act prompted the second line in the song's chorus: "Seven thousand years to sleep away the pain." Then comes the third, seemingly unrelated line "She will return," which some believe is another reference to Carol Levy.

In contrast with the aforementioned two songs, the inspiration for "Time After Time (Annelise)" was far from literary. The "water tower" referenced in the song was very likely a real tower in either the Barber Street neighborhood or nearby Baxter Hill that had become a popular spot for sexual assignations and other tomfoolery. Mike Mills managed to get himself arrested there on a charge of indecent exposure a couple of years after the song was written. Could it be, then, that this haunting song was in reality about an unspecified male in the scene (the "bull on his hooves") climbing up the water tower to get it on with women "time after time after time"? Not so fast! At the heart of the song is a tension—the push and pull between peer pressure and personal integrity. The "you" in the song (the Annelise of the title?) doesn't seem entirely comfortable with taking part in the water-tower shenanigans. "If your friends took a fall, are you obligated to follow?" Stipe sings in the first verse. Later, he asks, "If you try to refuse, will they judge your worth by the hour?" But then, as is typical with a Stipe composition, a later verse complicates, even contradicts, the emerging story: a first-person narrator emerges who invites the "tired" and "tried" "you" to his room. "You can stay if you want," he sings, "and the third time you can't lose." So is this narrative less the story of the moral uprightness of "Annelise" and more the story of a second seducer, cynically presenting a better offer masked as empathy? Suddenly we are back in ambiguous territory. Linear narrative was at this time either of no interest to Stipe, or was entirely outside his mode of thinking. As Patton Biddle puts it, "If you rolled Michael Stipe down a hill, he would not go in a straight line."

One other aspect of the *Reckoning* lyrics bears mentioning—their sense of place. We have previously seen that *Murmur* somehow conjured a mood of place even without specific references, but *Reckoning* makes the ties to Athens and the Southeast explicit. In addition to nods to the water tower ("Time After Time") and the storm that deluged Athens and Atlanta ("So. Central Rain"), the line "Vacation in Athens is calling me" pops up in the song "Letter Never Sent," and "Camera" mentions a "green light room," which former Athenian Lance Smith believes is a reference to a room in Stipe's house, the "green light" referring to an effect of the sun streaming in through the perpetually unmowed grass that grew to window height.

There is something quite remarkable going on in all these songs: the literary references, the insertion of small autobiographical details, the discarding of conventional rhyme structure in favor of words that simply sound good with the music, all anchored by a specificity of place. It really is "pure impressionism"; it is also the arrival of a wholly original voice. "Wrap your heel in bones of steel, turn the leg, a twist of color" may not actually mean anything, but the words have somehow pushed past the point where meaning is required. So yes, *Reckoning* is Michael Stipe's first fully realized statement as a songwriter.

The album was released on April 9, 1984, in the UK and on April 17 in the US. It was adorned with some truly baffling cover art, a collaborative effort between Michael Stipe—who provided the initial sketch—and Howard Finster. The finished painting depicts some sort of multicolored two-headed snake with the song titles scrawled along its length. "Part of it is rocks and part of it is the sun and part of it the sky," Stipe later said, in a typically unsuccessful attempt at clarification. The band were allegedly disappointed by the final cover, but at the very least it did nothing to hinder their reputation as the thinking person's rock band—the argument being that if one's album cover is cryptic enough to provoke confusion and debate, there must be something smart behind it.*

Reckoning did very well with its core college constituency, and university radio stations all over the US backed the album strongly enough to push it to a respectable mainstream sales level. It reached #27 on the *Billboard* 200 chart, and, even more importantly, sold consistently and remained on the chart through most of the year. I.R.S. had, as usual, been hoping for a bigger hit, but

---

* The counterargument is that they're having a joke at the audience's expense. I can't imagine that I'm the only person who feels that certain aspects of the "serpent" more closely resemble a condom than a snake.

they could hardly complain about an act that kept bettering its previous sales. It had become clear that R.E.M. were playing a long game.

Critically, the album performed equally well. It would have been hard to surpass the rave reviews that had greeted *Murmur*, but *Reckoning* came close. *Rolling Stone* gave the album four stars out of five. Joe Sasfy of the *Washington Post* wrote, "*Reckoning* proves that both Stipe's lyrical obfuscation and the band's textural haze, both of which are cleaned up here, are irrelevant to this band's wondrous music or its meaning . . . There isn't an American rock band more worth following than R.E.M." Going one better, Mat Snow wrote in his *NME* review that the album "confirms R.E.M. as one of the most beautifully exciting groups on the planet." A number of the reviewers did note that the album seemed to represent more a consolidation of previously established strengths than a bold leap forward, but the general consensus was that this was a sound well worth consolidating. Speaking from this mind-set, *College Music Journal* noted, "We are just beginning to see R.E.M. develop, and we look forward to the long exciting road ahead."

The release of *Reckoning* coincided with R.E.M.'s second European tour in as many years. This time around, some of the novelty had worn off both for the band and the critics. Chronic sound problems and even greater-than-usual alcohol consumption resulted in some ragged and oddly paced sets, though the band showed remarkable tenacity in completing its shows even when confronted with multiple PA failures. At the April 25 show at the Gallery in Manchester, the lights failed as well; undeterred, R.E.M. played on in total darkness.

Summing up this mini-tour, Peter Buck told Capital Radio, "Everyone was real nice to us last time we were here, the reviews were just totally positive, so we just assumed naturally that the second time we came over, everyone would hate us." He was exaggerating—Jack Barron of *Sounds*, among others, had praised the band on this outing—but his comments underscored a key frustration: despite their best efforts, and despite the fact that they were growing their European audience in pockets here and there, R.E.M. had failed to create a grassroots following in Europe the way that they had done in America. Put it down to cultural differences, or the fact that the UK was experiencing a musical renaissance of its own (the Smiths, New Order, and Echo and the Bunnymen were all in the ascendancy); in any case, R.E.M. found themselves unable to connect at the level that they, or their record label, desired. And despite their best efforts, this would remain the case until the very end of the decade.

Michael Stipe, Greek Theatre, Los Angeles, September 6, 1984. Photo by JoDe Dietsch.

Chapter Nine

Chris Edwards stands in the doorway of his Georgia Theatre office, a red baseball cap pulled low over his forehead. He gestures at a framed gold record hanging on the wall. "A gift from the guys," he says. "That's the *Green* album." He observes the record for a moment, then says, "I never once took it down and snorted cocaine off of it. I respected the work too much." He gives me a sideways gaze and the right corner of his mouth twitches upward slightly under his mustache.

Edwards leads me out to the main hall and over to the bar, where he presents me with a PBR longneck in a Georgia Theatre holder. "I have a lot of memorabilia from my time with R.E.M.," he says. "Some of it I had to sell during tough times, but most of it I kept. Like these." He fishes an overstuffed envelope out of his pocket and empties its contents onto the counter. Arrayed in front of me are dozens of VIP passes for R.E.M.'s 1986 Pageantry tour. They come in a variety of colors, each signifying a different level of access. All are adorned with Michael Stipe's primitivist artwork. "You can have them," he says.

This is Chris Edwards in a nutshell: almost comically laid-back (with his facial hair and low-register drawl he reminds me a bit of the actor Sam Elliott), paradoxically private and forthcoming, generous at unexpected moments. I came across Chris completely by chance. The night before, I had been sitting with Paul Butchart at a table outside the Globe. Chris walked by, recognized Paul, and said hello. Paul turned to me and said, "This is the guy you really need to talk to. He was on the road with R.E.M. for most of the '80s."

Talking to Edwards now, I discover his association with the band goes back to the very beginning. The New York native arrived in Athens in November 1978, on his way (so he thought) to Austin, where he hoped to enter the orbit of the "outlaw" country scene: Waylon, Willie, and the like. But meanwhile, his friends Bob and Macy Ramsey had moved to this little college town in Georgia, so why not stop by for a visit? It's sort of on the way, right? It turned out that Athens had everything he was hoping he might find in Austin, and was probably a hell of a lot cheaper, too. He never left.

In January 1979, Chris learned that a club called Tyrone's would be opening a couple of blocks from Sparky's, the seafood café where he worked. He interviewed for a bartending job but got turned down. Still, along with seemingly everyone else in town, he made his way over to Tyrone's on opening night and discovered the club's owners had completely underestimated demand. "The place was packed," Edwards says.

> There were about eight people behind a bar that was built for two. They were in the weeds, and I said, "You guys need some help?" They said, "Yeah, sure, come on back." 'Bout ten minutes later about six of them had vacated and gotten out of the way and I went to town and got busy. Made a lot of drinks and right afterwards one of the owners, John Schnell—his nickname was Tyrone—hired me and said, "When do you want to work? Days, nights, whatever?"

In a short period of time, Edwards ascended from bartender to co-owner of the club, and it was in this capacity that he met R.E.M. in spring 1980, when the band played their first full set that was not at a party, opening for Atlanta band the Brains. On the strength of that performance, Chris and Mike Hobbs (who handled much of the booking for Tyrone's and had been responsible for bringing the band to Chris's attention in the first place) offered R.E.M. a headlining slot, with a guarantee of 15 dollars apiece. The band members' eyes went wide in astonishment at such a generous offer. "I think about maybe three, four months later we had lines around the building," Chris says. Before long, he and Bill Berry had become best friends.

Tyrone's burned down in January 1982. It was one of the most disruptive events in the early years of the Athens scene; in addition to depriving many local bands of a steady venue, the conflagration consumed much of Pat the Wiz's sound equipment, derailing his career as a freelance sound man and music producer. Given its widespread impact on the community, it is perhaps not surprising that conspiracy theories about the fire's cause circulated in subsequent years. But in reality no one benefited from this calamity. The owners of Tyrone's, perpetually tight on cash, had let their fire insurance lapse four months previously. Over time, the explanation that gained the most traction was that the suspended space heater had come loose from its brackets and crashed to the floor. That seemed more persuasive than the competing idea that someone had gotten careless with a cigarette. At any rate, the loss of the club left Chris Edwards more or less a free agent.

In July 1984, Chris got a call from Bill Berry. R.E.M. were on the final stretch of the first leg of their epic Little America tour, in support of *Reckoning*. This was the first tour on which R.E.M. traveled in an air-conditioned bus rather than a van. It was the first tour with a name, for that matter, and the first with an official tour manager who was not Jefferson Holt. Bill wanted to see if Chris would like to meet the band in New York and hang out with them for the final week. You know, see the country in style, and partake in the opulent lifestyle of traveling on a real tour bus.

"I started to help out instead of getting in the way," Chris says.

It seemed simple to me because there's ten people doing the job I did running the club. It was like, somebody's on security, somebody else dealing with catering, somebody else, you know, etc., etc. Jeff Trump was the tour manager and we got along really well. On the ride back to Athens, Jeff invited me in the back lounge and said, "Listen, would you be interested in going out on the road with these guys next time and working?" Of course I said yes. He said, "Well, just keep a lid on it. Don't say anything to anybody because it's kind of taboo to hire good friends of the band, but you've really helped me out a lot, and I really need help because these guys are starting to take off and you seem well suited for it."

It was the start of a long run. Chris first hit the road with R.E.M. in the official capacity of assistant tour manager in 1985, and re-upped for 1986, 1987, 1989, and 1991.* "I started out being as much a gofer as anything," he says.

My nickname on that first tour was the Iceman, because I think there were 24 people on the road who required 12 cases of beer every day. I took care of all the catering and such. But as the years went on I got to the point where I was in charge of security in front of the house and backstage. I became the press liaison, setting up all interviews, phoners, photo sessions, stuff like that; I did all the guest lists and made out all the passes and such. I think the best year was when we had a production manager that was in charge of everything that plugged into a wall, and Jeff Trump—the "tour manager"—was actually the tour accountant; he was in charge of anything with a dollar sign next to it. I pretty much did everything else. Everything. That seemed to work out good.

---

* This last outing was a series of acoustic promo shows for the *Out of Time* album.

This was about as fine an example of someone being in the right place at the right time as there has ever been. The sheer amount of work Edwards found himself tasked with never detracted from his gratitude at having a front-row seat for something truly remarkable: the rise of one of the great American rock bands of the post-'60s era. These were, he says, "the best years of my life."

In subsequent years he went on the road with other bands. I ask Chris if, in the light of those other experiences, there was anything particularly different about how R.E.M. did things—anything that made them stand out from the pack. "I think the most unique thing about them is how little they asked of anybody," he says.

They each used to have a little backpack, instead of a whole bunch of luggage, that they carried themselves. Later on, of course, everything changed and they'd have two valets, two carts full of luggage and forty or fifty people sometimes, but the basic needs remained simple. In those years it seemed absolutely natural. Everything was in its place. Everything was right with the world.

Something that was amazing about them in those days: they would stay after the show and talk to everybody that wanted to talk. I remember sitting in a bus all the time, waiting for the crowd to thin out. You could always see after the show who was where, based on the number of people around them. Michael had the biggest crowd around him. Peter would be second. But then Mike and Bill might each have eighty people around them. They would stay there and talk and answer the same stupid questions and listen to everyone and converse until the fans were tired of talking. They were just so gracious with their time.

In time Chris's assistance to the band extended beyond the road. A 1986 *Spin* cover story on R.E.M.—one of the few places he has been mentioned in print—describes him as a sort of all-purpose chauffeur, host, and minder who shuttles the article's bemused author, Barry Walters, from one band member to another. Recounting his meeting with Michael Stipe, Walters notes Edwards's ruthless efficiency when it came to protecting the singer's privacy—and calendar. "Chris asks how long I will need [with Stipe]," Walters writes. "Thinking a whole afternoon, I hesitate. 'An hour?' he asks."

There seems to have been a mutual respect between Edwards and Stipe. A lot of that probably stems from just how far back the two go. Edwards worked closely with Stipe not just during his artistic peak but also back when the singer was merely a part-time band front-man, part-time art student who lived next door on Barber Street. Edwards's blend of admiration and realistic assessment becomes apparent when he talks about Stipe's lyrics and vocal presentation. "Back then [in the mid-'80s], I think a lot of people wanted to know what Michael was singing," he says. "Well, the Mona Lisa doesn't need a little cartoon bubble up there to tell you what she's thinking." But then he adds, "Personally, I think in a little way maybe it didn't serve the band when he decided he wanted to use his voice to be more purposeful. I mean, kudos to him for doing it. But I kind of like the whole 'art for art's sake' thing, you know?"

Edwards does seem genuinely in awe of Stipe's ability to stay grounded during the band's wildest road years. "Michael didn't drink very much," he says, reinforcing what others have said about the singer's habits.

In fact, he stopped. He quelled some of our drinking habits along the way without having to be mean or anything. I was responsible for all of the catering most of the time when I was with him, and he used to get the six-pack of Bass and would maybe drink two of them. He never really partied any other way that you might think rock stars should. He'd tend to get to sleep earlier and get up when the bus would hit the city and go see museums and things instead of sleep it off like most of us did.

It's probably just as well that at least one person in R.E.M. stayed in the slow lane, given that the lifestyle Chris describes—long days on the bus, shows nearly every night, hours spent talking to fans afterwards, hours and days spent talking to journalists when not talking to fans, 12 cases of beer a day plus whatever other recreational substances were on hand, constant plotting of the next move and the move after that—became the only life R.E.M. would know for most of the next two years, as the Little America tour segued into the recording of *Fables of the Reconstruction*, which led straight into the Pre-Construction tour, which begat the Reconstruction I tour, which begat the Reconstruction II tour, and culminated in Reconstruction III. They would not awake from this fever dream until the dawn of 1986, at which point they would discover that they—and the world—had changed considerably.

November 1984 found the band on their first-ever tour of Japan. A consequence of this overseas engagement was that none of the four members of R.E.M. voted in the US presidential election that year. It might seem astonishing now that one of the most politically oriented rock bands in history couldn't be bothered to line up absentee ballots in the year Reagan was up for re-election, but the truth is that—with the possible exception of Stipe—the guys still didn't really care much about politics. Even after the election, as the four band members gradually became more unguarded on the subject during interviews, Peter Buck said, "I don't ever see us being a band that preaches to anybody. Certainly none of us feel confident enough about our worldview to think that we're right."

In retrospect, 1984 was probably not a bad election for those of an even vaguely left-leaning disposition to sit out. Right from the start of the campaign season, Reagan's victory had been a foregone conclusion. Despite the fact that the Democratic challenger, Walter Mondale, ran a principled, issues-oriented campaign, and despite the excitement generated by his selection of Geraldine Ferraro—the first female vice-presidential candidate in history—as his running mate, the combination of Reagan's widespread popularity and an economic boom (for which the incumbent naturally took credit) proved an insurmountable hurdle. Mondale won only his home state of Minnesota plus the District of Columbia, making his the largest electoral-college loss by a Democratic candidate in history. Clearly, four pro-Mondale votes in Georgia wouldn't have made a difference.

While politics remained—for the moment—absent from R.E.M.'s list of concerns, the band found it harder to ignore the upheavals and innovations occurring in their chosen field. The year 1984 turned out to be a monster one for popular music. It was the year two envelope-pushing provocateurs, Prince and Madonna, exploded into the mainstream. The former's hit "When Doves Cry" sat astride the *Billboard* top 100 from the beginning of June all the way to the first week of August. The latter's "Like a Virgin" ruled the final two weeks of the year and the first four weeks of 1985. Van Halen, Culture Club, Tina Turner, and Billy Joel also had huge hits, and Michael Jackson's *Thriller* continued to dominate the charts, despite the fact that it had been released back in 1982. An essay on Billboard.com goes so far as to call 1984 "Music's Best Year." That is certainly an overstatement, but it was undoubtedly a fine year for pop songs. It was also the year in which the music video solidified its position as the dominant means of music discovery and delivery in the United States. Indeed, Prince's hits "When Doves Cry" and "Let's Go Crazy" rode on the back of his movie *Purple Rain*, which was itself essentially a long-form video—an ambitious answer to the challenge that had been laid down by the cable channel MTV, whose acronym originally stood for "Music Television." That upstart network had debuted in 1981 with an airing of the Buggles' "Video Killed the Radio Star" clip, and in the succeeding three years the channel had made good on the song's prophecy, creating a new type of image-oriented star. From the network's debut up through the end of the 1990s, videos were de rigueur accompaniments to single releases, capable of making or breaking any given record. Three hits of the era in particular— Thomas Dolby's "She Blinded Me with Science," the Eurythmics' "Sweet Dreams Are Made of This," and Duran Duran's "Hungry Like the Wolf" saw their chart positions (which were based on radio play) significantly bolstered by eye-catching MTV-hyped videos, and it's difficult to imagine Madonna's early career having been as successful as it was without MTV. A handful of more homely-looking artists—Phil Collins, Dire Straits, the Cars, Men at Work, for example—also carved out success during this period on the strength of innovative videos, but by and large the pop world of the 1980s belonged to the beautiful people.*

R.E.M., not an unphotogenic band by any means, remained defiant of these emerging trends. Sonically, they continued to eschew the synthesizers that featured in nearly all of the material mentioned above. It would have been hard to make an album more out of step with the 1980s zeitgeist than *Murmur*, and yet the band had managed just that with *Reckoning*, which was even more austere and less accommodating to current tastes than its predecessor. And once again the gamble had paid off, with strong reviews and respectable sales. Still, there was no way around the video conundrum. The current paradigm dictated that R.E.M. film something that—theoretically, at least—could be played on MTV. Three-fourths of the band (not coincidentally the three-fourths who did not attend art school) were dragged kicking and screaming into the process. Stipe, in contrast, came to see the medium as an additional avenue for artistic expression.

The first R.E.M. video out of the gate, for "Wolves, Lower," had been a standard mime job, notable mainly for its showcasing of Stipe's distinctive stage moves. But starting with "Radio Free Europe," the band began to have some fun. Directed by Arthur Pierson (who shortly afterward directed Madonna in her iconic "Lucky Star" video), the clip contrasts vaguely Kafkaesque imagery of anonymous clerks in a dimly lit room with scenes of the band members strolling through Howard Finster's elaborate, sculpture-infested garden. The narrative, such as it is, involves Bill Berry retrieving a mysterious object from the clerks and delivering it to Finster. Except that halfway through the video Stipe becomes the messenger. Anyway . . . the

---

*I can find no explanation as to how Toto fits into this theory. They are the Stonehenge of the 1980s—a completely unexplained phenomenon dropped smack in the middle of everything.

object is revealed at the very end to be a half-adorable, half-creepy home-made doll that Stipe sends tumbling down a miniature slide while Finster and the other band members gaze on in rapt attention. The only concession to MTV audiences is the grainy concert footage interspersed throughout. With its whimsy, aloofness, and emphasis on local color, this video was a comprehensive representation of the R.E.M. ethos circa 1983. Not surprisingly, it did not get a huge amount of airplay. But it did make an impression on those who saw it.

The biggest obstacle for the band (and their label) to surmount in this new medium was Michael Stipe's refusal to lip-sync, a stance he arrived at after filming that initial, perfunctory video for "Wolves, Lower." He explained the reasoning behind his approach in a 1990 interview with *Musician*'s Katherine Dieckmann, and in doing so essentially summed up his entire MO:

> I guess I've tried to alter the idea of commodity, to the extent that I don't want to see myself in pancake makeup lip-syncing with dancing girls and bears. Although I do like flashing lights. There's an incredible struggle inside of me that's been going on since I first stepped onstage, and has applied to everything I've ever worked on, and that is: although I do have a certain amount of integrity and won't do things I think are vile, I also have a great love for the big scam. And to me, for something subversive to move into the mainstream and be accepted by a lot of people is the ultimate victory.

Just as they had done with their "no synthesizers, no 1980s production elements" rule, R.E.M. turned their self-imposed ban on "lip-syncing with dancing girls and bears" into a strength. In the video for "So. Central Rain," Stipe insisted on singing the song live while the band mimed behind screens. The resulting video makes for a surprisingly powerful viewing experience, despite its near-total lack of dramatic flourish or, for that matter, movement of any kind. Stipe himself spends the entirety of the clip standing stock-still in front of the microphone, holding his headphones and concentrating as he croons his melody. When he lets out his final anguished cries at the end of the song, we, the viewers, feel like we have been given access to an intensely personal experience. "That's what you do in a studio when you're actually singing," he told Dieckmann during their interview. Then, perhaps in an effort to undercut his own boasting, he added, "But it looks like I was about to tear my head off and hurl it across the room."

Stipe hired his former professor Jim Herbert to film a clip for another

Reckoning track. Herbert elected instead to provide visuals for a complete album side, which could be broken up into discrete clips (as MTV did on the rare occasions they screened anything from it) or viewed as one continuous piece. This short film, which became known as *Left of Reckoning*, features artful footage of the band members wandering around R. A. Miller's whirligig gardens in Rabbittown, Georgia. Like Howard Finster, Miller was a folk artist whose work was inspired by his religious faith interspersed with elements of popular culture. The whirligigs were painted metal cutouts often depicting farm animals, dinosaurs, or iconic people, mounted on wooden supports. They spun wildly in the wind, often at different speeds depending on their weight and the height of the supporting pole. On a gusty day, the sight of hundreds of these whirligigs spinning around and around could be hypnotic.

As for Herbert's music video, it's tempting to think of it as exhibit A in Michael Stipe's "big scam." Viewed as individual music clips, *Left of Reckoning* contains some arresting images. Herbert plays around with speed, freeze-frame, and stop-motion. The picture comes in and out of focus. And somehow, through some primitive film trickery, the whirligigs sometimes continue to spin even as everything else in the frame becomes static. Those are the positives. On the down side, no effort appears to have been made to sync the visuals to the music. Occasionally the action in the film will line up to the beat accidentally, but more often than not, the two elements drift along completely independent of each other, making it hard to focus on either. The biggest strike against *Left of Reckoning*, however, is that it is simply too long. Three minutes of unshaven musos stumbling around, building sculptures out of bicycle wheels and looking at dogs, is about the maximum anyone should have to endure. Twenty minutes is just daring you to call bullshit on the whole enterprise.

I like to imagine the staff at I.R.S. Records on the fateful day that *Left of Reckoning* turned up in the mail. Picture for a moment a fresh-faced intern seeing the bulky package from Athens and thinking, *Cool, something new from R.E.M.!* But might there have been a touch of dread in the minds of some senior executives? I imagine them all crowded around a TV set as the intern ceremoniously pops the videocassette into the top-loading VCR. "Harborcoat" starts up as they all stare impassively. Perhaps someone taps his foot. Someone else begins to fidget. Then, as "7 Chinese Bros." kicks in and the band is still on the farm and that damned white dog keeps popping up on the screen, the throat-clearing begins. The image of Michael Stipe freezes, and a black frame appears around him. "Oh, that's interesting," says the intern. No one else says anything. Now we're on to "So. Central Rain," and the band members are in R. A. Miller's shop building a whirligig in earnest. Bill Berry has changed into a torn, sleeveless sweatshirt. Look at the pipes on that guy! Michael Stipe spray-paints "REM" on the wall. The freaking dog is everywhere. In the I.R.S. viewing room, coughs erupt intermittently like backfiring car motors. Finally, someone speaks—is it Miles Copeland?—saying, "What the hell am I supposed to do with this?"

For all I know, everyone at I.R.S. may actually have loved *Left of Reckoning*. But it's true that there wasn't much to be done with it other than appreciate the gesture. Fortunately, the label did have an outlet on MTV, albeit a tiny one buried in the late-night dead zone of the final Sunday of every month. A year previously, the network had reached out to Miles Copeland for programming ideas, and thus *I.R.S. Records Presents the Cutting Edge* was born. The show was a freewheeling hour-long showcase for the college rock genre with which Miles and Ian Copeland had become so closely associated. The episodes featured interviews, performance clips, and videos of artists from a variety of labels, but, as the show's title implied, pretty much anything on I.R.S. made the cut. Consequently, Jim Herbert's *Left of Reckoning* segment for "Time After Time (Annelise)" received an airing. On the July 29 episode, R.E.M. played a brief acoustic set in what appeared to be someone's bedroom. This sleepy performance was very much the opposite of the band's dynamic stage show, but it had a certain intimacy and homemade spirit that made a welcome change from the increasingly slick, high-budget videos that were beginning to fill up MTV. Perhaps most notably, R.E.M. played a new song titled "Driver 8," the music of which had been largely written by Bill Berry. Like a number of Stipe's more recent turns, the lyrics flirted with the idea of narrative before ultimately rejecting it. It's clear enough that "Driver 8" works on a train that passes through farm country. There's a wonderful line about children looking up to hear "sky-blue bells ringing," and a cryptic reference to a "tree house on the outskirts of the farm." But the lyric that stands out most strongly is the second half of the chorus:

> And the train conductor says
> "Take a break, Driver 8, Driver 8, take a break
> We can reach our destination, but we're still a ways away"

It's hard for anyone who knows the band's history not to read this as a plea to I.R.S.—and also as a declaration of intent: this is to be a gradual ascent, not to be forced; there may be breaks and reassessments; and it will all be conducted according to the band's timetable. Most listeners at the time would not have known anything about R.E.M.'s circumstances, of course, but like so much of Stipe's best writing, the lyrics here evoke universal feelings: a mixture of weariness and wistfulness, the desire to sink deeply into one place while simultaneously yearning for some unfixed destination far down the line. "Driver 8" was yet another breakthrough, moving Stipe one step closer to a cohesive literary vision.

"Driver 8" was just one of a whole batch of songs the band wrote while they were on the Little America tour. Since the material seemed to represent a new direction, particularly in the lyrics department, it seemed an appropriate time to think about a new producer for their next recordings. Peter Buck had his eye on Joe Boyd, the American-born, British-based producer best known for having overseen pivotal releases by Nick Drake, Fairport Convention, Pink Floyd, John Martyn, and Richard and Linda Thompson, among others.*

Boyd met up with the band in early 1985 and spent an afternoon recording demos with them in Athens. All went well, and the producer came away impressed with the new material. Arrangements were made to begin work on the new album at Boyd's London studio in late February.

We now arrive at the First Great Crisis in the history of R.E.M., a period during which the band allegedly came to the brink of breaking up. For many years the explanations the musicians gave for this made little sense. Bill Berry initially chalked this period of discontent up to a combination of homesickness and what sounds like Seasonal Affective Disorder. "Have you ever been to London?" he asked a journalist. "It's nothing but rain and fog. We had to drive thirty miles to the studio every morning, having had pork and beans for breakfast because that's all we could get." He complained that the TV in the hotel only got two stations. "One always had snooker on," he said, "while the other was showing a sheep-herding contest." The irony seems to have been entirely lost on Berry that he was making the kind of exaggerated generalizations about London that New York–based journalists often made about Athens. Furthermore, quite a lot of people *had* been to London and therefore found his comments puzzling. R.E.M. biographer Johnny Black breaks down the discrepancies:

> This was something of an exaggeration. Livingstone Studios was a converted church in the North London suburb of Wood Green. The band were staying in a more than acceptable hotel in Mayfair (central

---

* It would also not have been lost on R.E.M. that Boyd supervised the recording of the iconic "Dueling Banjos" for the movie *Deliverance*.

London), and the seven-mile trip to the studio took between 45 minutes and an hour, depending on traffic.

David Buckley, another of R.E.M.'s several British biographers, chimes in: "What did they expect to do in early March in the UK, sip caipirinhas beside the pool?"

Clearly something else was going on. Black speculates in his book *Reveal* that drugs may have played a role. "One of the best-documented side-effects of cocaine is its tendency to induce paranoia in users," he muses. And yet the crisis had its most visible manifestation in the one member of R.E.M. who was drug-free: Michael Stipe. His ongoing personal issues were readily apparent to the band's friend and former press officer Kelly Pike, who visited R.E.M. during the sessions. "The first thing I noticed was that Michael had shaved the crown of his head, like a monk, and he was behaving oddly," she told Black. "They were working on 'Wendell Gee,' and he would only listen to it while lying down under the mixing desk. The others made light of it, but it wasn't right."

Stipe subsequently admitted that he experienced a breakdown during this period, but it would be decades before he truly acknowledged the causes behind it. Finally, after years of giving pat answers along the lines of "I was just real tired," he opened up to Christopher Bollen of *Interview* magazine in 2011.

I went through this difficult time when we were making our third record where I kind of lost my mind. That's when the bulimia kicked in. And that's when I got really freaky. At that point we were playing our own shows and people liked us, but I was unraveling on the inside. I was also vegetarian, trying to eat from fast-food restaurants without meat. I didn't know how to eat properly and I was starving. I was adrenalized to the eyeballs from performing. I was afraid that I was sick with AIDS.

In this flurry of explanations, that last sentence may be the key. Stipe had in fact been wrestling with fears about AIDS ever since the first vague reports of the then-unnamed disease began circulating in 1981. "I'm afraid of everything," he told Bollen.

I'm not a naturally courageous person, but AIDS really brought it home. I mean, it was right when I was 21 years old and came to New York and saw the first billboard about AIDS. It was like, "Holy shit.

This is for real." It was scary. It was right at the time when I was in a band. Suddenly there were all these people who were available to me—men and women—and I was really having fun. But then there came responsibility and feeling afraid and being afraid to get tested, because you couldn't get tested anonymously. It was so fucked up.

By the time your [his interviewer's] generation was coming of age sexually, there was already this idea of safe sex. But that didn't exist for me. I came out of the free-swinging '60s and '70s. It was free love, baby. That was it. We had very liberal sex-ed classes in 1973, a yearlong environmental science class, and then Women's Lib and Gay Liberation. So it's insane to go from that to Reagan and AIDS. It was like, "What happened? Where's my future?" Our generation was supposed to be about trying to deal with nuclear concerns and environmental disasters. Suddenly, Reagan is in office, I'm 21 years old, and you can die from fucking. It was like, "I just started. I'm just hitting my stride. Are you kidding me? I don't want to die."

By 1985, Stipe's quite legitimate concerns had reached a peak, exacerbated by the general public's paranoia about the disease and the Reagan administration's apparent indifference to it. Indeed, at the time R.E.M. were recording in London, the US president still had not made any public mention of AIDS, despite the fact that the Pentagon was already moving to test all new recruits for the illness's retrovirus precursor—later to be named human immunodeficiency virus, or HIV—and to reject any applicants found carrying it. There were no commercially available HIV/AIDS tests, and it was impossible for a worried private citizen like Stipe to get tested anonymously. Meanwhile, more and more high-profile cases had been emerging. In 1983, the influential New York–based singer Klaus Nomi had died of AIDS-related complications. The following year, French philosopher Michel Foucault died of the illness in Paris. Closer to home, B-52's guitarist Ricky Wilson would pass away in October 1985.

In 2014, while introducing civil rights activist John Abdallah Wambere at Logo TV's "Trailblazers" event, Stipe elaborated on his early fears surrounding AIDS:

In the early '80s, as a 22-year-old queer man living during the Reagan-Bush administration, I was afraid to get tested for HIV for fear of quarantine, the threat of internment camps, and having my basic civil rights stripped away. I waited five years to get my first anonymous test. I am happy that attitudes have matured and changed, and I feel lucky that I live in a country where acceptance, tolerance, and policy toward HIV-AIDS and LGBTQ issues have advanced as far as they have.

This statement earned the derision of a number of conservative commentators. "You all remember the Reagan-Bush internment camps, right?" wrote Cain TV's Dan Calabrese. "Gay people with AIDS would be herded up by government agents in hazmat suits, put in the back of black vans and driven to camps with names like Stalag REM. There, they would be held by armed guards and fed porridge and drop biscuits three times a day until they simply wasted away, at which point their bones would be ground up and used to make more porridge for those who were still holding out against the inevitable."

Calabrese's sarcastic critique is highly insensitive, but he is correct to note that in fact "there were never any internment camps or government-mandated quarantines." Furthermore, Stipe's tendency, since the late 1980s, to blame the Reagan-Bush White House for all manner of societal ills—neatly summarized in R.E.M.'s 1992 track "Ignoreland"—makes it tempting to view his statements at the Wambere event as characteristic hyperbole. But such criticism ignores both the context and the emotional accuracy of Stipe's words. Whether or not the US government ever actively considered a quarantine program, such measures *were* openly discussed in the public sphere in the early to mid 1980s. In December 1985, the *New York Times* reported that, according to a recent national poll, "51 percent of the respondents supported a quarantine of acquired immune deficiency syndrome patients, 48 percent would approve of identity cards for those who have taken tests indicating the presence of AIDS antibodies and 15 percent supported tattooing those with AIDS." As someone who, like Stipe's interviewer Christopher Bollen, came of age during those years, I clearly recall the widespread perception, reaching far beyond the gay community, that the quarantine option was at least theoretically on the table. I also remember the discussions of camps, the prevalent AIDS jokes (which went as far up the chain as Reagan's press secretary Larry Speakes, who made insensitive cracks about the epidemic during press conferences in 1982, 1983, and 1984), and the nearly ubiquitous paranoia about catching the disease from kissing, or infected toilet seats, or casual skin-to-skin contact.

Is Stipe correct to link so much of his private turmoil from that time to the actions (or inaction) of the Reagan-Bush administration? At a practical level, probably not. The federal government did act quickly to fund AIDS research, and by the time Reagan left office the annual budget allocation for AIDS-related funding was $1.6 billion, having risen from an initial $8 million allotment in 1982. The figure would increase exponentially under his successor, George H. W. Bush. Furthermore, Reagan's Surgeon General, C. Everett Koop, was outspoken and aggressive on the topic even as the president remained silent; in 1988, Koop took the unprecedented step of mailing every household in America an information packet on the disease that advocated the use of condoms as the single best measure for avoiding infection.

However, if we accept the long-standing convention that one of a president's duties is to reassure and guide the public in a time of crisis, and if we measure this particular president against his reputation as the so-called Great Communicator, it's hard not to conclude that Reagan failed here and may have done real damage with his silence.

Contrary to popular belief, Reagan did not wait until seven years into his presidency to mention AIDS—he first discussed the epidemic during a press conference in 1985, and a year later called the search for an AIDS cure "one of our highest public health priorities"—but he did wait seven years before delivering a major address on the topic, an omission that seems almost incomprehensible in our current age, when something like swine flu can provoke an immediate response from the executive branch. In an article titled "Reagan's AIDS Legacy / Silence Equals Death," Allen White of *SF-Gate* writes, "The tragedy lies in what he might have done," and he laments the lack of a compassionate response from the administration. Such silence, he and other commentators have argued, allowed paranoia and hostility to swell unchecked in the public sphere. Again, anyone who grew up during that period would have a difficult time refuting that argument.

Significantly for Michael Stipe, Reagan's silence on AIDS seems to have triggered his own political awakening. As David Buckley notes, Stipe had always been of a liberal disposition, but it was not long into Reagan's second term that Stipe began to consider the idea of public activism. Such impulses would remain mostly private throughout 1985, but finally burst forth the following year when he sang, loudly and clearly, the words "Silence means approval," followed, in short order, by "Let's begin again."

All of this, however, lay well in the future as R.E.M. slogged through the recording of *Fables of the Reconstruction* in the winter of 1985. Already exhausted, they stood poised at the threshold of one of their toughest years— but also one of their finest.

R.E.M.

thursday · friday

march 8   march 9

with   with
the
art in the dark · nightporters

AT
THE # MAD HATTER

GEN. ADM. TICKETS **$5** NOW ON SALE AT

THE MAD HATTER   RECORD BAR,
WAX JR. FACTS and WUXTRY downtown

Poster for two March 1984 shows at the Mad Hatter in Athens.

Chapter Ten

> I'm pretty sure this is the band's first album with songs about identifiable people. Admittedly, "Driver 8," "Old Man Kensey," and "Wendell Gee" are more archetypal and symbolic than actual, but I believe their presence represents an artistic step away from abstractions. Also, not to overgeneralize, but my fundamental takeaway from this album is that people are sad and travel ends badly.
>
> —T. Kyle King, on *Fables of the Reconstruction*

Did *Fables of the Reconstruction* really "suck," as Bill Berry would put it, or was it, as Peter Buck later maintained, a personal favorite and one of the band's "stronger albums" in terms of songwriting? Perhaps it warrants both these reactions. Berry was, in all likelihood, referring more to the experience of making the record than the strength of the material itself. After all, this album included two of his more memorable composing turns, "Driver 8" and "Can't Get There from Here." But it's clear that both band and producer were largely disappointed by various aspects of the playing and the mixing, and those feelings colored their overall assessment of the album for quite some time afterward. Certainly, the band had less spring in its step than on previous efforts, with a few notable exceptions (the aforementioned "Can't Get There from Here" along with "Life and How to Live It" and "Auctioneer"). Berry's playing, in particular, lacked much of the creativity and nimbleness that had been so evident just two albums earlier. Similarly, Mike Mills had retreated from the song-propelling bass lines that had distinguished his work on *Reckoning*. Here his playing was more conventional and in places all but submerged in the mix. Michael Stipe sounded the way he was evidently feeling at the time—depressed and world-weary. Of the four musicians, only Peter Buck continued to innovate and expand—which he did in leaps and bounds, from the Andy Gill–inspired dissonance of "Feeling Gravitys Pull" to the haunting central motif of "Life and How to Live It" (a riff which, to my ears, seems to have directly inspired Sonic Youth's 1988 anthem "Teen Age Riot").

Three oars pulling in one direction with one pulling in the other can make for a disquieting listening experience, but there is more to *Fables* than its surface-level execution. For fans of compelling songwriting, this is indeed one of R.E.M.'s strongest albums, if not its strongest, and it may represent Michael Stipe's absolute peak as a lyricist.

When T. Kyle King observed that the album contained what sounded like "songs about identifiable people," he was closer to the truth than he realized. Old Man Kensey and Wendell Gee were not merely "archetypal and symbolic" figures, as King surmised—they were also actual individuals. Kensey was an assistant to the Reverend Howard Finster who, according to Stipe, had a penchant for kidnapping dogs for ransom and jumping out of coffins to scare people. Wendell Gee was the proprietor of an auto-repair shop the band drove past on the way to Rabbittown to film *Left of Reckoning* (though his connection to the song that bore his name was probably tenuous at best). And these were merely two of the more obvious examples from an album densely populated with real-life characters. The song "Maps and Legends" saluted Finster himself ("He sees what you can't see, can't you see that?"), while "Life and How to Live It" hewed closely to the life of Brivs Mekis, an eccentric who lived in a house on Meigs Street in Athens. Mekis, an alleged schizophrenic, had divided the house and furnished each side as a completely separate apartment, with separate pets and wardrobes. He would live on one side for a while, and then switch to the other when he felt another aspect of his personality take over. After he died, hundreds of copies of a self-published book titled *Life: How to Live* were discovered in one of his closets.*

Blogger Matthew Perpetua speculated on his *Pop Songs 07–08* website that Stipe's interest in the Mekis story may have had deeper roots than idle curiosity. "One could make an interesting argument," Perpetua wrote, "that the song reflects Michael's sexual confusion as a young man, and the intentionally separated home represents life in and out of the closet." This may be overreaching, and is perhaps one of the reasons Stipe later admonished Perpetua for reading too much of the author into the songs. "You confused and injected me [real Michael] in the work," Stipe told Perpetua. "That's the biggest mistake. I'm actually a better writer than all that." Stipe's claim that he stopped writing autobiographical material after *Reckoning* can be easily disproven, but it is true that *Fables* puts a greater emphasis on third-person

---

* *Life: How To Live*, a book of "personal philosophy" with allegedly fascistic overtones, went unloved and unread during Mekis's lifetime, but the R.E.M. connection has stoked posthumous demand: as of August 2018, a copy from the original batch will set you back $999 on eBay.

character studies, with Stipe acting as an opaque window through which we, the voyeuristic listeners, try to peek in.

There are only two songs on the album that give an autobiographical impression. "Feeling Gravitys Pull" has a discernible "I" that could be construed to be Michael. But what is the song actually telling us? It certainly sounds personal, with a streak of defiance ("I said 'I can too'!") crashing up against the inexorable pull of gravity. Factor in the reference to Man Ray, an iconoclastic 20th-century surrealist artist/photographer famous for pushing both creative and social boundaries, and the song takes on the shape of a manifesto—albeit a conflicted one. The artist becomes a god, able to suspend, for a time, the laws of physics: "Oceans fall and mountains drift." But inevitably it all collapses and he must return to reality: "Gravity pulls me down." And yet—in making the assumption that the "I" is indeed Michael, are we committing the same mistake as Perpetua? The song could just as easily be read as yet another character study, with the "I" being Man Ray himself, or another historical artist of his ilk. In any case, it's an appropriate kickoff for a hugely ambitious album—a thematically interconnected suite of songs that seeks to document some of the magic and mystery of the American South, as seen from the perspective of a native Southerner who spent almost the entirety of his life outside the region. Like the protagonist in "Feeling Gravitys Pull"—or any artist for that matter—Stipe may not be able to fully manifest his inner vision; he may not be able to truly "peel back the mountains, peel back the sky." But the art is in the attempt.

"Kohoutek" is the other apparently autobiographical track. This time, the notion of it being a character study is harder to sustain, given that its author inserts his own name into the lyrics ("Michael built a bridge, Michael tore it down"). But this song almost feels like a leftover from *Reckoning*—a reframing, perhaps, of the relationship from "So. Central Rain," or the documenting of an almost identical scenario. Once again, lack of communication is a theme: "I won't deny myself, we never talked." Once again, the narrator sings regretfully of a collapsed relationship: "Courage built a bridge, jealousy tore it down." Once again the relationship was short-lived, compared here to a much-hyped comet that flashed through the skies in 1973: "You were gone like Kohoutek, can't forget that." It's worth noting that the real Kohoutek was built up by astronomers as "the comet of the century," whose entry into the solar system was predicted to deliver some spectacular visual pyrotechnics. Yet when the comet did appear, it was barely visible and was considered a letdown.

Much has been made of the Southern thread on *Fables*. The South is certainly a key ingredient—from the uniquely Southern characters to the citing of exotic-sounding place-names (Philomath, etc.) to Stipe's liberal use of Southern colloquialism ("listen to the barter holler," "can't get there from here"). Plus there's that old Southern staple of a train, the Southern Crescent depicted in "Driver 8." Yet one wonders how much of this would have been picked up on by critics and listeners were it not for the album's title. Interestingly, the use of the term "Reconstruction" is, on one level, a bit of a red herring. There are no specific references on the album to the historical period that bears that name—a roughly ten-year span after the American Civil War during which the US government attempted to reintegrate the defeated South into the union by enfranchising freed slaves and promoting them to public office while barring former Confederate officials from holding government positions. All this while a flood of missionaries, teachers, and businessmen poured into the region with the intention of remaking both the Southern economy and the moral fabric of its society. Despite these generally noble aims (fueled, admittedly, by mixed motivations: altruism continually had to compete with the often stronger impulses of greed and the desire to exact revenge), this scheme played out like most US military occupations typically do. That is to say, after much effort, expenditure of treasure, and a brief, tantalizing glimpse of the desired utopia at gunpoint, the whole thing collapsed into violence, corruption, chaos, and intimidation. A virulent new terrorist organization called the Ku Klux Klan emerged, the northern carpetbaggers were routed, and the South reverted to a racial caste system with wealthy whites on top, poor whites several rungs lower, and the black population at the very bottom.

This history would seem ripe for lyrical exploration, and yet, if there are any actual references to the Reconstruction era on *Fables of the Reconstruction*, they are deeply buried. If I try really hard, I can make a tortured connection between the era and the album as two examples of outside forces attempting to impose upon the South a sort of idealized version of itself that doesn't always match up with reality. In Stipe's case, he highlights the eccentric pockets of the region while largely ignoring racial questions and more mainstream aspects of the culture. (One notable exception is Protestant Christianity, a dominant part of Southern culture with which Stipe was intimately familiar and which surfaces occasionally in the lyrics here, most notably in Stipe's offhand exhortation to "testify" in "Can't Get There from Here.")

Sidestepping such big issues seems something of a cop-out, or at best a demonstration of willful ignorance. After all, the racial legacy of Reconstruction was still very evident in present-day Athens, which remained deeply segregated in the early 1980s, albeit not by decree. For all its progressiveness, the music and arts scene was almost exclusively white. The town itself was still deeply divided along racial and economic lines, with the wealthy college students crowding the poorer parts of the community out to the margins. Not that addressing any of these concerns would have made for a better album. Churning on the racial questions would likely have obscured the many subtle delights and quirks that Stipe celebrates here.

All of this had come about by accident, for Stipe had never intended to stay in Athens once he finished school. His goal had always been to get to New York City as quickly as possible.* But like Chris Edwards before him, he had gotten waylaid. Most obviously, the band happened. But also, Stipe had looked around and seen all the crumbling-down beauty, the strangeness, the luminescent souls of all the holy fools—people like Ort, Finster, Kensey, Mekis—that other people took for granted because of their familiarity with that world. Stipe was just Southern enough to deploy his accent with authenticity, but he was also enough of an outsider to be able to see the hidden specialness in a lot of the things full-time Southerners simply accepted as normal.

It must also be said that the combination of Stipe's outsider status with his youthful idealism made him prone to romanticize—a tendency he was probably well aware of, hence the other significant word in the title. Fables are not history, nor are they meant to represent all aspects of a culture. And Stipe had been reading up on his fables, specifically Joel Chandler Harris's "Brer Rabbit" stories. *This* aspect of the title seems to suit the album quite well, for Reverend Finster, Old Man Kensey, Wendell Gee, Brivs Mekis, and even the mysterious Driver 8 are all rendered in the simple, whimsical language one might find in that mode of storytelling. Furthermore, each song seems to have an instructive quality, a feeling of "learn by this," even if the actual moral of the story, in typical Stipe fashion, is not always clear.

An additional clue as to Stipe's intentions may come from the album's alternate title, *Reconstruction of the Fables*, which adorned the cassette and CD versions of the release. Here *reconstruction* is shorn of its historical overtones and employed to describe the fables. And what are these songs if not reconstructed fables—that is, fables for a new era, reconstituted by the lyricist out of timeworn elements to make something original?

Beyond the Harris stories and the surfeit of local inspiration, Stipe was also fixated on the novels and travel writings of British author Lawrence Durrell during this period. A protégé of Henry Miller (author of *Tropic of Cancer*

---

* He did eventually reach this goal in the 1990s, when Manhattan became his primary home.

and other acclaimed/controversial novels), Durrell was cut from the same cloth as many of Stipe's other heroes; like Patti Smith, John Barth, Man Ray, Lou Reed, and Lillian Hellman, Durrell was a freethinker who challenged prevailing social norms in both his life and his work—particularly those related to religion and sexuality. But what Durrell also brought to the table— and what undoubtedly influenced Stipe—was his strong affinity for place (in Durrell's case, the Mediterranean and Egypt), his impressive vocabulary, and his lyrical, somewhat ostentatious deployment of that vocabulary in the service of his muse. In an interview a few years later, after the bloom was apparently off the rose. Stipe seemed to rue his fixation with this author. "Oh my God," he said. "He's so sappy and thick, I'm embarrassed. Lawrence Durrell. Before I traveled to Greece. His prose was so thick and tactile, no country could live up to that." But during 1985 Stipe cited Durrell frequently. In an August 1985 television interview in Toronto, Stipe claimed that he had read "everything" by the author.* The fact that he made a routine of publicly name-checking Durrell, much as he had done with Patti Smith a couple of years earlier, may be seen as some indication of the depth of Durrell's influence on the songwriter.

Lawrence Durrell is definitely something of an acquired taste. Like D. H. Lawrence, his dense—some might say flowery—prose can be initially off-putting. And yet, once a reader becomes attuned to his rhythms, it is easy to fall under his spell. Take this passage from his first major work, *The Black Book*:

> Lost, all lost; the fruiting of green figs, apricots. Lost the grapes, black yellow, and dusky. Even the ones like pale nipples, delicately freckled and melodious, are forgotten in this morning, where our one reality is the Levantine wind, musty with the smell of Arabia, stirring the bay into a muddy broth. This is the winter of our discontent.

And that's just two paragraphs in to the first page. On the surface, such overwrought language seems ripe for parody, but in the context of the book it

---

* During that same interview, Stipe and Buck also mentioned that they had both read *The Wasp Factory*, the controversial debut novel by Scottish author Iain M. Banks, and had written a song inspired by it. As for the identity of that song, take your pick. The book documents the inner life of a murderous, emotionally troubled young man who lives in semi-isolation on a small island off the Scottish coast. Given how deeply buried Stipe's John Barth tribute was in "Laughing," I'd say there are probably half a dozen potential *Wasp Factory*–inspired tracks among R.E.M.'s publicly released material from 1985 and 1986. The band also allegedly attempted to purchase adaptation rights to the book so they could be involved in composing the soundtrack to a potential *Wasp Factory* feature film. This project never progressed beyond the idea stage.

becomes one evocative passage in a larger hallucinatory symphony. Perhaps it is not a surprise that place-specific sensory details began popping up in R.E.M. songs such as "Driver 8," "Green Grow the Rushes," and "Wendell Gee," and that Stipe began using words like *lachrymose* in interviews. At any rate, 1985 marks the point at which the fragmentation in his writing began to recede, replaced by a dense, lyrical flow that conveyed a sense of some underlying, though still largely inscrutable, narrative.

R.E.M. may have had misgivings about the way *Fables of the Reconstruction* turned out, but happily for them—and for I.R.S.—those concerns were not reflected in its sales. The record reached #28 on the *Billboard* 200 album chart and a more than respectable #35 in the supposedly indifferent UK. US sales were bolstered by moderate MTV rotation of the "Can't Get There from Here" video clip, co-directed by Stipe and Rick Aguar. Although it didn't feature any lip-syncing, this strange creation hewed closer to the MTV aesthetic of the day than previous R.E.M. videos had done. It featured the band members in costume, mugging for the camera and acting out a story, in this case one that involved them going to a drive-in movie in classic old cars and throwing popcorn at each other while images of low-budget monsters and abstract landscapes ran across the screen. Intercut with this "narrative" were shots of local signs advertising boiled peanuts and footage of Michael Stipe and Jefferson Holt jumping over hay bales. Most unusually for R.E.M.—and contravening previous statements that they would not publish their lyrics—many of the words of the song appeared onscreen to accompany the action. It also helped that the song itself was an upbeat funk/soul pastiche with horns and a clipped/gravelly vocal that seemed to pay homage to both Ray Charles and Joe Cocker. Anyone who bought the *Fables* album expecting more of this sort of thing was probably disappointed, though for some casual consumers the surprise may have been a pleasant one—the equivalent of purchasing a paperback that you assume is a light beach read and instead finding that you've bought a quality work of literary fiction.

The critical reaction to *Fables of the Reconstruction* was largely positive, though the album was greeted with few of the over-the-top plaudits that had accompanied the release of *Murmur*. Parke Puterbaugh, writing in *Rolling Stone*, echoed many of his fellow reviewers in his attempt to reconcile his love of the band with what was clearly a confusing listening experience: "R.E.M. undermines our certitude in reality and deposits us in a new place, filled with both serenity and doubt, where we're forced to think for ourselves."* John Platt's somewhat more critical review in *Bucketfull of Brains* still strove mightily at the end to accentuate the positive. "It's a progression along existing lines," he wrote, "and with such a high proportion of good songs, that's fine with me." Still, journalistic integrity compelled Richard Defendorf of the *Orlando Sentinel* to admit his disappointment, even as he reiterated the band's importance: "One senses that something great is brewing. The problem is that it rarely simmers to the surface . . . I'll admit that much of my disappointment is the fault of high expectations. Standing alone, *Reconstruction* is a respectable effort."

In July 1985, *Musician* magazine published a lengthy profile titled "History of R.E.M.," which may have been one of the first major pieces on the band that did not describe Athens in tones of either breathless hyperbole or Northern condescension. "Forty-five years ago, maybe Athens, Georgia, did look like a shooting location for *Gone with the Wind*," Scott Isler wrote. "But in 1985 Athens (775 alt., c. 50,000 pop.), like most of the formerly deep South, has pretty much joined the cultural mainstream . . ."

> The Joseph Henry Lumpkin House, built in the 1840s in Classical Revival style, is next door to the Athens Podiatry, in fallout-shelter-revival style. The stately-columned house of Mrs. Peninah Thomas (1835) looks down on a jaggedly geometric wing of the Emmanuel Church (1962). These and a few other elegant mansions, long converted to institutional use, are a dwindling breed reduced to rubbing shoulders with fast-food outlets.

This lengthy piece, which captured the band during a brief pause between the recording of *Fables* and the start of the Pre-Construction tour, was the most nuanced assessment published so far of the band's four personalities and its composing and performing process. Isler highlighted the band's long-standing democratic tradition of crediting all compositions to "Berry, Buck, Mills, and Stipe," even though, in the case of *Fables*, Berry had written two songs "completely from beginning to end, just about." (Although the drummer politely declined to identify which two, Isler correctly guessed that the "good-timey 'Driver 8'" was one of them.)

---

*Puterbaugh's doubts did not prevent him from awarding the album four stars. This, too, was characteristic of a larger trend. The enormous goodwill the band had built up with the music press early on in its career arguably resulted in a sort of "grade inflation"—with *Rolling Stone* leading the pack—that reached its apex in the late '80s and would affect many of its reviews well into the mid-1990s.

Berry was particularly candid in his interview, admitting that he had at first considered Stipe's lyrics to be "silly" and "kinda pretentious," but had subsequently come to appreciate their artistry. He admired Stipe's ability to improvise on a nightly basis. "It's really funny," Berry said. "He'll throw in current events; he'll see somebody in the front row and I can tell if he's responding to them. It's great, very spontaneous." Such fluidity kept R.E.M.'s performances fresh and unpredictable, even as the set list inevitably became more rigid over time.

Another interesting detail Isler captured—almost inadvertently—was that Stipe had become something of a real estate mogul. "He provides a critical tour of the houses of Athens," Isler wrote, "many of which he's apparently lived in." Billy Holmes confirms this. "R.E.M. were smart with their money," he says.

> One reason is because Michael Stipe's mother—my wife knows her real good—was a real estate agent; she got all of them to buy real estate early on. And so Michael Stipe and Peter Buck in particular bought a lot of real estate around town. I think the band as a limited partnership now owns a good bit of Prince Avenue and downtown. Not too shabby for some guys who threw together a funky new-wave band in a rundown church!

Any impression the members of R.E.M. conveyed—in this piece and others—that they still lived quiet, laid-back lives in their adopted hometown was either wishful thinking on their part or a carefully constructed illusion. In reality, the band spent most its brief break between album and tour rehearsing for the impending shows and entertaining out-of-town journalists. Indeed, Mills, Stipe, and Buck all invited reporters (from *International Musician, Xtra,* and a number of other publications) into their homes for refreshments and, on a couple of occasions, impromptu musical performances. Here we arrive at one of the rarely acknowledged keys to R.E.M.'s early success: the band could play the media game without it seeming like a game at all. And perhaps it wasn't; Peter Buck could easily have switched places with any of the journalists tasked with interviewing him. With his massive record collection, his encyclopedic knowledge of rock history, and his forceful opinions, he spoke their language. Add the fun-loving Mills and Berry into the mix, and Stipe for some artsy seasoning, plus the seeming exoticism (to Yankee writers) of a Southern small town, and you have a music writer's dream band. The Replacements may have been just as exciting musically, but in the socializing department there was no way they could compete with R.E.M., nor did they

Michael Stipe backstage with two former Collinsville High classmates, Foelinger Auditorium, Champaign, Ilinois, November 16, 1985. Left: with Jeff Wendler, photo by Michael Edson. Right: with Michael Edson, photo by Jeff Wendler.

understand the value of cultivating long-term relationships with members of the press. R.E.M.'s early efforts in these areas would go a long way in keeping the media on their side for many years to come.

R.E.M. performed 121 documented concerts in 1985, ranging in size from a bar gig (at the Uptown Lounge in Athens, playing under the name Hornets Attack Victor Mature) to several massive outdoor festivals in the UK and Europe, appearing alongside U2, Joe Cocker, and Depeche Mode to audiences in excess of 50,000. Michael Stipe underwent a startling visual metamorphosis over the course of the year, beginning Pre-Construction as a bald "hobo" in a black trench coat, porkpie hat, and round black sunglasses, with vertical lines shaved into his eyebrows, and ending Reconstruction III as a manic, wiry "elf" with bleached blond hair. Somewhere along the way, he went through a transitional "backwards hat" phase. Chris Edwards explains how this came about:

> During the Pre-Construction tour we played Regents Field and then got on the bus and drove overnight to some little college in Pennsylvania or something, in the middle of nowhere. I stopped at this little country store and saw this guy with a Genesee Light hat on. It was a blue corduroy hat but it said "Genesee" and I thought it was really cool. I grew up on Genesee beer—Genesee Cream Ale in New York State. I loved the stuff and hadn't seen it since I'd moved to Georgia. It took me a while but I talked him out of it. I loved that hat and wore it every day.
>
> Michael liked that hat too. Not because it said "Genesee" but because it was blue corduroy. He asked me if he could wear it

onstage . . . He turned it around backwards because he didn't want a corporate logo in the front. I thought, humph, yeah, that's pretty weird, but okay. As we would do right when doors would open in the early days, myself and some of the guys from the crew would hang around at the sound board to check the chicks coming in the door. Just to check out the local talent. About a week after Michael started wearing my hat on backwards, we started to see guys coming in with their hats the same way and we thought it was the craziest-looking thing you'd ever seen. It's like, look at this guy—he's got his hat on backwards because Michael does.

We'd stand out there and see these guys walk in and we'd say, what a bunch of idiots. Looking like doofuses. They have no idea why Michael wears the hat backwards . . . they're doing it because they think it's cool. We laughed at them. *No one* wore their hat backwards back then. It's just not something that was done. Now, I swear *that* hat started the whole backwards hat trend that became so popular in the late '80s!

What Edwards offers here is an early sighting of a certain type of R.E.M. fan, who came to be known around Athens and elsewhere as a "Distiple." Billy Holmes also witnessed the phenomenon: "We used to joke that you could tell what Michael Stipe looked like this week by going downtown and seeing all the people who were trying to copy him," he says. "And it was the honest-to-God truth; Stipe would change his look, and then every kid downtown would have the new Michael Stipe look." In one sense, this was nothing new: Michael had been attracting hangers-on all the way back to his days at Collinsville High, when a couple of fellow misfits began adopting his dress style. But as his looks became more and more off-the-wall—particularly on the *Fables* tours—and as R.E.M. became ever more popular, the Distiples became more numerous and more easily identifiable, and their proliferation in the band's hometown was yet another indication to local residents that the onetime cover band was getting a lot bigger than anyone had ever expected.

As for the bleached-blond elf look, Chris Edwards was there for the inception of that style as well, at the Greek Theater in Los Angeles:

The Greek was a huge outdoor amphitheater with a path you had to walk down . . . to get to the stage. Michael and I walked into the dressing room at the same time. He looked at the catering, and there's a bowl of mayonnaise and a bowl of mustard—really nice, round, silver bowls. He looked at me and he said, "Doesn't it make you want to stick your head in it?"

"No, Michael. No, it doesn't."

Michael was always the last one to come out of the dressing room . . . Not much longer after everyone else, but he wouldn't leave until everyone else did. We waited on the porch for him and he came out and we started to go down the path. He goes, "Chris, wait, I'll be right there." I knew exactly what he was doing. He ran back in and stuck his head in the mustard, right before he went onstage. You've never smelled Michael Stipe like he was that night after being under the hot lights for a couple hours onstage. Especially after getting back on the bus and doing a runner after the show. He was pretty nasty.

After that he had me advance about every different mustard we could think of and he'd wear a different mustard on his head every night . . . his favorite was French's. That went on for a few weeks and finally he ended up dying his hair blond. It was rough for a while.

With the new hair color came a more liberated persona. Stipe dropped the reserved, minimal-movement shtick he'd employed since the latter half of the *Murmur* tour and returned to the frantic dancing that had so enthralled audiences during the Tyrone's days. Only now his movements were even more unhinged, and often incorporated long-forgotten styles such as the Mashed Potato and the Chicken. This new approach was perhaps best exemplified in a performance of "Can't Get There from Here" on UK television show *The Tube*, in which Stipe came across as an overcaffeinated hybrid of Joe Cocker and David Byrne. Audiences found it difficult to take their eyes off of him.

A major turning point in R.E.M.'s development occurred during an April show at Barrymore's Music Hall in Ottawa. After running through their regular set list, the band was heckled with cries of "Fuck off!" when they encored with "Moon River." This almost resulted in a fight: Mills allegedly had to be restrained from attacking the heckler. A couple of songs later, Buck couldn't let it go. "The guy who yelled 'Fuck you' during 'Moon River': Meet me backstage, you asshole." Further heckling ensued, but instead of storming off (which the band had sometimes done in similar situations), R.E.M. elected to play an entire second set of mostly cover songs—including punishing, shambolic versions of "Smokin' in the Boys' Room" (originally performed by Brownsville Station but mistakenly attributed by Mills to Bachman Turner Overdrive), "Sweet Home Alabama," and "God Save the Queen," interspersed with deranged monologues from Stipe and Mills. While this harked back to the band's days playing covers-heavy sets at Tyrone's, on this occasion it fell well short of the standard they'd set back then. It was, frankly, a train wreck, and even though the band had performed almost an entire set of their own material before this, in the eyes of some audience members they were only as good as their final song—and by the time R.E.M. careened and caterwauled through their 34th and last song of the evening—their own "Carnival of Sorts (Box Cars)"—they weren't very good at all, at least on a technical level. Uninhibited? Yes. Embodying the spirit of punk rock? Perhaps. But certainly not "good" on the professional level that a paying attendee at a concert far from the band's home might expect.

The Ottawa gig was not quite the end of the old fly-by-the-seat-of-their-pants R.E.M.—impromptu, often strange cover versions still found their way into their encores at later shows, and Peter Buck had a few more tantrums up his sleeve before the tour wound down at the end of the year—but it can be considered the culminating moment of that earlier, more carefree incarnation. It is probably not a coincidence that an emergency band meeting was convened a few days later with the purpose of determining the band's future. Nor that their subsequent (post-1985) tours would be very different affairs—more scripted, polished, and often incorporating additional musicians into their onstage lineup. In the future, R.E.M. would be a band that could be relied on to deliver a solid, crowd-pleasing performance night after night.

This was probably a necessary transition for a rising band to make, but some of the mad, combustible energy that had helped forge their greatness in the first place was inevitably lost. Reconstruction (if I may be allowed the liberty of grouping the Pre, I, II, III, and End installments of the tour under this umbrella name) was by comparison all over the map, with transcendent highs and soul-crushing lows. It may very well have been R.E.M.'s greatest tour. This was the last time the original four members took the stage night after night without the safety net of a second guitarist, the last time that they would play—and live—together for a long, uninterrupted span of time, and it was the last time, save for a smattering of secret gigs in Athens and elsewhere in subsequent years, that a person could walk into an R.E.M. concert with little idea as to how the evening would unfold. In this particular group's case, these factors were the prerequisites for magic.

R.E.M. toured with a number of supporting bands in 1985. These included the Three O'Clock, True West, Faith Brothers, 10,000 Maniacs, and the Minutemen, all of whom received encouragement and generous treatment from the main act. At a fair number of these shows, it was not unusual for Peter Buck to jump onstage during the opening band's set to accompany them on one or two songs. He did this mainly for his own enjoyment, but his de facto endorsements were not lost on the audiences, who typically afforded the openers more attention than supporting groups are used to receiving.

The band 10,000 Maniacs, who supported R.E.M. at 14 US shows on the Reconstruction III tour, already went back a ways with the group. Both had recorded albums with Joe Boyd in 1985, and Stipe and 10,000 Maniacs' singer Natalie Merchant had been intermittent lovers since the previous year, as Merchant revealed in a 1998 "How We Met" piece for the *Independent* to which Stipe also contributed. The depth and duration of their romantic involvement remains unknown, but Merchant's artistic and personal influence on Stipe, and vice versa, cannot be overstated. Perhaps most significantly, Merchant helped nudge Stipe's nascent political stirrings into actual activism. "Natalie was really the reason my work became politicized in the late Eighties," Stipe wrote in the *Independent* piece. "The work she was doing was real and important—all about the human condition. It was a very accurate reflection of the power and greed of the time, and I was impressed by her understanding. Through our conversations, I got to thinking that the plight of the native American Indians was a very important issue."

Merchant confirmed this. "We talked about music and had a great time," she said of one of their earliest meetings. "I was doing a lot of research about the genocide against the native American Indians, and we made a pact that we'd both write songs about their plight. Michael wrote 'Green Grow the Rushes' and I wrote 'Among the Americans.' Both songs appeared on our next records. I look at that as the beginning of our friendship."

The desire to make some kind of meaningful political statement created an interesting tension in Stipe's writing and public persona that would take a few more years to sort itself out. Initially, he had to reconcile the activist impulse—which by its very nature requires clear, forthright statement—with his ingrained inclination toward metaphor and fragmented narrative. The meaning of "Green Grow the Rushes" (on *Fables of the Reconstruction*) may have been abundantly clear to its author, but it was lost on most listeners. The general consensus among those who diligently tried to parse its meaning was that the song addressed the plight of Mexican migrant workers in the US—an interpretation that finds considerable support in the actual lyrics. Furthermore, the line "They've found some surplus cheaper hands" could be interpreted as the lament of a poor white farmhand who has seen his job outsourced to the very migrant/Mexican/Native American workers the song supposedly celebrates. The song itself is quite lovely—but it's not the sort of focused, forceful statement likely to influence hearts and minds.

On the Reconstruction II and III tours, Stipe attempted to up the ante by literally wearing his issues on his sleeve. At the band's October 2 show in Bochum, West Germany, the singer came onstage with a Xeroxed photo of the McDonald's mascot Ronald McDonald—on which the words *No Cruise* were scrawled—duct-taped to the back of the suit he was wearing. This was probably intended as a protest against the US government's installation of cruise missile launch facilities in six European locations (including Germany), with the McDonald's clown symbolizing how Michael felt about President Ronald Reagan. It was a clever swipe, but given Stipe's reputation for general oddball behavior, the political reference was lost on many in the audience. They simply saw the R.E.M. front man wearing a picture of a clown—a fitting fashion accessory to the singer's yellow hair and purple eyebrows. At some later shows Stipe sported a T-shirt with the words *The amber waves of GAIN* (a line from "Green Grow the Rushes") scrawled on the front in Magic Marker. To those who had failed to grasp the song's critique of American materialism—which was just about everyone—this bold-faced clarification was hard to miss. The era of Stipean sloganeering had officially commenced.*

R.E.M. were supported on the final 16 shows of Reconstruction III by the Minutemen, and the two bands became quite close. Despite the differences in their musical styles—the San Pedro, California–based Minutemen leaned toward short, fast-paced experimental punk songs that made R.E.M.'s more melody-based compositions sound conventional by comparison—each group saw its ethos mirrored in the actions of the other. Independently of R.E.M.'s earlier Ian Copeland–derived thrift-tour strategy, the Minutemen had developed a similar, albeit more extreme, approach to touring—and recording—that they called "econo-jamming." Just as R.E.M. had done in their earliest days, the Minutemen structured their tours around long weekends—to accommodate their day jobs. They played small clubs off the beaten path and all but lived out of their Ford Econoline van (unlike R.E.M.,

---

* This tendency would reach its culmination when Stipe wore a T-shirt emblazoned with the words *USE A CONDOM* at the 1991 MTV Video Music Awards. We must remember the context: the AIDS epidemic was at its peak at the time, as was Stipe's influence on the public. Safe sex had become an issue of life or death for many people. What may have been an admirable, and possibly even effective, plea for public awareness was not a particularly rock 'n' roll move (try to imagine Keith Richards wearing such a shirt), but it was at least a more actionable command than the one on another shirt Stipe wore that evening: "White House Stop AIDS Now"—a policy recommendation that rather overestimated the executive branch's abilities.

they held on to their day jobs well into their career). They carried their own gear and teched their own shows. In the recording studio, the Minutemen opted to save money by utilizing used or leftover tape, and they tracked the songs after midnight, when studio rates were lowest. They also recorded their songs in the sequence in which they would appear on the finished album, so as not to waste money and tape during the mastering process. Needless to say, overdubs were kept to a minimum. R.E.M. had not operated at quite this level of austerity, but their sympathies had always been in this direction.

At the final concert of Reconstruction III, on December 13 in Charlotte, North Carolina, all three members of the Minutemen joined R.E.M. onstage for a raucous version of Television's "See No Evil." It was a great moment, fraught with significance: two like-minded bands, pioneers in a revolution that would transform rock music, joining forces to create a mighty roar. Tragically, this would turn out to be the Minutemen's final performance; nine days later, Minutemen singer/guitarist D. Boon was killed in a van accident, a loss that sent bassist Mike Watt into a deep depression and led a shaken R.E.M. to host a tribute/benefit concert at the 40 Watt the following month. Watt and Minutemen drummer George Hurley would eventually regroup and form the band Firehose, but the ghost of D. Boon continued to haunt—and perhaps guide—the indie rock community for many years, well after R.E.M.'s ascension to major-label stardom. Mike Watt has dedicated every subsequent record he has released—either with Firehose or solo—to Boon's memory.

For R.E.M., the death of D. Boon was a tragic endnote to the band's most turbulent year, dampening the fact that the Reconstruction tours, alongside the album that had spawned them, had turned out to be the band's biggest successes thus far. Many people saw R.E.M. live for the first time in 1985, and quite a few of these first-time attendees would become long-term followers. It was the beginning of something.

But first, it was time for a real break.

1. RADIO
2. SECOND
3. HARBOR
4. FALL ON ME
5. HYENA

6. DREAM
7. DRIVER 8 - Bill
8. SWAN, SWAN   Acoustic
9. TIME AFTER TIME
10. ROCKVILLE - BILL

11. AUCTIONEER
12. 7 BROS.
13. SITTING
14. KENSEY
15. JUST A TOUCH
16. PRETTY

1. GRAVITY
2. WIRE SONG
3. GOOD TIME

1. SEE NO EVIL
   PASSION
   LIFE + HOW

Set list for D. Boon tribute/benefit show at the 40 Watt Club Uptown, January 20, 1986, written for Pat the Wiz, who did the sound. He comments: "Michael pointed out in Sharpie the two songs that Bill sang on. He knew I was aware of that, but I suppose he'd been doing that for other soundmen he worked with, and he did it for me out of habit. He also mentioned the acoustic guitar on 'Swan, Swan Hummingbird'." Courtesy T. Patton Biddle.

Atlanta Civic Center, December 31, 1984. Photo © Joanna Schwartz.

Chapter Eleven

Velena Vego lives in a house straight out of a C. S. Lewis novel. The grayish-green early-20th-century residence has a huge front window that wouldn't disgrace a cathedral and is ringed by crepe myrtle trees and a wrought-iron fence covered in ivy. A winding stone walkway leads to a door on one side, where Velena greets me by saying, "We know each other, don't we?"

It turns out that we do, though I am taken aback. As the booking manager for the 40 Watt, Velena has worked with literally thousands of artists since she first assumed that position in the early 1990s. These include Nirvana, Foo Fighters, Bob Mould, the Flaming Lips, Drive-By Truckers, Kenny Chesney, and Cracker—whose primary songwriter, David Lowery, is Velena's husband. So it's somewhat surprising that she would remember a jittery, unsigned singer-songwriter who played the Watt just once in the late 1990s. But that's the kind of person she is: she keeps track of everything, and she has time for everyone.

Velena leads me through the house, whose interior has a magic to match its outside. Perhaps this is heightened by the fact that we're only a few days away from Christmas and the front room is filled with colorfully wrapped gifts and a well-decorated tree. But I suspect I would find the wall-mounted guitars and framed concert posters beguiling during any season.

Given Velena's confidence and poise, it would be easy to believe that her path from struggling musician to industry mover and shaker (she also manages Cracker and Camper Van Beethoven) was inevitable. But that was not the case. Her career journey was unplanned and fraught with periods of uncertainty, not to mention unemployment. And, like a lot of people, she ended up in a place she did not expect—both physically, in Athens, and careerwise, as a booking agent. She began as a self-described city girl, living in Atlanta and playing with her sister Vanessa in an all-female goth/new wave group called Mystery Date. In 1982, Vanessa began dating Mike Richmond and moved to Athens. Velena followed, officially taking up residence there around 1983–84. Thinking back to one of the earliest gigs her band played in Athens, opening for Limbo District at the Last Resort, Velena recalls being horrified at first at the changes the town had wrought in her sister. "I remember my sister having her shoes off," she says. "She's barefoot onstage and I was so appalled. I'm like, 'What are you doing? You've completely turned into a hippie; this is so ridiculous!' All these years later I'm still living here and still in the music business, so it's just so funny that I had no clue that this would be my home back in 19-whatever . . ."

One of my interviewees for this book joked that Mystery Date was a band that "everyone followed but no one liked," which seems unfair. Quite possibly they were stronger on image than substance initially, but by the time they recorded the song "Seance" at John Keane's studio in 1986, they had developed a distinct, brooding sound that in some respects (particularly Vanessa's guitar work) anticipated the paranoid swirl of My Bloody Valentine's *Loveless* by five years. Jeff Walls of Guadalcanal Diary was a fan and supporter from early on. "Loved Mystery Date," he wrote recently on Facebook. "One of the few post-REM Athens bands that had an over-the-top outré image & sensibility." Peter Buck was also a fan and served as the band's unofficial roadie whenever he was in town. At the very least, the Vego sisters made an impression. "They were amazing," Chris Edwards tells me. "They used to dress up like China dolls . . . They were just so precious and gorgeous. It was totally out of left field. It's not like that was a trend or anything going on. They were just doing their own thing, but it was really neat. I really enjoyed it; I liked to see them out and about."

Velena eventually became romantically involved with Jefferson Holt, which brought her more directly into R.E.M.'s orbit. In early 1986, R.E.M./Athens Ltd, which had previously operated from a P.O. box address, opened a two-story business office/rehearsal space on Clayton Street in downtown Athens. The second floor was split between management and fan club functions, and Velena and Robin Edwards (Mystery Date's bassist) were brought in to work the phones—Velena taking the ten to two shift and Robin working from two to five. "I had no idea just how big R.E.M. were until I started working for them," Velena says.

It was supposed to be, like, maybe the phone rings every once in a while. But they had to get two of us to work full-time Monday through Friday because people were asking from all over the country, "When are they playing? What are they doing? Where do I find the tickets?" I remember Peter Buck being up there in the office because we all hung out. He answered the phone. He's like, "This is Peter Buck." They're like, "No, it's not." He goes, "It is. What do you want?" The person on the other end said, "No, it's not." He said, "Fuck it. You don't believe me."

We would answer the phone and people would say, "Oh my God! I can't believe it! You're in Athens. I can't believe it!" These people were so blown away that they actually got a person on the phone . . . somebody from Athens, Georgia, because it was so mystical to them. These are college kids from Michigan, from Ohio, I mean, all over. Not just the South, but all over. I learned more about the states and the cities from working for them because I had to know where all these places were . . . That was a lot of fun. Those are good memories.

The band members and management often made a big show of the office's recycling practices for visiting journalists. This might seem a bit ostentatious now, but it's important to remember just how far ahead of the curve R.E.M. were. "The offices are run on an 'environmentally conscious' basis," noted Marcus Gray in his 1992 book *It Crawled from the South*, "using recycled materials, and employing a series of labeled bins to separate their own garbage for recycling purposes." This is now the preferred waste-sorting method for many businesses, restaurants, and private residences in the US, but that was not the case in the 1980s. R.E.M.'s vocal enthusiasm for such innovations probably influenced a lot of people at the time, especially at the local level. Many were already sympathetic to such ideas, but R.E.M. demonstrated methods for implementing them. As we will see, environmental awareness is one political cause that R.E.M. can legitimately claim to have played a role in popularizing.

Adjacent to the fan club office where Velena and Robin worked was an executive office shared by Jefferson Holt and Bertis Downs. Velena remembers Bertis being "on the phone quite a bit. He was their legal counsel and he certainly was there the entire time."

He was a big part of that band. Jefferson I would call a cheerleader and I think all that he did was fantastic, but I'm sure they needed someone legally to know about contracts and all that because that's where bands get screwed. [R.E.M.] own all their publishing, they never sold their publishing, so when you hear "The One I Love" or whatever, they made lots and lots of money way before their big Warner Bros. deal. Sincerely, even with the back records, it's unbelievable. They were smart from the get-go.

As much as she enjoyed working with R.E.M., Velena didn't have much of a sense, at the time, of being any kind of witness to history. "Although I was involved because my boyfriend at that time was managing them," she says, "I really had my lead-singer thing going on in my head."

Right now it seems like I probably would have been more involved because I'm a manager and I book a club, but at that time, remember, I was just a young girl. I was home-based and trying to figure it out. One of the stories I have is that being in an all-girl band and being so young, I was dealing with a situation that was probably like it is now too: every dude in the room had the attitude of "Which one do I want? Do I want the lead singer, the guitarist, the whatever?" I did not like that feeling. I remember asking Stipe, "How do you do it? You play in front of a bunch of frat dudes. How do you do it, because I'm losing my shit here!" This was early on; I'm talking about '84, '85, you know. He said that he just looks at the audience and tries to pinpoint one person that's interesting to him or he can connect with in some weird way and he just plays to them. He just enjoys playing for that one person. I was like, "God, that is so smart of him to do something like that." Instead of me being like, "Why aren't they listening to my lyrics? Why do they only think of me as a sex object?" Do you know what I mean? He just embraced it.

In the short term, this advice helped Velena become more comfortable onstage. But in the long term, it was Holt who had the lasting influence, given the career path Velena eventually took. She remembers Holt coming home from the R.E.M. office, having dinner, and then getting back on the phone to do more work. "That's another thing I learned," she says.

If a band member calls you, it doesn't matter what time it is, you pick up the phone. There's no hours, there's no nine-to-five. Whenever they need you, you'd better be there or they'll find somebody else. You don't wait until the next day to make a return call or a return e-mail or you will be replaced. It is what it is. There are tons of people that are hungry for any of our positions.

Velena recalls one conversation between Holt and Stipe that occurred around 2 a.m. "I don't know what year it was."

Stipe was in New York. He was doing some kind of show: a photography show or something like that. I do remember Jefferson getting a little upset and saying, "You need to come home. The reason why they are looking at you is because of the band you're in, so you do need to focus. At this present time you need to come and write songs . . ." It was the first time I ever saw him get kind of angry or frustrated with him.

Michael Stipe had been involved in side projects from the very beginning. But only in 1986 did people outside of Athens begin to take serious notice of his extracurricular activities. In January and again in March and July, Stipe hit the road with drummer/composer Anton Fier's band the Golden Palominos, singing lead on several songs. These shows were in support of the album *Visions of Excess*, which had been recorded the previous year and featured significant songwriting and vocal contributions from Stipe. The Palominos were a loose entity—only Fier, Bill Laswell, and Nicky Skopelitis were constant members—and the *Visions of Excess* project brought Stipe together with such luminaries as John Lydon, Jack Bruce, Richard Thompson, Chris Stamey, and newcomer Syd Straw. Significantly, though, it was Stipe's powerful and distinctive vocals that dominated the first three songs of the album and set the tone for what followed.

Musically, the project put Stipe firmly back in art-rock territory and functioned as a logical extension of his work with Tanzplagen. In contrast to R.E.M.'s ensemble playing, the Palominos' songs were characterized by virtuoso, often atonal guitar workouts courtesy of Skopelitis and Thompson, funk- and dub-influenced bass from Laswell, and loud, heavily processed drumming from Fier. These three elements managed to maintain their distinctness even when layered atop one another, with the vocals adding a further individual part.

Peter Buck, too, had a difficult time winding down, though he was not involved in anything quite so polished as the Golden Palominos. Early 1986 saw him popping up onstage with Love Tractor, Hüsker Dü, Jason and the Scorchers, and his own ragtag side band, Full Time Men.* He also went back to work at Wuxtry, accepting free records in lieu of wages.

Even Mike Mills and Bill Berry, who had considerably higher capacities

---

* Fun fact: Velena Vego joined the Full Time Men onstage at their February 7, 1986, Athens show at the Uptown Lounge to contribute lead vocals to "One More Time."

for taking it easy than the others, felt compelled to throw a group together—the Corn Cob Webs—which played a bewildering array of obscure and classic rock covers (including several by Led Zeppelin) and became the unofficial house band at the Uptown Lounge. And if that weren't enough, Mills, Berry, and Buck revived the Hindu Love Gods—another side band, also primarily focused on covers, that had formed during a break back in 1984 and had alternately featured Warren Zevon and Athens musician Bryan Cook as lead vocalist.

All this might lead one to believe that R.E.M. didn't take much of a break during the first half of 1986, but the key difference here is that all of these activities were relatively spontaneous and of the participants' choosing. At no point from January through August did any of the four members of R.E.M. find themselves locked into a packed itinerary with no end in sight, and this afforded Bill, in particular, the opportunity to take a significant step in his life—one that was not without collateral damage. He and Kathleen had continued to be involved on and off since 1981, though the relationship had been complicated at times. "We maintained our relationship for years," Kathleen says,

> but as R.E.M. started getting more successful, that's when the groupies and the [other] women started popping up and I really couldn't handle that so well.
>
> He came back from one tour and we . . . Gosh, at that point, was it 1986? We'd been together for about seven years at that time, pretty much off and on, but together. He said he wanted to talk to me. I swear to God I thought he was going to come in and ask me to marry him and instead he came in and told me he was engaged to somebody else. I didn't even know who this was. I never knew about Mari. I was like "Oh God!" And I said "Okay then, well I guess you should go then, and best of luck." And that was that and I ended up leaving Athens shortly thereafter, because when she moved to town I could not deal with it, because I was still in love.*

Let us pause here to give Kathleen O'Brien a proper send-off. I always

---

* Tony Fletcher states in his R.E.M. biography *Perfect Circle* that Bill had begun dating Mari after ending his relationship with Kathleen. These two accounts are not necessarily in conflict, given that the participants were all in their twenties and one of them was a touring rock musician. It's not overly difficult to believe that Bill and Kathleen had divergent interpretations of their relationship status by 1986.

found it disconcerting when she disappeared abruptly from the narrative in earlier R.E.M. biographies—usually at the point when Jefferson Holt comes in. But that is largely what has happened here, too—and there is some reason for it. Although she remained very much in Bill's life for a number of years, Kathleen's roles as de facto co-manager and booking agent ceased when the band's official administrative structure began to coalesce. As her relationship to the band became more personal than professional, and given the band's long-term reticence regarding such relationships, she has, perhaps inevitably, receded from our narrative. This doesn't seem quite fair given her importance to the R.E.M. story, but Kathleen herself remains respectful to the memory of her relationship with Bill, so there is really not much to divulge.

Kathleen completed her degree at the University of Georgia, moved to Atlanta, co-founded a business, got married, had two kids, and later divorced. Her daughter attends her alma mater in Decatur—the same high school that first brought Kathleen into proximity with Peter Buck and thereby kicked our story into gear. In October 2007, she returned to Athens to participate, alongside Bertis Downs, Tony Fletcher, and others, in an "R.E.M. in Perspective" seminar hosted by the Athens Historical Society. There she received a long overdue public acknowledgment on behalf of the band (via Downs) for her role in the band's founding. Fans owe her . . . oh, just about everything, because, as has hopefully been made clear, it is unlikely that the four young men would have connected either socially or musically were it not for her intervention. So—a very fond farewell to Kathleen O'Brien, with my deepest gratitude.

Spring of 1986 was a season of endings. When Barry Walters arrived in Athens in July to interview the band for a *SPIN* magazine profile, Peter Buck commented, "The girl I've been dating for six years broke up with me last Saturday." He was referring to Ann Boyles, with whom he had been involved since the early Barber Street days.

This event, coupled with Berry's transition from one long-term relationship into another, underscores a key difference between the two halves of R.E.M. As band friend Diane Loring Aiken puts it, "Peter and Bill always had steady relationships, unlike the other two." Velena Vego adds, "I think Bill has always had a girlfriend or someone in his life . . . He's that type of person that needs someone in his life." This is not to say that there weren't shenanigans on the road, but Peter's and Bill's situations were markedly different from those of, say, Mike Mills and Jefferson Holt, as Velena explains:

> My friend Lauren used to date Mike Mills and somehow these two huge R.E.M. fans that worked at KUSF . . . invited us out to

San Francisco because they had been here for one of Peter Buck's New Year's parties. I'd never been out of the South, and so in 1987 Jefferson and Mike flew us, me and Lauren, to go and just hang out for a week.

Back in the day, on each tour, we used to have tour jackets like high school letterman jackets, so I wore my letterman jacket. I was in San Francisco for the first time. People would come up . . . We'd be at bars, we'd be at clubs, really trendy happenings in San Francisco. They're like, "Oh! Do you know R.E.M.?" Lauren said, "Yes, I live with Mike Mills." I said, "Yes, I live with Jefferson Holt." And people were telling us these stories about all of their little escapades, especially Mike Mills. Lauren was furious because she had dated him for a while. Me and Jefferson had this handshake. I knew there was . . . You know what I mean, he's on the road, right? I certainly was on the road, so that's neither here nor there, but I called Jefferson at the R.E.M. office and I'm like, "Oh my God! What the hell is going on? We're over here and . . . Damn, you little sluts!"

Mike Mills happened to be sitting in the office and said, "Oh man, that's not even one of my good towns." And I thought, that's so awesome. Because everybody thinks he's such a nerd. You know what I mean? They think, "Oh he's the nerd. He's not getting shit." It's Michael Stipe or Peter Buck. Well, you know what? *No.* It's Mike Mills, saying, "Oh, that's not even one of my good towns." I'm telling you. You know what I did, though? I took that damn jacket off and I put it in my suitcase, because I just didn't want to hear about it anymore. It's kind of embarrassing. You think you're like a rock wife and then you're hearing about, you know . . .

As for Michael Stipe, his fears concerning AIDS plus his introverted disposition constrained his behavior on tour during the mid to late '80s, at least relative to the other band members. Still, as Velena puts it, "I promise you, on the road, there was nobody not having a good time."

By mid-1986, it's quite likely that Peter Buck was itching to get back on the road. In the short span of time he'd been home, he had been forced to deal not only with the end of his relationship with Ann but also with the death of his father, with whom he'd had a somewhat problematic relationship, at least when it came to discussions of his career. Whereas the parents of Stipe and Mills had been tremendously supportive of R.E.M. from the beginning, Buck's parents had not hidden their disappointment at their son's chosen occupation. Buck's father ultimately came around to a kind of bemused pride at R.E.M.'s success, but the way he chose to express this to his son proved hurtful. "We weren't really close in a lot of ways," Buck later told an interviewer. "The last thing he said to me before he died was, 'Make sure you make a million, because there's nothing else on earth that you are able to do.' He was trying to kind of say 'Stick with it,' but he was saying it in the nastiest possible way."

Somehow, in the midst of all the life changes and side activities, the members of R.E.M. found time to work on new material and also to participate in a documentary about their hometown scene: *Athens, GA: Inside/Out*. Although the film's California-based director, Tony Gayton, was generous (and wise) enough to involve many of the scene's key players—Sandra-Lee Phipps, Jim Herbert, Paul Lombard, Jeremy Ayers, and John Keane, among others—and although he gave Ort prominent on-screen time (a clear indication that he and producer Bill Cody had done their homework), the project was not without controversy. Many longtime Athenians groused that it was an unsuccessful attempt to relaunch a ship that had already sailed. Armistead Wellford, who appeared in the film alongside his bandmates in Love Tractor, later told Denise Sullivan, "The greatest time here was from '77–'81. That was when you would have liked to have had a camera rolling . . . Most of the bands that made it into [*Athens, GA: Inside/Out*] aren't around anymore. They just clicked on a camera and those bands happened to be there. They never even talked about the Side Effects." Lance Smith pointed to the inclusion of the Flat Duo Jets as a major flaw, referring to the North Carolina natives as "musical carpetbaggers." He did seem to have a point; that band's residency in Athens was not long, and it was widely believed by locals—rightly or wrongly—that the Jets had moved down to the Classic City solely to appear in the film. If true, the calculation paid off, at least in the short term. The band's singer, Dexter Romweber (brother of Let's Active drummer Sara Romweber), got singled out by the *New York Times'* Janet Maslin, who commented in her review that the "crazed-looking" Romweber "should consider a movie career." The band released its debut album in 1990 on Jefferson Holt's Dog Gone label, scored an appearance on *Late Night with David Letterman* shortly thereafter, and subsequently signed to a major label (Outsider, a subsidiary of Geffen) and recorded with R.E.M. producer Scott Litt.

The documentary presents an interesting, perhaps unintended contrast between the Flat Duo Jets' apparent opportunism and Pylon's complete lack of any such tendencies, and this functioned as a pretty accurate summary of the major divisions within the scene itself. Pylon, who had broken up at the end of 1983, chose not to do a reunion gig to provide new footage, even though re-forming in time for the movie's filming and release would almost certainly have created opportunities for them.* "I never planned on being a musician, so it's not like any big loss in my life that I'm not in a band any-more," Vanessa Briscoe says in the documentary. "I never made any plans. I never planned to be in a band. I never planned anything." She comes across as a guileless artist with no commercial aspirations—truly a living embodiment of the ideals of the early Athens scene.

In truth, R.E.M. had always been rather closer to the Flat Duo Jets than to Pylon in this respect. The worst that can be said about the Flat Duo Jets is that they made the most of the opportunities that presented themselves to them, just as R.E.M. had done. The "carpetbagging" charge, which had also plagued Matthew Sweet during his time in Athens, carried a lot of weight in the 1980s, but by the time bands such as the Drive-By Truckers, the Olivia Tremor Control, and Neutral Milk Hotel relocated to the town in the 1990s and became part of the third great wave of Athens bands, the accusation had lost any relevance. By then pretty much everyone was from somewhere else.

One of the more charming features of *Athens, GA: Inside/Out* is its egalitarian nature. High-profile bands like R.E.M. and the B-52's share equal screen time with relative unknowns like the Bar-B-Q Killers and Kilkenny Cats. The absence of the Side Effects and any commentary from Paul Butchart is indeed unfortunate, but on the plus side, Love Tractor finally get the at-tention they're due. The live footage of that band, some of which features Peter Buck guesting unobtrusively on rhythm guitar, goes a long way toward showing why the Tractor was so revered by its peers. But it is Laura Carter of the Bar-B-Q Killers, an obscure group that might otherwise have been lost in the sands of time, who steals the movie with her stage charisma and completely unforced insanity. Here again, the comparison with Dexter Rom-weber is instructive; Carter operates at a similar level of batshit crazy as the Flat Duo Jets' front man, but there doesn't appear to be anything calculated in her presentation.†

---

* After much cajoling, Pylon did finally re-form in 1989 and opened for R.E.M. on the closing leg of the *Green* world tour.

† Stewart Voegtlin of *Stylus* described the Bar-B-Q Killers' sound as "guitars as malfunctioning lawn equipment . . . Carter lasciviously bucked into the blade, straddling it—her lyrics a mélange of truck-stop sex, Dadaist nonsense, and pure unintelligible noise." Aesthetically, if not sonically, the band had much in common with Drunks with Guns, Mike Doskocil's St. Louis–based band mentioned in an earlier chapter. Indeed, song titles such as "Her Shit on His Dick" and "His and Hearse" (both Carter compositions) would be right at home on the back of a Drunk with Guns

And then there's Stipe, who falls somewhere in the middle. He appears with R.E.M. to perform the then-new song "Swan Swan H," holding a cane and vibrating to the music like a Civil War pensioner (albeit one with bleached-blond hair and purple eyebrows) in the first stages of Parkinson's. His shtick comes across as calculated, but it is also oddly compelling. R.E.M.'s version of the Everly Brothers' "All I Have to Do Is Dream" is something else entirely. Here Stipe starts off in much the same manner but quickly gets lost in the song's lovely melody and sense of sweet longing.

For his brief interview segments, Stipe goes into full-on oddball mode, nattering on about "people who can smell ants" and demonstrating "how Popeye exercises," tap-dancing and whistling in his layers of thrift-store clothes. Leave it to Stipe's former art teacher and current collaborator Jim Herbert, a powerful presence in the film, to surreptitiously explain Stipe better than Stipe could. About midway through the film, Herbert gestures at one of his massive abstract canvases. "This is a reclining figure," he says, pointing to a chaotic riot of bright colors and squiggled lines. "Young people can tell, crazy people can tell. It's based on this whole idea of searching your way through the painting, building up layers of space, almost painting from the inside out, is really what it's about." Herbert was describing his own work, but this might also be the single best summation of Stipe's approach to songwriting—which further underscores Herbert's central importance both to Stipe's early artistic formation and to that of the early Athens scene in general. If anything, the early bands were an outgrowth of this philosophy, married to a dance beat.

The criticism from the scene's old guard that greeted *Athens, GA: Inside/Out* on its release in 1987 was not without a certain irony: this group of art-school students and their fellow travelers, who had originally sought to upend all conventional notions of music-making, had themselves fallen into a sort of conservatism by the late '80s, adopting an attitude that nothing in Athens post-1982 could have been any good, and if a band wasn't of the generation of Pylon and the Method Actors and Love Tractor, it wasn't worth hearing. Yet although this view demonstrably ignores many great bands who came later, it is not without some foundation, as the truly electrifying archival footage of Pylon included in the movie attests.

LP. In terms of uncompromised rock 'n' roll purity, these are the two most "authentic" bands mentioned in this book. Tragically, Carter died in 2002 at age 37. Athens musician David Barbe, who played bass in the band Sugar with Bob Mould, said of Carter: "There was no one like her. She had an unbelievably positive impact on me; she changed the course of my life. She was the kind of person who challenged you, and there are not enough people like that."

Despite its flaws, *Athens, GA: Inside/Out* remains a valuable time cap-sule. As the only documentary film about the Athens scene, it has come to be regarded as the definitive statement. It certainly had an impact on me. I saw the movie a year or two after its release, and it was pivotal in my deci-sion to move to Athens. Trapped in the middle of my high school years and chafing under a social and religious (Catholic) culture that I felt to be stifling and conformist, I saw in this film an invitation to a beguiling place where all the artistic opportunities of a big city could be found without the attendant crush of people. The fact that it had a Southern accent sealed the deal, since a Southern thread also ran through my family (my grandparents on both sides lived in the South, North Carolina and Mississippi, and my father was a North Carolina native). Thinking back on this now, I am aware that it seems a little ridiculous of me to have been pining for the creative opportunities to be found in a backwoods town when I was living in Minneapolis, which at that time had, arguably, the most exciting music scene in the country. The Replacements and Hüsker Dü were still together, Prince had just released *Sign o' the Times*, local heroes the Suburbs had recently disbanded, and cult favorites Trip Shakespeare were hitting their stride. It would have been a good time to stay put.

But such decisions are generally not reached on the basis of logic, and my experience has been that the dictates of the heart and soul—which rarely present themselves as clearly as they did in this instance—ought to be heeded. I'm grateful that my teenaged self took the call seriously. On a surface level, the Athens I found did not quite sync up to the one presented in the film. For one thing, the documentary gave the impression that downtown Athens was a happy melting pot of racial diversity, which was not exactly the case. For another, the real Athens music scene was not nearly as harmonious as the mutual appreciation society I saw on the screen. And the second half of the film's title is misleading. The musical and arts aspects of Athens—perhaps its greatest cultural exports—have *always* existed on the periphery of the town's essential culture. Athens, Georgia, is first and foremost a college town whose rhythms are set by the class schedule of the university and, most significantly, by its football season. And the party and nightlife scene continues to be dominated by the fraternities and sororities.

Still, the *magic* of Athens—that combination of landscape, people, ideas, and some ineffable quality, "something in the air," that made it such a fertile environment for creative endeavor, or, as Ort puts it in the movie, "the most Zen place on Earth"—was very much a real presence. Despite all the grum-blings from the old guard, it was still there in 1986, when the documentary was made, it was still there when I arrived in 1992, and it was still there when I left in 1999. Athens was, is, and, I suspect, always will be a great place to make art and be inspired. So not only did I find what I was seeking, but it exceeded my expectations.

That ineffable quality must have had something to do with R.E.M. deciding to remain in Athens instead of moving to New York, Los Angeles, or Nashville. And perhaps it's no coincidence that the band created its most commercially successful work during a two-year period (1990–92) when Berry, Buck, Mills, and Stipe remained largely at home. In a way, 1986 was a test run for that. The band was obligated to tour in support of its new album, but this time the tour would be restricted to a three-month North American jaunt instead of a yearlong around-the-world slog. Again, I suspect that the extended time the band had to rest, regroup, and rediscover home played a direct role in the quality of the resulting music, because *Lifes Rich Pageant*, the album R.E.M. released in July 1986, is arguably the strongest record of their I.R.S. years. It may not be their best collection of songs (that would be *Fables of the Reconstruction* or *Murmur*); nor is it their most sonically adventurous release (a toss-up between *Murmur* and *Chronic Town*); nor does it rock the hardest (1987's *Document*); but *Lifes Rich Pageant* boasts a near-perfect union of sharp production, quality material, and bold, confident execution. Its dynamic range extends from the hushed, reverent "Flowers of Guatemala" to the propulsive, distortion-drenched "Begin the Begin," with plenty of midtempo fare along the way—the wistful "Cuyahoga" and the relatively straightforward "What If We Give It Away" (a repurposing and rebranding of "Why Don't They Get on Their Way"—one of the band's earliest songs). *Lifes Rich Pageant* is a statement of purpose and a calling card: the ideal entry point into the R.E.M. catalog for someone new to the band.

The title for this effort had already been circulating for some time before R.E.M. began tracking the new material. Chris Edwards was a big fan of Peter Sellers movies (an obsession he had picked up from band friend Tony Eubanks) and had brought a bunch of Pink Panther videocassettes along on the 1985 tours. One evening, while watching *A Shot in the Dark* as the tour bus crossed eastern Canada on the way to Portland, Maine, he and the band got to a scene that made quite an impression on Stipe.

In the scene, Inspector Clouseau (Sellers) is interviewing a key witness (played by Elke Sommer). She touches his trench coat and says, "You're all wet. Is it raining?"

"No, it's just that that stupid driver of mine parked too close to the fountain," Clouseau replies.

"You should get out of these clothes immediately. You'll catch your death of pneumonia, you will."

"Hmm. Yes, I probably will, but it's all part of life's rich pageant, you know. We police have to put up with a lot of things in the course of our duties that in private life one wouldn't normally tolerate."

Most viewers laugh at what happens next: Clouseau accidentally sets his coat on fire and then gets accidentally pushed out the window. But it was the "life's rich pageant" line that sent Stipe into a laughing fit.

"Stipe rolled off the couch watching it on the bus," Edwards says. "He started laughing and laughing, and he said we've got to name the next album that. That's what he said. Eventually they did exactly that."

Don Gehman deserves a significant amount of credit for the strength of *Lifes Rich Pageant*. On the surface, John Cougar Mellencamp's go-to producer might have seemed like an odd choice to produce an R.E.M. record. R.E.M. had, up to this point, worked almost exclusively with producers who shared their musical tastes and left-field artistic vision; Gehman fit into neither category. He had begun his career as a live sound engineer, working extensively with classic rock acts such as Loggins & Messina, Chicago, and Crosby, Stills, Nash & Young. As a producer, he had spent most of the decade in a fruitful collaboration with Mellencamp. The iconic "Jack and Diane," with its muscular guitar riff, handclaps, crisp vocals, and dramatic peaks and valleys, was Gehman's calling card. It sounded simultaneously modern and timeless, and perhaps here was the meeting point between Gehman and R.E.M.: neither party had any interest in synthesizers, gated reverb, or any of the other production gimmicks that were then in vogue. Their preference was for the tried-and-true mixture of electric and acoustic guitars, cleanly recorded drums, unadorned vocals, and occasional piano and organ. These elements had always been present on R.E.M. records, but what the band left behind now was the murkiness that had distinguished both *Murmur* and *Fables of the Reconstruction*: the sense of hidden layers, the haze. Most significantly, *Lifes Rich Pageant* left behind the indecipherable vocals that had been such a key element of R.E.M.'s sound and persona up to that point. Never again would Michael Stipe's powerful voice be buried beneath the guitars. And rarely again would his words be difficult to discern.

Interestingly, it was Gehman who sought R.E.M. out, not the other way around. The producer was only vaguely aware of the band, but then a mutual acquaintance mentioned that he could make an introduction. As Gehman later told radio documentarian Sam Coley, "I was interested in doing something in my career that would put me back into the cutting edge of things."

> I think it was an odd call for them—and for me. Neither one of us knew each other that well. And I represented almost the establishment to them, even though I was a relatively new record producer. They weren't accustomed to working with people who had any kind of commercial success, and that was something they were very afraid of. I don't think they really wanted a successful commercial record, but I think behind it all they wanted to make enough money to be able to continue doing what they were doing. They just wanted it on their own terms. And they were leery of record companies, and they were leery of anyone who would be answering to a record company, and so that made them leery of me.

Despite hesitation on R.E.M.'s part, it was clear that Gehman's specialty in recording "acoustic rock bands," as he puts it, made him a strong candidate to oversee their next record. With Gehman, there would be no threat of behind-the-scenes insertions of synthesizers onto tracks, as had occurred with Stephen Hague. Mills, in particular, was a fan of the John Mellencamp records Gehman had produced. The performances on those albums had an energy and a clarity that stood in marked contrast to R.E.M.'s restrained work on *Fables of the Reconstruction*.

Still, Gehman did not get the job right away; he had to audition first, just as Joe Boyd had done. And the audition had two aspects, because the band wanted to be sure it could get along with Gehman on a personal as well as a professional level. So the first step was to fly the producer in to meet them at a North Carolina performance at the tail end of the Reconstruction tour. The situation proved disorienting for Gehman. "It was very awkward," he told Coley.

> Because the band—I don't know how to describe it. They all kind of go off in separate directions until they play. They're not really "hanger around" kind of people. So when I got to their bus, as I recall, Peter was off riding with somebody, Michael was out with a friend . . . Bill was the only guy that was there. Maybe Mike was there. But I had flown all the way across the country to have a sit-down meeting with them and no one was there. And that's just the way they always were.

Gehman was able to roll with it, though. As it turned out, his personality was an ideal fit for the band at this stage in their career. He was friendly and easygoing, while at the same time quite forthright in his opinions. He may have been young and a relative newcomer to production, but his spectacularly successful work with Mellencamp had instilled in him a confidence that R.E.M. probably found reassuring at this critical juncture. The two parties reconvened in Athens from March 10 to March 14, 1986, to record demos at John Keane's studio. Although the new track "Fall on Me" received the most attention, 18 other songs in various stages of completion were committed to tape. These included the older compositions "Just a Touch," "Mystery to Me," and perennial runner-up "All the Right Friends," as well as new, mostly instrumental tracks such as "March Song" (later renamed "King of Birds"), "Cuyahoga" and "These Days." The sessions went well and Gehman was officially hired to record the next R.E.M. album.

The band decamped in April to Bloomington, Indiana, to record at John Mellencamp's new studio. This was Gehman's suggestion, and it derived from his observation that R.E.M. tended to write while recording. Someone in the band (usually Buck, but occasionally Berry or Mills) would arrive with a partially completed piece of music. The band would run through it a few times, record it, and then start laying parts on top of it. Only after all the music was recorded would Stipe work up his lyrics and add vocals. Gehman found this approach interesting but somewhat nerve-wracking. In his experience, artists usually arrived with their songs more or less complete, which allowed all parties to spend their time in the studio attending to the minutiae of arranging and tracking that material. He was certainly open to the idea of using the studio as a compositional tool (an idea R.E.M. probably got from Mitch Easter, and one that Easter probably picked up from the Beatles and other studio-oriented groups of the 1960s and '70s), but he argued that the process might work best if R.E.M. situated themselves in an environment where they would be free of distractions—which is where Bloomington, Indiana came in.

It ended up being a sound decision. The band completed *Lifes Rich Pageant* in three weeks of focused activity, and all four musicians brought their very best efforts to the process. The performances did indeed have that jumping-out-of-the speakers quality that characterized Gehman's previous projects, and yet the material remained unmistakably R.E.M. Like Easter, Gehman was always on the lookout for extra flourishes—a banjo here, an accordion there—that might accent the material and help build dynamics. But whereas Easter and Dixon tended to perform those parts themselves,

Gehman wanted all of the playing to be done by the four musicians. "I was looking for other colors," he told Coley.

> Typically, within bands I worked with, I tried to draw on whatever anybody in the band could play. In this case, Peter pretty much was just an electric guitar player. There wasn't much else he could do. Michael could sing, and that was about it. Whereas Bill and Mike both were a little bit more fluid. I could get Bill going out and shaking rattles and hitting glasses and even doing melodic things with percussion. And Mike was really my "producer's friend" in the whole project because he had the ability to play just about anything.
>
> Most of those extra colors were me looking for some instrument that I could throw in to make the bridge sound different than the chorus, and then Mike would figure out how to play it. A lot of the overdub time was spent with Mike. Same thing with the background vocal parts. Mike did all of that stuff.

One aspect of the making of *Lifes Rich Pageant* that is not well known, and that may have indirectly contributed to its overall cohesion, is the fact that it was originally intended to be a concept album, similar in some ways to *The Who Sell Out*. That 1967 album had included fake commercials and transitional passages between the songs to convey the impression of a pirate radio broadcast. R.E.M.'s intention was not quite as specific, but they nevertheless recorded nearly a dozen brief instrumental passages that were meant to provide bridges from one song to the next. Don Gehman eventually prevailed on the band to remove much of this material; he felt that the many connecting sections diluted the strength of the actual songs. Just three passages remained, two of which were fused to the beginnings of their respective songs: a brief banjo snippet that functioned as the lead-in to "I Believe" and a recording of a Japanese pull-string Godzilla doll that kicked off "Superman." The third bridge piece, "Underneath the Bunker," was given some hastily composed lyrics and sequenced on the album as a stand-alone song.*

Gehman pushed the band hardest in an area where no previous producer had made any headway: Stipe's vocals. Perhaps his lack of familiarity with

---

*Interestingly, this aspect of *Lifes Rich Pageant* mirrored yet another Who album: 1971's *Who's Next*. The songs on that release were originally intended to be part of a sprawling rock opera titled *Lifehouse*. In circumstances similar to those R.E.M. later experienced, the Who's lead songwriter, Pete Townshend, was persuaded to remove the connecting framework and release the album as a collection of stand-alone tracks. *Who's Next* has subsequently come to be regarded by many critics as that band's strongest and most cohesive album.

R.E.M., coupled with the fact that he had no background in punk rock or the avant-garde, allowed him to make a hard assessment of Stipe's approach without being blinded by the "art for art's sake" argument. And it may well have been his easygoing demeanor that allowed him to challenge Stipe on such an important point without getting himself fired. At any rate, Gehman called it like he saw it. "Michael had a reputation of writing things that were gobbledygook," he later said. "And I really didn't want to make a record that was gobbledygook." The two men had a series of "heated but respectful" conversations regarding Stipe's process and finally reached an accommodation: Stipe could continue to be obtuse, but Gehman insisted that the words at least be discernible and the vocals clearly audible. He slyly appealed to Stipe's vanity, noting quite rightly that Stipe was a powerful singer and that his vocals ought to be more central to the production than they had been in the past.

To hear Gehman tell the story, this process of nudging Stipe toward articulation was fairly low-key and nonthreatening. For Stipe, it appears to have been more traumatic. He later told MTV that Gehman "made life hell for me during the making of the record." He eventually rose to the challenge and later came to regard this event as a major breakthrough that pushed him forward as an artist and singer. It seems telling, however, that R.E.M. never hired Gehman to do another album, though the two parties briefly danced around the idea in the wake of *Lifes Rich Pageant*'s success. (Gehman has described his failure to push harder for the opportunity to record the follow-up as "one of the biggest regrets of my life.")

What happened next was probably inevitable, and was likely Gehman's not-so-secret intention: now that Stipe's words were naked for all to hear, the singer began giving more thought to their meaning and began a gradual shift toward more linear songwriting. And Stipe made another shift around this time that may or may not have been related: he stopped reading books. At least, that is what he claims; as with Stipe's mythical "year of silence" in the late '70s, his statement should perhaps be taken as more emotionally than literally true. Nevertheless, the singer made a pronounced move away from his solitary, bookish ways toward more outgoing behavior. "Loud shy" was back. Correspondingly, the literary references that had heretofore saturated his lyrics began to slip away. And into that void came politics.

This was all a very gradual process. *Lifes Rich Pageant* itself was still very much in the classic Stipe "arty" mold. There was nothing on the album that would have shocked Stipe's longtime listeners other than the front-and-center vocals, and for many fans that was a welcome change. During his marathon attempt to catch up on the R.E.M. albums he had ignored during his youth,

T. Kyle King remarked that *Pageant* "has the band's highest concentration of songs that make me say, 'I understood the words clearly, and I enjoyed the song immensely, but I haven't the faintest idea what it means.'" Stipe had held Gehman to his end of the bargain and remained obtuse. Yet change was clearly afoot. The song "These Days," while fairly incomprehensible to most listeners, represented for Stipe a line in the sand. "This is a song that means a huge amount to me, because I wrote it when I came out of a very bad, a very dark period," he told a Dublin audience in 2007. "Which we all have. I was 25. But this was a little bit of an epiphanal song for me, and that's written into the lyric, especially in the chorus."

This was Stipe moving away from his persona of the entertaining "other" toward an almost messianic presence. It was not a perfect fit, as Stipe well knew; he would never be Bono. At one point he sang, "We have many things in common: name three," which undercut somewhat his preceding declaration that "I wish to meet each one of you." Still, his line "All of a sudden, these days" seems appropriate. It's inconceivable that he would have sung "We are hope despite the times" even a year before on *Fables*. Can this "all of a sudden" change be attributed solely to Gehman's prodding? Probably not. As we have seen, Stipe had already begun adopting a more extroverted stage persona during the second half of 1985. But Gehman can at least be credited for pushing Stipe to sing about these changes in a clear, confident voice.

Not surprisingly, and probably not coincidentally, this greater clarity in the vocals made R.E.M. more palatable to mainstream radio. I.R.S. seized on this, and pushed hard to release the track "Fall on Me"—which they rightly perceived to have the makings of a hit—as the lead single. According to Gehman, there was some grumbling and pushback from within R.E.M. over this. The band apparently bristled at the record company's attempt to capitalize on that song's commercial potential. In retrospect this seems unfathomable. If ever there were a song that represented a perfect balancing act between exquisitely wrought pop songcraft and artful, multilayered lyrics, it would be "Fall on Me." It was a triumphant synthesis, not a compromise, and getting something this interesting onto pop radio would have been like getting the wooden horse full of soldiers through the gates of Troy. It presented no downside, which is more than can be said for some of the band's later singles, such as "Shiny Happy People." The executives at I.R.S. were right to be excited.

Stipe, at least, came to understand why everyone had gotten so fired up. Introducing the song at the band's 1991 *MTV Unplugged* performance, he said "This may well be my favorite song in the R.E.M. catalog." Over the following three minutes he proceeded to demonstrate why, giving one of the most impassioned live vocal performances of his career. Stipe's original lyrics had centered on acid rain, but by the time the band recorded the album version, the verses had been rewritten and thematically expanded. Like the best of his work, the lyrics could be about many things: spiritual longing, the fragility of hope in times of despair, the futility of human progress in the face of nature, or whatever else the listener might want to bring into it. Stipe himself later claimed that the song dealt with oppression but to his great credit did not elaborate much beyond that. T. Kyle King shares Stipe's opinion that this is R.E.M.'s best song, but he adds that he has come to this conclusion "for reasons I cannot articulate." Ultimately, he's right to not attempt an explanation; magic, by its very nature, cannot be quantified, and most R.E.M. fans would agree that this song is imbued with a special kind of magic.

Still, there are some compositional and performance flourishes in the song that are worth examining. There is Mike Mills's background vocal, which provides extra lyrics and a counter-melody during the chorus. Mills also sings the lead during the bridge. His work here may be the strongest example of something he had been doing almost since the beginning of the band: on many songs, instead of simply echoing Stipe's lyrics when he harmonized, Mills often wrote his own words and melodies without consulting Stipe as to the meaning of the song. He had done this on "Harborcoat," "Letter Never Sent," "Can't Get There from Here," "Wendell Gee," and "Hyena," the last of these a *Pageant* track that had already been a live staple for some time. Furthermore, when the band performed the *Reckoning* track "Second Guessing" live, Mills often sang his own lyrics (which did not appear on the record) in a call-and-response with Stipe. Here on "Fall on Me," Stipe might very well have been singing about acid rain, but it's not clear that Mills had that in mind when he sang, "But I would keep it above / But then it wouldn't be sky anymore / So if I send it to you / You've got to promise to keep it home."

These subtle but distinctive contributions from Mills, based on what he *thought* Stipe might mean, often added a just-below-the-surface deepening of Stipe's already cryptic lyrics. Berry too would sometimes get in on the act. Here he sang "It's gonna fall" over and over during the chorus and provided ghostly "Ooohs" during Mills's bridge. Further adding to the layers, Stipe sang his own alternate lyrics and melody* alongside his lead vocal, a contribution that is barely audible without headphones. For his drum part, Berry

---

* These are actually the original, acid rain–themed lyrics from the demo.

delivered a spare, powerful beat, accented by tambourine, reminiscent of Phil Spector's "Be My Baby," and then shifted to a double-time pattern during the chorus (another Spector hallmark). Mills rounded out the song with a subtle but distinctive organ part.

While delving into the nuances of this song, I had a conversation with my friend Paul Lickteig (a Jesuit priest and writer) that brought home just how integral the supposedly peripheral elements are to its power. When I mentioned that I was writing about "Fall on Me," Paul immediately began singing Mike Mills's backing vocal. I remarked that I found it interesting that he had zeroed in on Mills's part rather than Stipe's, to which Paul replied, "What stands out to me in R.E.M. songs is rarely Michael Stipe, to be honest. I'm more drawn to those little nooks and crannies you can crawl inside that make the song habitable. That's the magic."

Clearly the band had a potential hit on their hands. Yet, just as they had done every previous time they stood on the cusp of major success, they tapped the brakes. For the music video, Stipe offered some upside-down black-and-white footage of a rock quarry and railroad tracks, with the lyrics, sometimes misspelled, superimposed over the images. This was the exact opposite of the type of direct, band-centered video Miles Copeland had continually urged R.E.M. to make, and yet it didn't seem to matter. As Stipe later boasted to *Interview* magazine, MTV "played the living shit out of ["Fall on Me"] . . . We were a big enough name and we had enough cachet that MTV wanted to play us, so, along with Michael Jackson and Madonna, they played our upside-down, black-and-white, backward, single-camera unedited footage of a rock quarry with orange letters over the top of it and called it art." Still, the song itself only reached number 94 on the *Billboard* Hot 100 chart. We can only speculate on how much higher it might have climbed had it been accompanied by a video that looked like it gave a damn.

Reflecting further on his tendency to present the network with difficult videos such as the one for "Fall on Me," Stipe told *Grantland* in 2015:

It's one of my great regrets that I didn't key into [the potential of music videos]. I'll compare myself to certain artists at the time, people I think really got it, the power of the image: Madonna and Michael Jackson. They were like, "Holy shit, we can do something with this. This is a great tool." I had a little bit more of a punk rock attitude toward MTV, not realizing the power of it as a marketing tool and as a way to get yourself out there. I think I recognized it slowly. Mine was an adversarial relationship. Theirs was more embracing . . . I was presenting stuff to [MTV] and I thought, Well, let's see what they do with this because they're not gonna fucking show it. Then there was a point where they *had* to show it.

There's a related thought that Stipe doesn't voice here, although it was clearly beginning to dawn on him by the end of the 1980s, which is that artists who mastered the video medium could afford to tour less, or not at all. Michael Jackson did not tour behind *Thriller*, yet that album was until recently the biggest-selling record of all time, bolstered in part by its ground-breaking videos. Madonna did tour, but she seemed to do so out of genuine enjoyment and a desire to express herself artistically rather than to sell more records. Her first tour did not occur until 1985, two years into an already hugely successful career.

Touring was beginning to wear heavily on two members of R.E.M. Bill Berry, while still an enthusiastic participant in the "rock 'n' roll lifestyle," had lost interest in traveling, and was happiest when at home and in close proximity to a golf course or fishing pond. As we have seen, he had been the great driving force in the band's early quest for success, but by the late 1980s he'd concluded that the music business "sucks." He began urging his bandmates, loudly and sometimes publicly, that they should ditch all the tour trappings, get back in the van, and do a series of unannounced club gigs. Anything to rekindle the magic that had hooked him in the first place. He also started floating the idea that the band should break up after some kind of blowout performance on New Year's Eve, 1999. At the time these comments were not taken very seriously.

Stipe had more of a love/hate relationship with the road. He clearly didn't mind it—after all, he'd elected to spend a significant amount of time in 1986 performing with the Golden Palominos—but there seemed to be a big difference between the low-pressure situation of chipping in with a pre-existing collective and fronting his own band. With R.E.M., it usually took him a few shows to regain his "loud shy" performing persona, and the transition phase could sometimes be awkward. At the band's first show of the Pageantry tour, at Oak Mountain Amphitheatre in Pelham, Alabama, Stipe told the crowd, "If anybody's read the back of the T-shirts that are up there, this is our first show, and we haven't played in a bit of time, since, um . . ."—Berry broke this pause with an impatient tapping of his cymbal—". . . seems like about a hundred and fifty years. The, um . . ."—another pause—"I'll tell you later." Stipe had become adept at accentuating his awkwardness for humorous effect, but it was nevertheless clear that this was an off night for him. Later in the show he commented, "Everything's kind of falling apart up here," and, still later, "We're hoping by next week that we'll be able to keep the time between songs down to under five minutes . . ."—more impatient drum taps from Berry—"This is our showcase song for the evening, featuring the inimitable . . . Bill Berry!" Stipe gave an embarrassed laugh; the song in question, "Superman," featured lead vocals by a different member of the band. "I mean Mike Mills!" he yelled over Buck's guitar intro.

To be fair, the entire band was pretty shaky during this first performance, even with an additional guitarist—band friend Buren Fowler—backing them on several songs. But a couple of gigs into the tour, they were on firmer footing and Stipe was back in his element, prowling the stage in a long black overcoat and top hat, dragging his mic stand to and fro, howling out his lyrics as if he were possessed by the muses themselves—or at least by coyotes. "Let's begin again," indeed.

L.E.A.F. (Legal Environmental Assistance Foundation) benefit, Moonshadow Saloon, Atlanta, February 18, 1985. Photo © Joanna Schwartz

Chapter Twelve

The interior of Jeff Walls's house is tricked out in early-'60s retro-futurist chic: lots of white, curvy plastic, squiggly glass, and white shag carpets, incongruously set against brick and wood-paneled walls. It is a house entirely befitting the lead guitarist of the Woggles, Athens' premier garage-soul rave-up combo. Walls himself is an imposing presence: stocky, broad-shouldered, decked out in a tan jacket and a cap bearing the socialist red star.* His hair is jet black, an indication of either excellent genes or a ready supply of hair dye. If it went gray, he would look a bit like Southern author William Styron, with his full cheeks and round nose. He leads me from one room to another, shuffling along with a certain lumbering grace. We arrive finally at a den overstuffed with guitars and books on all manner of pop-culture detritus: a Robert Mitchum biography, a critical study of film noir, biographies of various '60s icons (the Who, the Beatles, etc.). Walls motions me to a seat, produces a bag of weed and a pipe, and asks, "Do you smoke?"

This sort of question always puts me in a quandary. I'm not overly fond of pot, but I've learned that it can be a good icebreaker in interviews. So I say, "When it's offered to me."

Walls loads up the pipe and hands it to me, along with a lighter. "I'm offering." There seems to be a carefully scripted protocol to this; I am reminded of the story of a vegetarian friend who spent a semester studying in an African country and was given the considerable honor of butchering the goat for her host family's evening meal: it was a tense situation, but she managed. In comparison, what I'm facing here should be easy, and I get through the first section of our ritual fine. I tilt the pipe forward slightly so the flame licks the dried leaves, thereby avoiding the common mistake of angling the lighter down and singeing my thumb. I drag the smoke deep into my lungs, holding it there for a good five to ten seconds before exhaling. So far, so good; I may actually look like I know what I'm doing.

---

*Although he looks on this day as if he has walked out of the Cuban Revolution, this is more a fashion statement than anything; Walls is suitably jaded on the subject of politics.

But then I place the pipe on the small table between us, and as our conversation gets going and the pipe goes cold, I realize that I was supposed to hand it back to my host. There it sits, glowering at me in inanimate rage, and I am paralyzed with indecision, like a clueless Westerner lost in the middle of a Japanese tea ceremony. Whatever Emily Post's rules of pot etiquette may be, they apparently prevent Jeff from reaching down and grabbing the pipe for himself. My host's act of beneficence is inadvertently spurned, and so here we sit.

Some ice-breaking would have been helpful. Jeff is a man of few facial expressions; he oscillates between a poker face and a sleepy smirk, and has the professionally aloof demeanor of someone who has been interviewed often. Yet as a son of the South, born and bred in Marietta, Georgia, he is also unfailingly polite in that way true Southerners are with complete strangers. One thing that I appreciate about Walls is his honesty. Like Mike Richmond, his genuine affection for R.E.M. does not lead him to sugarcoat his experiences. Still, on the occasions when he gives the band a ribbing or offers up a tantalizing, slightly risqué tidbit, he does so with a light touch and a twinkle in his eye.

Jeff has a long and impressive musical history, some of which dovetails with R.E.M.'s. An unheralded master of the 12-string electric guitar, he came to prominence as a key member of Guadalcanal Diary, a critically acclaimed college rock band that recorded with Don Dixon and supported R.E.M. on the Pageantry tour. During the '80s, the playing styles of Jeff Walls and Peter Buck displayed some marked similarities: above all, both shared a fondness for the arpeggiated jangle sound first popularized by the Byrds in the mid-'60s, though Walls is quick to explain to me that he and Buck did not influence each other. The two men have discussed their similar styles "many times" and have concluded that the similarity is due to them both mining the same influences: the Byrds' Roger McGuinn, the Beatles, the Monkees, and the great garage bands of the 1960s. Walls, in fact, doesn't listen much to his contemporaries—R.E.M. or anyone else.

Guadalcanal Diary was one of many bands of that era that seemed destined for the same sort of slow-build success R.E.M. had experienced. They had all the right ingredients: hook-filled songwriting, intelligent lyrics, crisp and emotive vocals, and an instantly recognizable guitar sound. Yet, like nearly all of the other contenders of that era (including Camper Van Beethoven, another Pageantry opening act), they never made it beyond cult status. This was to some degree by choice; by the close of the 1980s, Jeff had married Rhett Butler, the group's bassist, and the two had started a family. Walls and lead singer/guitarist Murray Attaway agreed to dissolve the band, stating that they would rather keep their friendships intact than chase success. This was a move

R.E.M. themselves had contemplated more than once during the recording and touring of the *Fables of the Reconstruction* album.

Walls elaborates on this dilemma:

I'm convinced there's a point—and I remember feeling like this when we were out with R.E.M. and the Cars—when you see the wheels that are having to turn to make all this stuff happen, and the publicity, all the people that are scratching each other's backs . . . Any thinking individual trying to become a superstar has to sort of acknowledge that all this stuff is going on on their behalf, and who knows who's getting crushed in the process? You just have to look yourself in the mirror and say, "I'm just going to turn a blind eye to that and let it happen." You have to.

I was struggling with that a little bit. Kind of feeling like . . . at that point I'd been around enough famous people to feel like I kind of know what fame does to people and I'm not sure I want that. It changes people.

Guadalcanal Diary joined the Pageantry tour on September 22, 1986, and went on to play 12 shows with R.E.M. before Camper Van Beethoven took over the opening slot on October 9. This was hardly the first time they had opened for R.E.M. Walls's association with the Athens scene predated the band's formation, and Guadalcanal Diary had first supported R.E.M. at a gig in Marietta, Georgia, back in February 1982. "I'll be up front and say I've never been the biggest R.E.M. fan," Walls says. "But those first few shows we played with them, I thought they were great. They were real energetic onstage."

Walls recalls getting on well with everyone in the band. "I would say I knew them all kind of equally," he says. "Probably Michael the least just because he deliberately makes it that way . . . It was funny because several times over the years I would get the impression I would have to re-introduce myself to Michael. I think it's a game that he does or something. He knows who I am."

The Pageantry slot came about as a natural extension of Walls's friendship with Jefferson Holt, the member of the R.E.M. team with whom he was closest. "They were always giving friends a chance, for sure," he says. "They were always pretty nice about that."

That's one thing I will say about them too: we were on tour with them, and of course they were playing amphitheaters and stuff, whereas we would not have been. It was a bigger level than we were used to, and it was kind of interesting to see how they had their shit rolled up in a tight little ball. The first day on the tour it was like they gave you a sheet, all this information about yourself you have to fill out, and it was all this stuff like your shoe size. We were like, "Why do they need to know all that?" Next day there was a package at the front of our hotel room with shoes, T-shirts, all this stuff. It was their merch T-shirts and stuff, but it included tennis shoes, socks, just stuff that was useful on a tour. It was much appreciated.

The one aspect of the R.E.M. machine that irked Walls was the concerted effort to bring everyone's behavior in line with the band's emerging standards of political correctness. "I remember that we were admonished for asking for Coors beer on our rider," Walls says.

That was back when you couldn't get it east of the Mississippi. It was kind of a special treat for us. Plus, it was supposedly spring water, which Rhett was interested in. After the first day's show, I remember Jefferson coming to us and going, "I need to talk to you about your rider; you all know Coors means Nazi," or something like that.*

"No, I guess we didn't know that." I kind of couldn't help but feeling like, *Does that mean we have to be concerned about the drug lords we're keeping in business with all the coke that's being consumed around here??* But we switched to, I think, Rolling Rock, which also has spring water. I thought that was kind of funny. It was so politically correct.

I remember one time Michael Stipe having some article in *Rolling Stone* or something: "How to Spend Your Eco Dollar." I'll be damned if I'm going to have somebody like that telling me how to spend my money. Never mind that a scientist that would really know something about that wouldn't even rate a mention. I'm not faulting Michael for that, but I'm not really into mixing politics and rock 'n' roll too much.

---

* This was apparently a reference to the company's full name—the Adolph Coors Brewing and Manufacturing Company—as well as to the then-ongoing AFL-CIO boycott of Coors over its heavy-handed response to a labor strike in the late '70s. Coors had also been sued in the 1970s for alleged discrimination against racial minorities and gays. The company did demonstrate a willingness to evolve, however, and it should be noted that in the mid-1990s, Coors joined the earliest wave of major US corporations to extend employment benefits to same-sex partners.

Various passes for the Pageantry tour, featuring artwork by Michael Stipe.
Courtesy of Chris Edwards.

It's interesting to note that Michael Stipe, while still very much a political activist, has in recent years come to rue some of the band's heavy-handedness during those early days of emerging political awareness. "There's a live R.E.M. recording that, I think, is from 1989," he told the *New York Times* in 2011. "And between songs I make a comment to some guy who's holding a cup. I said, 'That better not be Styrofoam, bud.' We decided to include that. Not cool. That was embarrassing."

The Pageantry tour featured some tentative steps toward the soapbox, but Stipe was still feeling out how he could best address his areas of concern in public. There were some anti-Reagan harangues from the stage—not an entirely new development. And there were occasional comments about acid rain before they played "Fall on Me," and some even more oblique references to atrocities in South America in an attempt to offer context to the otherwise inscrutable "Flowers of Guatemala." But for the most part Stipe was content to rely on the few but noticeable "sound bites" (Gehman's phrase) of discernible meaning he had strewn across the new songs: phrases like "Silence means approval" (from "Begin the Begin") and "The only thing to fear is fearlessness / The bigger the weapon, the greater the fear" (from "Hyena"). Offstage, the band had apparently sent Greenpeace flyers out to members of its fan club. *SPIN* magazine's mixed-to-negative review of *Lifes Rich Pageant* derided this move, and said of the band:

> The freshmen at the University of R.E.M. were holy defenders of their school spirit, that soft-focus, Pre-Raphaelite, dance-barefoot-in-the-kudzu utopian vision. *Murmur* demanded that. It was intoxicating. But soon that class will graduate to the real adult world, where self-righteous rock bands lie that they are Superman, that they can do anything, even preserve our faith in romance.

Stipe, to his credit, either ignored or never saw this snarky warning, and continued to follow the dictates of his conscience. This led, for better or worse, to a full and public realization of the sort of political advocacy that Jeff Walls had witnessed in private. By the start of the Green tour in 1989, Greenpeace had both the band's sympathies and a promotional stall by the door at every venue—perfectly placed to capture the maximum number of mailing-list sign-ups from R.E.M. fans.

It might seem easy to accuse the band of hypocrisy here: For all its emerging sensitivity to the plight of the oppressed in South America, for instance, the band and its entourage (along with most rock acts of the day) seemed relatively untroubled, as Jeff Walls observed, to be bankrolling South American drug cartels via their cocaine consumption. It is a critique that carries some weight, yet it misses the fact that much of the advocacy was driven by Stipe, who was not involved in the drug scene and generally tried to walk it like he talked it. No one questioned his sincerity on environmental issues, for instance, because Stipe was well known around Athens for living a relatively simple, low-consumption lifestyle. He had never followed his bandmates in purchasing a fancy car for himself, and his home was not noted for any expensive appliances (or indeed for much consideration toward its upkeep at all). He had begun showing up at Athens City Council meetings to speak out on certain local issues, usually involving land development or historic preservation; Peter Buck commented that Stipe's interjections at the meetings were "fairly amusing to say the least, totally befuddling to these old Baptist guys that run the city council."

Stipe should certainly be commended for exercising his rights as a citizen and attending local government meetings, but I tend to side with Jeff Walls in feeling that politics and rock music often make for an awkward—and distracting—mix. It is a delicate balancing act that requires a polished touch—not something Stipe was known for. *Lifes Rich Pageant* manages to squeak by due to its somewhat veiled approach to political concerns, but subsequent albums became more specific, a move that has tended to date some of the material.

And yet I must also concede that my own emerging environmental awareness in the late 1980s had a lot to do with R.E.M. I definitely began to take recycling and pollution seriously after hearing the band members speak passionately on these subjects during interviews. I was very much one of those teenagers who would have signed up for the Greenpeace mailing list because R.E.M. said I should. Now, in my forties, I may wince a bit (as Stipe himself does) when I look back at the band's air of self-righteousness during that era, but I remain concerned about the environment and sustainability to this day. Clearly an important seed was sown. Does it matter that the gardener was clumsy? Perhaps from a music critic's standpoint it does: this sort of thing rarely makes for great rock 'n' roll. But if young people were shaken out of their complacency a bit, maybe that's not such a terrible trade-off.

Velena Vego, too, credits R.E.M. with getting her to take politics seriously—and she was not exactly an impressionable teenager at the time. "Just remember this," she says. "R.E.M. got me to vote. My first time voting for a president was because of them, because they were very politically aware. As a young person in a punk rock band, I didn't even think about it."

Even Walls, who—as we have seen—has little taste for overt political posturing, commends the band for its effective advocacy and hands-on involvement at the local level.

> They kind of bought into the downtown area a little bit financially. Kind of went on to have an influence on local politics in good ways, trying to keep the downtown area from getting either too strict or [having] a bar on every corner. They helped preserve the quality of life, so to speak. You hear about some big celebrity somewhere buying something in their hometown, but with R.E.M. it seemed to be a very long-term kind of thing.

Velena believes that R.E.M.'s management played a role in nudging Stipe, and the rest of the band by extension, from latent concern into outright activism on a variety of issues. "I could be wrong," she says, "but I swear it was Bertis's house we were all at when there was all the fundraising and all that stuff. It was Bertis, Bertis, Bertis, Bertis. To be honest with you, I always thought Bertis was going to get to win an office. And Jefferson came from a political family, so I think with the combination of that, it maybe grew on the guys." Jeff Walls concurs, though he points to Holt as the driving force: "He was probably the one that initiated a lot of the politically correct stuff. He was way into that. I think he probably was pushing that."

For Stipe, the Pageantry tour was probably the point at which the temptation to influence the masses, which had already been building for some time, became impossible to resist. The "Distiples" had been a fixture on tour, and in downtown Athens, for a few years already—perhaps even since the beginning, if we count the small pack of followers Pat the Wiz observed when he first met the singer in 1981. But on the Pageantry tour their numbers swelled, and their fervor became more intense. "I remember at one of the first couple of shows," Jeff Walls says,

> we pulled up in our Winnebago at a big venue and there were all these Distiples hanging around and maybe it was a cigarette butt or cigarette pack got thrown out and these girls were all atwitter over the cigarette pack. I think they thought it was Michael's. So Rhett and I were saying, "Maybe we should start getting Pete's old guitar strings and cutting them into inch-long segments and selling them."
>
> Or when we were in either Portland or Vancouver, somewhere up there, it was an old theater, a really neat place. The dressing rooms

were upstairs and they had balconies that were out over the street. It was about three stories up. At some point we ducked out on our balcony and saw the Distiples down there on the street below and they were obviously waiting for a glimpse of Michael. Pat, our roadie, was standing around and I was like, "Pat, check them out, they're waiting for Michael to step up there." Pat took all of his underwear and wrapped it all around his head and stood out on the balcony. Everybody's cooing, "Oh, that's Michael." [*laughing*] A guy with sunglasses with literally underwear wrapped around his head . . .

As the members of R.E.M. would discover, this sort of frenzy was here to stay. It came with the new territory—a place considerably higher in the atmosphere than they were accustomed to, for *Lifes Rich Pageant* had nabbed them their first gold record. In November, the track "Superman"—a cover of an obscure '60s-era song by the Clique—was released as the album's second single. It climbed to #17 on the *Billboard* Mainstream Rock Tracks chart. The band members may have been allergic to the word mainstream—and Michael Stipe said in an MTV interview around this time, "I don't think the mainstream is ready for us"—but that's exactly what "Superman" was. And it was toward a mainstream audience that R.E.M. were headed, whether they liked it or not.

Atlanta Civic Center, December 31, 1984. Photo © Joanna Schwartz.

Chapter Thirteen

We appear to have begun to take percussion a tad more seriously.
—T. Kyle King, on hearing *Document* for the first time

February 10, 1987. Keith Joyner looked on with a mixture of pride and disbelief as Peter Buck put Keith's guitar amp through its paces on the stage of the 40 Watt. Just a little while earlier, Keith and his band Seven Simons had been performing a sweet and suitably off-kilter rendition of "The Rainbow Connection" (from *The Muppet Movie*) to a small audience, warming up the crowd for the evening's main act, Mystery Date. Behind the soundboard sat Pat the Wiz, bearded and resplendent in his West Point jacket, working his magic and ensuring that everyone sounded good.

Keith had anticipated that there would be at least a couple of members of R.E.M. in attendance. Jefferson Holt was partial to Seven Simons. And Velena from Mystery Date lived with Jefferson and was friends with Peter Buck—who liked to roadie for the band when he was in town. What Keith hadn't counted on was R.E.M.—or at least three-fourths of R.E.M.—getting up onstage and tearing into an impromptu set with Mystery Date's instruments and Keith's amp. Dreams So Real drummer Drew Worsham filled in for the absent Bill Berry on drums, providing an interesting swing to the songs that opened up fascinating possibilities while at the same time highlighting Berry's essential rightness for the band's sound. Mike Mills handled Robin Edwards's bass with aplomb, but Buck had a more vexing time with the gear he had commandeered. Playing through Vanessa Vego's chorus pedal and Joyner's solid-state amp, Buck sounded choppy and heavy-handed, as if his fingers were tripping over the unfamiliar guitar strings. He sounded, in other words, far removed from the clean-toned minimalist he had been the last time he had played at the 40 Watt. For that matter, R.E.M. didn't sound like the same band that had cut *Lifes Rich Pageant* just a year before. They sounded meaner, more paranoid, a bit more dangerous. After kicking off with a snarling rendition of "Begin the Begin," they worked through two new songs that seemed to mix the dissonance of the New York noise band

Sonic Youth with the hard funk of their old friends Gang of Four. With Stipe's raspy vocals laid over the top, the "acid *e*" more pronounced than ever, this made for a unique and bracing hybrid. The lyrics themselves were clearly still works in progress.

R.E.M. did not engage the audience. They simply got down to business, pushing at the walls of their stylistic boundaries and rocking hard. It was a public rehearsal. Then, midway through a deranged take on "Just a Touch," Keith's amp—which had clearly been struggling under the weight of Buck's onslaught—finally gave up one last scratchy cough before going silent.

And just like that, R.E.M.'s set was over. Buck, Mills, and Stipe—at that point three of the four most famous men in Athens—faded back into the audience with nary an acknowledgment of what had just happened. As Seven Simons bassist William Mull later put it, "History was happening before our eyes . . . until it wasn't!"

About a week later, Keith Joyner received a delivery from Peter Buck: his crappy old Peavey amp, freshly repaired and ready to go.

If *Athens, GA: Inside/Out* was one of my primary inspirations for moving to Athens, the other was Keith Joyner—at least, Keith Joyner's music. To this day I regard him as one of the finest guitarists to have emerged from the scene, despite the man's disparaging attitude toward much of his own work. It is true that Seven Simons were never a band you would hear cited alongside the town's legends. As Joyner puts it now, "Seven Simons were part of the latter tier of bands to ride the coattails of R.E.M. I was keenly aware, and eager to do something different. But I had learned to play guitar only by listening to songs by R.E.M. and the Church. It was kind of unavoidable." In my view, Joyner does himself a disservice; Seven Simons had a keener ear for melody and harmony than just about anyone else in town, before or since. They were simultaneously more psychedelic and more pop than R.E.M., and Joyner and bassist/band co-founder William Mull's strong interest in the Paisley Underground bands, Australian psych-rock, and British new wave, coupled with the powerful and dynamic singing of Nathan Webb, ensured that the band did not come off as an R.E.M. clone, however much Joyner may have been influenced by Buck.

And influenced he was. The Decatur native had first become aware of R.E.M. in the early '80s via a show on local Atlanta TV called *Cousin Brucie's Jukebox Video*. "The video was 'Wolves, Lower,'" Joyner says. "And I was mesmerized. It was familiar, but strange and mysterious at the same time. It was almost as though I had been waiting for this band to happen." Prior to this discovery, Joyner had subsisted on a diet of top 40 radio, his sister's Donny & Marie collection, and "a slow-burning obsession with the Beatles." But "that band," he says, "was literally and figuratively dead at this stage. I wanted something new."

> Better yet, Athens was a mere sixty miles up the road. But it may as well have been China. I was too young. I couldn't drive. I had homework to do. I lamented the fact that I couldn't be a part of what was going on up there. But I listened to every note this band played. I waited patiently for them to play a show that I could attend. It seemed it would never happen. Then, finally . . . R.E.M. played Atlanta's Fox Theater for the Reckoning tour.
>
> I showed up early in the day with my friend Peter, hoping to catch a glimpse of my guitar hero, Peter Buck. It never occurred to me that they'd have no reason to be there at two in the afternoon. We did see Jefferson. He seemed bemused at the two fanboys waiting outside the backstage door. Little did I know, this guy would put out my first record a few years later.

It took Keith little time to insinuate himself into the heart of the Athens scene once he got his driver's license—he was already a fairly experienced musician by that point. Seven Simons was not his first band; from 1985 through 1987 he had played bass in Mr. Crowe's Garden, an early version of what became the Black Crowes. As Velena Vego puts it, a desire "to impress R.E.M." was one of the factors that spurred Mr. Crowe's Garden onward and eventually led to the success of the Black Crowes, even as that band found its own voice in a decidedly non-R.E.M. classic rock–soul hybrid sound. After Keith's departure, the Black Crowes played Athens numerous times and got to know the key players in the scene—including R.E.M. Diane Loring Aiken has several pictures in her collection of a lanky, well-scrubbed, and quite innocent-looking Chris Robinson— future bad-boy singer of the Black Crowes—hanging out at the 40 Watt with various Athens musos and scenesters in the mid-'80s.

Joyner's entry into the Athens scene occurred via Seven Simons rather than Mr. Crowe's Garden, but his experiences in that earlier band had given him both chops and onstage confidence. When the Mystery Date/R.E.M. show happened, Keith was still in high school. But shortly after graduating that spring, he and the rest of the band moved to Athens. Given his already-established connections, it seemed quite natural that Keith would spend some of his idle time hanging out at the R.E.M. office and occasionally answering the phone. And while he hadn't played in Pylon or the Method Actors, he wasn't perceived as a hanger-on. Jefferson Holt, in particular, had high hopes for Seven Simons. Toward the end of 1987, Holt signed the band to his Dog Gone label. The label's roster already included Flat Duo Jets, the Squalls, and Sara Romweber's post–Lets Active band Snatches of Pink, but Holt apparently envisioned Seven Simons as a sort of crown jewel. "I don't want to speak ill of Jefferson or for Jefferson," Joyner says, "but I think he thought of us as the flagship band for the label, the one that was going to get Dog Gone a distribution deal with a major. And we did have a demo deal with Atlantic, and ultimately a pretty mediocre demo produced by Scott Litt. But alas, it didn't happen in the end."

Billy Holmes tells me a story that seems to confirm Jefferson's intentions regarding Seven Simons, while providing an interesting twist:

> I saw him one night at the Uptown Lounge, where he was saying, "I got a new racehorse." And I said, "Oh, you do?" You know, he had had a few beers. And, he says, "Yes, I have a championship racehorse, and it is winning all of the races." You know, using R.E.M. in the metaphor, and he goes, "But, my championship racehorse is getting a bit old, and I am going to have to put him out to pasture. And I've got a new racehorse." And he was talking about Seven Simons, Bill Mull's band. And Jefferson swore up and down that Seven Simons was going to be as big, or bigger, than R.E.M. And he worked hard for them, and nothing ever happened. He also tried to start his own record label, and that was a big hassle, and he recorded some people, and they were flops. He got in a spat with somebody who had the same record-label name as his, and he had to change it. So, you know, he went through a lot of crap there, I think, and then he finally just said, "Screw this business, I am sick of this, I hate this."

Was Jefferson already sick of R.E.M. by 1987, even while he was giving Michael Stipe a hard time for engaging in too many outside projects? His alleged horse metaphor was more likely the byproduct of excessive alcohol intake mixed with excitement over his new signing than any true fatigue concerning his "championship racehorse"—a horse which, at that point, had just begun an incredible winning streak. And yet his comments to Billy may have contained a kernel of truth. Years later, after his acrimonious parting with R.E.M. in the mid-1990s, Holt ran into Velena Vego and the two reminisced about the old days. "When I talked to Jefferson," Velena says, "I said, 'When did it stop being fun?'"

> Because, you know, I had the fun years. We always did stuff together. It was New Year's at Peter's house, it was going to the movies, it was everything. It was together. We were always together, all the band members. We all ate lunch together and all that kind of stuff. When did it just stop being fun? I think it was right before the Warner Bros. deals. Then maybe it got a little bit more serious because of the money and because of all that stuff. So I really feel blessed that I had those three solid years of just, every day, us goofing off and doing stuff and them coming over to our house or us going over there and stuff. I do think I got prime time.

The year 1987 was the end of "prime time." That much was clear from the band's tour arrangements that fall. Stipe and his entourage got their own bus—"the tea-drinking bus," Chris Edwards calls it—while the rest of R.E.M., along with the road crew, rode "the fun bus"—i.e., the drugs and alcohol bus. In many ways this arrangement benefited the performances: the separation gave Stipe the peace and quiet he needed to prepare himself psychologically for the shows. Yet it also, unavoidably, contributed to a loosening of the bonds of camaraderie that had been so vital to the band's chemistry. This development was probably inevitable; back in 1985, Don Gehman had observed that the members of R.E.M. tended to go their separate ways whenever possible. The opportunities for doing so at that stage of their career had been limited, though. At the end of the day they were all still on the bus together; they all still lived in the same small town; their social circles still overlapped. By 1987, the members of R.E.M. could afford to become individuals. This probably kept the band together for longer than would otherwise have been the case—but it also meant that some of the fun went away.

For I.R.S. Records, 1987 was a very good year: it was the year in which R.E.M. finally delivered the sort of unequivocal mainstream success Miles Copeland had long desired. The irony is that they did so with one of their most difficult releases. *Document* had little of the warmth or intimacy of *Lifes Rich Pageant*. It was loud and angry and dissonant. It had a lot to say about American politics—little of it positive; the one upbeat call to action, "Finest Worksong," seemed out of place, almost like a carryover from *Lifes Rich Pageant*. But *Document* also contained a single, "The One I Love," that sounded tremendous on FM radio. Its confidence and snarling energy—coupled with a killer guitar riff—caused it to practically leap out of car speakers; most of the surrounding songs in the top 40 seemed lifeless by comparison. This too was a subversive move on R.E.M.'s part, for the content of the song was anything but ingratiating. "This one goes out to the one I love," Stipe sings at the start of each verse. "This one goes out to the one I've left behind." Apparently, many listeners tuned out at this point, missing the bit that turned the song's meaning on its head: "A simple prop to occupy my time." (The third verse varies the line slightly: "Another prop has occupied my time.") The chorus consists of Stipe howling the word *fire* over and over while Mills once again supplies his own lyrics in the background: "She's coming down on her own now / Coming down on her own." (Berry also contributes to the chorus, though his words are indecipherable.)

Stipe later performed some public hand-wringing over the lyrics, describing them in *Musician* magazine as "incredibly violent" and "about using people over and over again." In *Talk About the Passion*, Denise Sullivan's oral history, a onetime associate of Stipe's, Geoff Gans, opines that "the whole 'The One I Love' scenario was a very Stipe-type thing . . . using people, meeting others, and moving on. I think that was the only time Michael came clean about one of his personality traits. It was true." From his quotes in the book, it seems clear that Gans himself felt he had been discarded, much like the "prop" in the song—an ironic twist given that Gans played guitar on an acoustic version of the song that was released as the B-side of the 12-inch single for "The One I Love." More importantly, Gans collaborated with Stipe on R.E.M.'s album art in the 1980s, then went on to earn multiple Grammy nominations for his work designing album packaging for Bob Dylan from 1995 onward.

Gans had apparently missed, or chosen to ignore, the commitment-phobic subtext of much of Stipe's early writing on the subject of relationships. It had been a while since Stipe had addressed the topic in his songs, but when he had done so in the past, the material had almost always had a misanthropic edge. Even "So. Central Rain" and "Kohoutek"—his two most tender, fully realized love songs—depicted the aftermath of one partner discarding the other. In an otherwise veiled life, this was one aspect of Stipe's personality that had always been clear as day, though human nature dictated that each new friend/confidante/lover would believe that he/she was different from those who had come before.

Despite Stipe's rotating cast of casual acquaintances and romantic interests, the singer remained fiercely loyal to both his family and a small circle of longtime friends. He never missed a Christmas with his family, and, as Velena Vego observes, he has had "the same friends forever. He has connected, and he stayed, and even when he's here with his family, he's very, very loyal to his friends . . . The people that he adores and loves are still in his life." Velena notes, though, that she herself is not part of this circle. "Even today," she says, "I just never know if he's going to give me a huge hug when he's at the 40 Watt or is it just going to be 'Hello'? I'm sure he loves me in his own way, but I always knew to not take offense."

In terms of hooks and melody, "The One I Love" is a near-perfect pop song. It even features a rare guitar solo from Peter Buck that tips its hat to the work of Bob Mould, guitarist in Hüsker Dü. And despite the acerbic nature of the lyrics, the public responded. The single got to #9 on the US *Billboard* Hot 100 chart and the album itself spent 33 weeks on the *Billboard* 200 chart, peaking at #10. *Document* was the first R.E.M. album to go platinum, selling in excess of a million copies.

The year 1987 was a diverse one for pop music. R.E.M. shared the charts with the likes of Whitney Houston, whose sophomore *Whitney* album yielded four number-one singles; George Michael; and INXS; as well as familiar faces such as U2, who broke into the mainstream in a big way with their iconic *Joshua Tree* album. It was a good year for Don Gehman, too: John Mellencamp's *Lonesome Jubilee*, which Gehman produced, proved to be the singer-songwriter's commercial and critical peak. Prince and Madonna continued their winning streaks: Prince released what was arguably his best album—*Sign o' the Times*—in March, and Madonna embarked on her hugely successful Who's That Girl tour from July through September. But it was R.E.M. who were on the cover of *Rolling Stone* at year's end, trumpeted as "America's Best Rock & Roll Band." It turned out that the mainstream was ready for them after all.

One thing *Document* had in common with its predecessor was clarity of sound. In this, something of the spirit of Don Gehman persisted, even though the album was produced by his colleague Scott Litt (Gehman had recommended Litt for the job). Litt had already demonstrated his commercial acumen with his engineering work on Katrina and the Waves' hit "Walking on Sunshine." Where the two men differed was in Litt's tolerance for experimentation; it's hard to imagine Gehman signing off on *Document*'s "Fireplace," for instance. As we have seen, Gehman had initially floated a compromise of letting Stipe stay weird as long as he enunciated his words. But in truth Gehman had also pushed Stipe to adopt a more direct style of songwriting. Litt, in contrast, was content to let the singer be as weird as he cared to be. Still, the mandate for recognizable words remained.

Among Litt's primary sonic contributions was a massive drum sound, helped in part by Berry's reinvigorated playing. The drums on *Document* are loud and unrelenting and propel the music. This is closer to the John Bonham school of "heavy" drumming than the lighter, more inventive playing on the first two R.E.M. releases. Yet it is still unmistakably Berry, and it perfectly suits the music. The hard, militant snare hits and accentuated bass pedal are as right for *Document* as the rolling toms and sly nods to disco and reggae were for *Chronic Town* and *Murmur*.

Lyrically, *Document* remains the most overtly political album in the R.E.M. canon, although Stipe's fondness for quirky metaphor may have obscured this aspect for many of the new listeners. "Disturbance at the Heron House" remains a mystery, despite Stipe's insistence that the song's narrative was one of his most direct pieces of writing. Well, yes and no:

> *Just a gathering of the grunts and greens*
> *The cogs and grunts and hirelings*
> *A meeting of a mean idea to hold*

Some impressions come through clearly enough: the frenzy and ignorance inherent in the mob mentality, and their manipulation by "party central." From there it's a short leap to Stipe's narrow list of political obsessions: Republican skullduggery, environmental degradation, and all things Reagan-Bush. It is a striking piece of writing, but "Welcome to the Occupation" is a bit clearer in concept and execution. The line "Fire on the hemisphere below" refers to the Reagan administration's repeated interventions (overt and covert) in the internal affairs of several South American countries—particularly Nicaragua. In a rare peek behind the veil of R.E.M.'s songwriting process, it emerged that Bill Berry had felt one of Stipe's original lyrics— "Hang your freedom fighters"—went too far and asked that it be removed from the song. Stipe had been referring here to the Contras, the right-wing Nicaraguan paramilitaries that Reagan repeatedly lionized as "freedom fighters," but Berry felt the line was too heavy-handed, too militant. In its place, Stipe substituted the superior "Hang your freedom higher."

The closing verse, in which Stipe pinpoints what he believes to be the true motivations behind these conflicts ("Sugarcane and coffee cup / Copper, steel, and cattle"), is arguably one of his finest lyrics, marred only ever so slightly by the closing line: "Listen to me." Rather innocuous in the context of the song, it nevertheless highlights the Achilles heel of much of Stipe's advocacy. He would become known for aggressively cajoling his listeners both to think for themselves and—paradoxically—to listen to and agree with him. This tendency reached its apex—or nadir—the following year when the singer took out ads in college papers in California and Georgia that read, "STIPE SAYS / DON'T GET BUSHWHACKED / GET OUT AND VOTE / VOTE SMART / DUKAKIS." There were several valid reasons why one might have wished to support Michael Dukakis over George H. W. Bush in the 1988 presidential election, but hopefully "Stipe says" was not the guiding motivation for anybody. Otherwise, Stipe's fans would have become "cogs and grunts and hirelings" with simply a different set of allegiances. One would hope that was not his intent.*

Taken on its own, divorced from any knowledge of R.E.M.'s late-'80s public soapboxing (Buck had some awkward moments of his own during his emergence as a politically opinionated individual†), *Document* stands as a quite sophisticated and largely on-point body of topically oriented songwriting. Don Gehman had previously spoken positively of Stipe's ability to write in "sound bites," and *Document* contains some of the singer's best: "What we want and what we need has been confused" (from "Finest Worksong"); "Standing on the shoulders of giants leaves me cold" (from "King of Birds"); "By jingo, buy American" (from "Exhuming McCarthy"); "It's the end of the world as we know it and I feel fine" (from the song of that name). As noted, both "Welcome to the Occupation" and "Disturbance at the Heron House" are impressively written. Stipe stumbles a bit in "Exhuming McCarthy": here, too, the writing is arresting, but the connection between the late '80s and the McCarthy era is somewhat tortured. T. Kyle King cuts to the heart of the problem: "I'm not really sure what the critique of capitalist culture contained in 'Exhuming McCarthy' has to do with Joseph McCarthy." Stipe had apparently ended his self-imposed reading ban: a 1987 photo of the singer, taken by Sandra-Lee Phipps in the Nashville recording studio where

---

*In a 2001 interview with the London *Daily Telegraph*, Stipe cut his younger self some slack while acknowledging his shortcomings as a political agitator: "I couldn't not be political in that environment. It was a little before that stuff had become its own franchised adjunct to entertainment and I became this spokesperson for all these things that I really didn't know much about. You hear a story and respond to it from Joe Grab-a-Sandwich's point of view. Which is what I am. And it's not a very good sandwich, I might add. Some good songs came out of it but there are other musicians that do it much better. I happen to think that the songs I'm writing now are much stronger in terms of how they can change someone than anything I wrote that was overtly political."

† Buck's comments to *Melody Maker* after the 1988 US elections make Stipe look like a model of restraint: "We're pigs! Americans are pigs! You can quote me on that . . . I'm so fucking furious, I feel like shooting people—George Bush first and then the people who vote for him."

Document was tracked, captures two books by his side: David M. Oshinsky's *A Conspiracy So Immense: The World of Joe McCarthy* and a book simply titled *McCarthy* (the author's name is obscured). This research probably led to the inclusion, during the song's bridge, of a clip of US Army Chief Counsel Joseph Welch rebuking the anti-Communist senator for casting aspersions on one of Welch's junior attorneys during the 1954 Army-McCarthy hearings: "Let us not assassinate this lad further, Senator. You've done enough. Have you no sense of decency, sir? At long last, have you left no sense of decency?"

The story of the meteoric rise of Joseph McCarthy, a Republican senator from Wisconsin, and his highly publicized attempts in the 1950s to purge alleged Communist sympathizers from the US government, is a fascinating one. A connection could have been made between the anti-Communist fervor of that era and the renewed anti-Soviet rhetoric of the Reagan era (even if the timing was a little off; relations between Reagan and Soviet leader Mikhail Gorbachev were friendly by 1987), but that did not happen in Stipe's lyrics. Instead we get, as King notes, a vague critique of capitalist culture, which is further confused by the line "Enemy sighted, enemy met / I'm addressing the realpolitik." The term *realpolitik* has a long history, but in the context of US foreign policy in the 1980s, it is often used to describe, in a pejorative sense, the US government's willingness to partner with countries and/or movements with questionable human rights backgrounds in order to preserve its power or protect its interests. The Reagan administration's support of the Nicaraguan Contras, a topic Stipe tacitly addresses one song over in "Welcome to the Occupation," would be a prime example. But what is a line about realpolitik doing in a song about corporate greed and Red-baiting? Mills's lyrical contribution—"Meet me at the book-burning"—merely adds to the mess. To suggest that the United States was in the midst of an era of suppression and censorship (similar, perhaps, to the McCarthy era of blacklisting), even while R.E.M. themselves enjoyed a large and unrestricted platform for their views, also seems a bit of a stretch. And yet, despite these flaws, "Exhuming McCarthy" might be the catchiest song on *Document*. At the end of the day, this is pop music.

It is instructive to compare "Exhuming McCarthy" with the song that closes side A of the album: "It's the End of the World As We Know It (And I Feel Fine)." If the former suffers due to its pretension to coherence, the latter triumphs by abandoning all such pretensions, instead floating on its lyricist's unfiltered stream of consciousness. Is this a celebration of the impending demise of the planet, a concerned call to arms, an exhortation to listeners to tie one on and forget about it, or a critique of people who do just that?

How about all of the above? And what does Leonard Bernstein, celebrated composer and conductor, have to do with all this? Who cares? Stipe "vomits out" (his description) a free-association riot of names, events, and phrases over an unrelenting punk backbeat. Familiar tropes poke out from the barrage of language—"world serves its own needs," "a government for hire," and, once again, "book-burning," juxtaposed against snatches of dreams and even a reference to Stipe, Buck, and Paul Butchart's run-in with Lester Bangs back in 1981 ("Lester Bangs, birthday party, cheesecake, jelly bean, boom!"). Significantly, Stipe implicates himself in the world's imminent collapse: "Offer me solutions, offer me alternatives, and I decline." Yes, the "I" might very well be a character, or a personification of the US population, but the implication of personal culpability keeps the song from becoming overly preachy, as does his background lyric at the end: "Time I had some time alone."

Surprisingly, "It's the End of the World As We Know It (And I Feel Fine)" didn't make a huge splash at the time—it peaked at #69 on the *Billboard* Hot 100 chart—but it has gone on to become arguably the highest-profile song in the R.E.M. catalog. It is certainly the one R.E.M. song that younger music listeners immediately recognize, which may be the result of its appropriation over the years by DJs and TV presenters as the go-to anthem for every near-cataclysmic event of the last quarter century—the most recent being the Mayan "apocalypse" of December 21, 2012, a non-event (as it turned out) that prompted the Alberta-based radio station CFEX to play the song 156 times in a row.

It would be difficult to imagine *Document* working as well as it does without this song. Remove it from the track listing and you are left with one album side filled with overly serious political harangues plus a Wire cover, and the other comprising four oddities plus a subversive hit single ("The One I Love") with nothing to tie it all together. But "It's the End of the World As We Know It" incorporates all these elements within one song and leavens them with a sense of humor. Stipe blends the universal—apocalyptic anxiety spurred by earthquakes, environmental destruction, and political malfeasance—with the deeply personal: the contents of his own dreams. He doubles down on his most oddball writing tendencies and in the process somehow emerges as Everyman.

This defining track makes the political material more palatable. But what of the impetus behind that political material? Here I must make some personal observations. Perspective is everything, and my perspective on Ronald Reagan is inevitably somewhat different to Stipe's because of our age gap. Stipe was a teenager in the mid to late '70s; I was a teenager in the late '80s.

Reagan was president during a large portion of my childhood, and I have fond memories of him as an avuncular, comforting figure. I must balance those memories, however, against the historical data. And that data lends support to Stipe's criticisms.

There are still aspects of Reagan's presidency that impress me. Many historians—quite a few of whom, like Douglas Brinkley, are not usually inclined to sympathize with the political Right—concur that his negotiations and eventual friendship with Mikhail Gorbachev played a role in the thawing of the Cold War. Now that he is routinely lionized by the Right for "winning the Cold War," it is easy to forget that this outreach of Reagan's was, at the time, bitterly opposed by many conservative pundits, as well as by members of his own cabinet. So there's that.

However, as successful as Reagan's direct dealings with the USSR may have been, his administration's escapades in Central and South America are largely perceived to have been reckless and morally compromised, and tend to come in for criticism from those same historians who praise Reagan in other areas. In addition to interference in the Nicaraguan civil war and the subsequent Iran-Contra scandal, there was a controversial and arguably unnecessary incursion in Grenada in 1983 that involved heavy combat and civilian casualties. And, for all of Reagan's stated concern for democracy and freedom, he seemed to have no issue with those rights being violated elsewhere—Chile, Argentina, and Guatemala being the most notable examples—provided the oppressors were supportive of or subservient to US interests.

As adults in the 1980s, Stipe and his bandmates found these developments deeply troubling. Add to that Reagan's confused and muted reaction to the AIDS epidemic, a policy of deregulation that reduced the social safety net, a military spending policy that escalated the national debt, a not-quite-real program called the Strategic Defense Initiative (or "Star Wars") that promised to bring down enemy missiles with lasers, publicly bellicose language toward the Soviet Union, and the takeaway image for these young liberals was of an out-of-touch president and an out-of-control executive branch. They were not privy to the kind of nuanced historical assessment that could be made only many years later, and their political convictions might well have prevented them from agreeing with such an assessment even if it had been available at the time.

It is useful to separate Stipe's and Buck's public statements on political causes—which could sometimes come off as shrill or naïve—from Stipe's politically oriented lyrics, which more often than not were intelligent, rich in metaphor, and provocative in the best sense. There would be some duds (1992's "Ignoreland" springs to mind), but there were many triumphs, such as "Welcome to the Occupation" and 1989's "World Leader Pretend" (one of Stipe's best overall compositions). And even though *Document*'s political songs largely concern themselves with people and situations specific to the 1980s, the material has aged surprisingly well, thanks to its inventiveness and implicit universality; a modern listener can substitute the Middle East for the South American milieu of "Welcome to the Occupation" without much difficulty. That is a mark of good songwriting.

Despite the exponentially greater success R.E.M. experienced in 1987, the year followed essentially the same trajectory as the previous one: the band members spent January through August working on their new album and attending to various side projects. And while the album work took them to both Nashville and California, they could be found in Athens much of the rest of the time. A typical evening for Stipe was an August 21 appearance at the 40 Watt, during which he and a couple of friends took the stage prior to Love Tractor's scheduled opening act (Cowface) and proceeded to make an unholy racket. The R.E.M. Timeline describes the performance as consisting of "Stipe playing a guitar drone, while other musicians bash sheet metal with sledgehammers."

Buck, as usual, was apt to get onstage with just about anyone who would hand him a guitar. That winter and spring he performed with the Feelies, the Fleshtones, and Charlie Pickett & the MC3. The surprise came in May, when he married Barrie Greene. Just one year previously he had lamented to Velena Vego that all of their friends were getting hitched, but now the guitarist himself was tying the knot.

Greene was a well-known, and well-liked, local who bartended at the 40 Watt. She lived in the house off of Barber Street in which Billy Holmes's mother had been born: yet another example of Athens's small-town insularity. "I loved Barrie," says Holmes.

> She was sweet, and smart, and when Peter started dating Barrie, I thought that was awesome. And there is a funny quote. I saw Pete one day. I said, "So, you're dating Barrie Greene?" "Yes." "Well, what turned you on to her?" And, he said, "Because she is six foot barefoot." Because Pete is what—six four, six five? And he will stare down at you. If you argue with him in a recording studio, he will use his height advantage.

The new Mrs. Buck moved into her husband's quasi mansion just outside of downtown: a large, turreted house with a long wraparound porch that Billy Holmes refers to as "the Ghost and Mr. Chicken house," due to its resemblance to the haunted mansion in the Don Knotts film of that name (it was more popularly known as "Buck Manor"). Perhaps in an effort to complete the gothic vibe, Buck purchased a hearse from a local funeral home, which passersby would often see parked in the driveway.*

All these years later, Barrie is no longer married to Peter Buck, but she still lives in the house. She owns and manages the 40 Watt, as she has done since the late '80s—first in partnership with Jared Bailey and later on her own. Her ex-husband still plays at the Watt from time to time. The current whereabouts of the hearse are unknown.

R.E.M. commenced the Work tour at London's Hammersmith Odeon on September 12. The name of this new jaunt was aptly chosen, for touring was now very much a job, and had been for some time. However, as Stipe had implied in "Finest Worksong," there could be dignity, and even joy, in work. And R.E.M. played exceptionally well on this tour, trading some of the looseness and playfulness of earlier outings for a vigorous—one reviewer called it "tumescent"—hard-rock energy well suited to the new material. Peter Buck went further into the realm of guitar effects than he ever had before, and once again, Buren Fowler played rhythm guitar on several songs, adding to the wall-of-sound effect.

I.R.S. had been hoping for a yearlong tour in support of the album, but the band tapped the brakes once more. The tour lasted just two months. This didn't seem to matter so much for the US dates; the success of the album ensured they could play larger venues than before, and so in a month and a half of stateside gigs they performed to a larger number of people than they had on 1985's three lengthy tours combined. But R.E.M. probably set themselves back in Europe when they elected to play only four shows on the continent. These were well attended and served to stoke the existing fan base, but the band was hardly on the ground long enough to make any gains.

In truth, R.E.M. were already thinking ahead. *Document* represented the last installment of the band's five-album contract with I.R.S. Earlier in the year, they had also released a compilation of B-sides and outtakes titled

---

*Observant fans may be wondering what happened to the black '57 Chevy that Buck had purchased with his first flush of earnings, and that had been featured in the music video for "Can't Get There from Here." According to Holmes, Buck traded this car for a "pretty good" Fender Telecaster guitar. "Even trade," says Holmes. "I mean, it was a pretty good Telecaster, obviously, but ... "

Dead Letter Office, which sold surprisingly well despite limited promotion; it reached #52 on the *Billboard* 200 chart, and the song "Ages of You" peaked at #39 on the *Billboard* Mainstream Rock Tracks chart, which further underscored the selling power now inherent in the R.E.M. brand.

Quite understandably, I.R.S. wished to continue the partnership, and Miles Copeland was willing to be exceptionally generous in his re-up offer. But the major labels were also "sniffing around," as Jeff Walls puts it. The band had never been opposed in principle to a major-label deal, as we have seen; they had come very close to signing with RCA back in 1982. What was most crucial to them in any proposed deal was the level of creative control on offer. Despite the occasional disagreement over marketing strategy or choice of single, I.R.S. had afforded R.E.M. a level of artistic independence relatively unheard of at the time. No major label would have granted such power to an untried band in 1982. But how did things look now, at the close of 1987, when the band in question could drop an album of B-sides and throwaway covers into the marketplace and watch it chart, and when the band's current single—"The One I Love"—competed with Whitney Houston on Casey Kasem's *American Top 40* and dominated MTV via the Robert Longo–directed video? If R.E.M. could land a deal with a major equal to or better than what they enjoyed with I.R.S., then they would be well positioned for major success on their own terms. Perhaps they could even transform the mainstream itself. A major label would also have the resources to better target that ever-elusive overseas market.

Warner Bros. Records piqued Peter Buck's interest right away. In addition to its stewardship of esteemed legacy artists such as Neil Young and Elvis Costello, the label had proven friendly to left-of-center acts (and R.E.M. friends) like Hüsker Dü and Gang of Four. Perhaps most important, the label's co-presidents Mo Ostin and Lenny Waronker were true-blue music geeks of the sort rarely found in the upper echelons of an entertainment corporation. Ostin had helped transform Warner Bros. in the 1960s from the relatively staid home of Frank Sinatra and Peter, Paul & Mary into a more exciting, rough-and-tumble outfit that released challenging work by Jimi Hendrix and the Grateful Dead. Waronker, as an A&R exec at Warner during the Ostin era, had signed James Taylor, Ry Cooder, and Van Dyke Parks (another Buck favorite). He also made the seemingly out-there decision to bring John Cale of the Velvet Underground, an eccentric and erratic individual at the best of times, into the fold as an A&R rep. Waronker understood artists. A veteran producer himself, he knew exactly how to create the environment crucial to artistic creation. And as a businessman he knew how to sell the result of that alchemical process without diluting it.

Warner Bros. offered R.E.M. an appropriately artist-friendly deal. The band would have complete artistic control over its output—not just over the music itself, but also the album artwork, videos, and selection of singles. As with the previous deal with I.R.S., the Warner agreement was for five albums, which R.E.M. would deliver to the label completed and ready to go.

None of this was particularly new for the band. They already enjoyed a similar degree of freedom with I.R.S. What was different was the far greater promotional capabilities (and budget) Warner Bros. could offer, as well as a guarantee that I.R.S. would not have been able to accommodate: R.E.M. would own their master recordings. This marked a break with industry tradition: typically, the record label owned an artist's recordings as a kind of insurance for the label putting up all the money in the first place. Whatever might transpire down the road—a falling-out, a public meltdown, even the death of the artist—the label could potentially recoup at least some of its investment via long-term sales of the recorded work. Under the R.E.M./ Warner deal, the band agreed only to lease its recordings to the label for a predetermined period of time. Thereafter the band could either re-up with Warners for another stretch or take its product elsewhere.

It would have been difficult for any artist to walk away from such a deal. Warner were required to release whatever R.E.M. gave them. And R.E.M. could decide how much, or how little, they wished to promote that work; they wouldn't have to tour, do interviews, or make videos if they didn't feel like it. And, at the end of the day, R.E.M. would own every note of music they produced while under contract to Warner Bros. These factors, plus the warm relationship that had developed between the band and Lenny Waronker, gave Warners the edge over I.R.S.

In time, Jay Boberg would come to respect the band's decision, but in the short term he felt betrayed. I.R.S. had been willing to meet R.E.M. on all of the above points except for the one over which they had no control: the ownership of the masters (the label's various distribution and licensing arrangements precluded such a concession). They had also been willing to stake a very large percentage of their current and future income in order to hold on to the band. But it was to no avail. "I think injustice occurred," Boberg later said, "in that the little guy got beaten out for no apparent, no obvious reason."

He ought not to have been too surprised. R.E.M. and their management had always been exceptionally clearheaded in their decision-making. Loyalty was important, but it went only so far. Case in point: the deal that Boberg himself had brokered with the band back in 1982 had necessitated R.E.M.

breaking their previous agreement—and friendship—with David Healey. Boberg had also been a witness to the band's fair-but-tough tactics in getting the rights to "Radio Free Europe" and "Sitting Still" back from Jonny Hibbert.

It was likely the combination of such shrewd business decisions with their consistently high-quality output that enabled R.E.M. to vault into the American mainstream at the close of the 1980s. They had been jockeying at the starting gate with a number of other college rock artists who all seemed poised for breakout success: the Replacements, the Smiths, Hüsker Dü, Robyn Hitchcock, the Church, and the Cure, to name a few. But of that class of '87, only R.E.M. and the Cure broke into the big time. Hüsker Dü and the Replacements imploded not long after securing their major-label deals. The Smiths, whose guitarist Johnny Marr had been so often compared with Peter Buck, likewise succumbed to internal strife before they could break through. Robyn Hitchcock remained locked in cult status (his insistence on titling his A&M major-label debut *Globe of Frogs* might have had something to do with it), and the Church "fumbled the ball" (in singer Steve Kilbey's words) by following their breakthrough album, *Starfish*, with the interesting but muted *Gold Afternoon Fix*. The Cure may not have sounded anything like R.E.M., but in singer-songwriter Robert Smith and manager/label head Chris Parry they had the same mixture of ambition and business chops that characterized R.E.M., and it was probably not a coincidence that the Cure enjoyed a similar run of sustained success in the late '80s and early '90s.

In 1988, R.E.M. ceased to be an independent, cult-level rock band—though you wouldn't have known it around Athens. Michael Stipe could still be seen out and about most any night of the week. And Peter Buck still got up on-stage with practically any band that would have him, and continued to throw his weight behind various doomed side projects—such as the Nasty Bucks (a band featuring members of the Georgia Satellites and the Swimming Pool Q's) and the Upbeats, a non-band fronted by "this crazy drug addict around town," according to Billy Holmes, "who just got a who's who of Athens musicians [including Peter and Kenny Buck along with Holmes himself] to play on a record together." Bill Berry, too, did some recording. In May, he went into John Keane Studios and tracked an enjoyable but somewhat throwaway country original titled "My Bible Is the Latest TV Guide" and a heartfelt rendition of New Colony Six's "Things I'd Like to Say." These were released the following year on Dog Gone under the name 13111—a move that seemed calculated to bury the project in obscurity for perpetuity, or at least until the dawn of YouTube and SoundCloud. Even Jefferson Holt got in on the act, demonstrating with his Vibrating Egg project (recorded with Mike Mills) why he had chosen the path of manager over rock musician all those years previously. These were the actions of men who seemingly had nothing better to do.

In other words, R.E.M. held on to life as they knew it. For the time being. But for those looking closely, it became clear that a shift had occurred. For eight years, Billy Holmes had never seen his friend Mike Mills without his brown bomber jacket. Any night, any bar, any party, there he was, always with the jacket. It had been on every tour of duty, from the club circuit in 1981 through the Work outings of 1987. Every year it looked a bit more worn; every year the leather at the shoulders and the elbows grew lighter in hue. Still, it hung in there, becoming, over time, an extension of Mills's body. Then, one day in 1988, Holmes saw his old friend walking along the street and thought to himself, *What's different here?* It was difficult to pick out at first. It was still the same old Mike—same bowl haircut, same glasses, same friendly demeanor, but . . . *where's the jacket?* That day Mike was wearing a brand-new black coat resplendent with colorful patches of Elmer Fudd, Bugs Bunny, and the rest of the *Loony Tunes* crew. And on the back was a giant Warner Bros. logo.

Epilogue

Michael Lachowski's loft party, October 1992. The room shook with the bass notes of the techno and soul music coming out of Lachowski's turntables. Lynda Stipe danced just a few feet away from me, shaking her long, dark, curly hair. I attempted to dance with her, which amounted to dancing near her. Elsewhere in the room, her brother burned up the floor, shaking and whirling around as if he were on the stage at Tyrone's in the fall of 1981. On all sides, the movers and shakers—in both senses—of the town's musical history pressed up against me. Paul Butchart, Kurt Wood, and Mike Richmond were probably there, though I wouldn't become aware of—let alone meet—any of these personalities until years later.

And yet, in the immediate aftermath of this brush with greatness, my recollections of the party primarily centered around my disastrous attempt to make a move on the young woman with whom I had attended. I had gone in for a kiss at the exact moment her body lodged a complaint against the excess alcohol in her system. Moments later, I stood in Michael Lachowski's driveway holding my date's hand as she vomited all over the pavement. And that was the end of that particular beginning.

I tell this story to highlight something about Athens, and about history. It is difficult to spend any time in the town without becoming aware of the significant events that occurred there in the late '70s and early '80s—events that impacted the course of popular music. And yet the town's population always contains a disproportionately high number of college students teeming with lust and confusion and dreams. Many of the old guard still live there, even now—but the kids are not inclined to notice. And why should anyone expect it to be otherwise? What 18-year-old has any interest in living in the past? Even those students who are actually R.E.M. fans—and there are fewer and fewer among the college-age set nowadays—quickly get caught up in the experience of living and loving in the now, growing into themselves. They have only just recently broken free of their parents. The members of R.E.M., the R.E.M. story, the tales of the early scene, and even rock 'n' roll itself, come to seem old, like their parents. It is usually out of this dissatisfaction with, or disinterest in, the past that new scenes are born. "Let's put our heads together and start a new country up," someone once sang. Certainly there were very few members of the Athens art school crowd in 1979 obsessing over local resident Randall Bramblett's impressive contributions to music just a decade earlier. Randall who?

Standing on the shoulders of giants left them cold.

I returned to Athens twenty years after I first arrived there in order to conduct research for this book. You may recall my description in an earlier section of the pretty girl who walked up while I was interviewing Ort and asked to have her picture taken with him—not because of his formidable status in the town's history, but because she really liked his smile and his long white beard. I probably cracked a joke, like, "You are standing next to a legend," and "That picture will be worth a lot of money someday." But it occurs to me now that she was approaching the world precisely as a young person should: with open eyes and a clean slate.

The story of R.E.M.'s early years, on the other hand, belongs to those of us still afflicted by history. As the participants die and memories fade, the flame necessarily diminishes.

Even R.E.M.'s business model—the manner, accidental or calculated, in which they ascended from independent college rock band to global pop sensation in slow, incremental steps—has largely disappeared from practice. With the ongoing upheaval in the music industry, artists now tend to be on one side of a great divide or the other; there are those who, like Lady Gaga and Katy Perry, follow the world-domination plan and work from within the ever-dwindling corporate machine. Then there are the vast majority of artists, some quite successful, who either remain on independent labels (or on the indie fringe of major labels) throughout their careers, or follow an even purer DIY approach—using the recently developed tools of YouTube, Bandcamp, and various streaming services to take their music directly to consumers.

Back in the 1990s, though, many bands (most famously Nirvana) attempted to duplicate the R.E.M. template. It turned out to be not quite as easy as it looked. In Nirvana's case, the impossible-to-refuse major-label deal came just a few short years into the band's career, brokered by, of all people, Sonic Youth. Emboldened by R.E.M.'s example, Nirvana demanded, and got, complete creative control. They even got DGC (part of Geffen Records) to partner with their previous independent label—Seattle's Sub Pop—and display both labels' logos prominently on each release, thus retaining some degree of connection with the world of independent music. But despite these visible instances of brake-tapping, success rapidly overtook—and overwhelmed—Nirvana.

R.E.M., it turned out, were an anomaly. Their musical legacy is also something of an anomaly. Whereas Nirvana's reach has stretched, Hendrix- and Beatles-style, beyond their generation, R.E.M. remain largely locked into their time period—an odd turn of events given the self-consciously timeless production and arrangements on their records. For whatever reason, the vast majority of R.E.M. fans in 2015 are the people who grew up listening to R.E.M. Perhaps the band's catalog, particularly the material from the I.R.S. years, must remain, for now, a carefully curated time capsule waiting to be opened by later generations hungry not for nostalgia, but for something deeper and more substantial than what they encounter all around them— some kind of hidden knowledge. Perhaps, in the end, R.E.M. will come to be much closer in spirit and legacy to their heroes the Velvet Underground than they anticipated.

Whatever the age of their current audience, R.E.M. sold enough records in their day to ensure that, at any given moment, someone somewhere in the world is listening to *Murmur*. Which means that, at least for now, someone somewhere is being engaged rather than just entertained. And that seems to me a fine legacy.

R.E.M.

RAPID.EYE.MOVEMENT.TOUR.1981

«Best New Athens Band»
—CREATIVE LOAFING–ATLANTA

"You can't sit down"
— NEW YORK·ROCKER

March 27·Cantrell's–Nashville
March 28·the Milestone–Charlotte
March 31· Fridays– Greensboro
April 2·NewYorkNewYork–Augusta
April 3·Vanderbilt–Nashville
April 4·the Station– Carrboro
April 6 the Pier–Raleigh

Acknowledgments

This book owes its existence to my longtime editor and friend Steve Connell. Our first collaboration, *No Certainty Attached*, was barely off the presses when I expressed the desire to work with him again. Steve asked if I had ever considered writing about R.E.M. The answer at that time was no, but afterward I thought of little else.

A subsequent conversation with my friends Angela Albright and Jim Doerfler pushed me out of the realm of daydreaming and into the writing chair. They completed the process that Steve began.

Keith Joyner and William Mull, formerly of the great Athens band Seven Simons, helped immensely in the early stages. William provided a detailed list of contacts that I used throughout the project. We can thank him for putting Pat the Wiz, Billy Holmes, and Diane Loring Aiken, among others, on my radar; I think all would agree that the book is richer for these voices.

I wish to thank Jesse Waters and the Bowers Writers House at Elizabethtown College for providing a working space during the completion of the book.

Thank you to Amy Hairston at R.E.M. HQ for the assistance and open line of communication.

While writing the book, I thought often of childhood friends who shared my love of R.E.M.: Andrew Beccone, Pat Curry, Michael Ellick, and Patrick Liddiard. This volume is my attempt to answer the half-verbalized questions we asked each other all those years ago while listening to *Murmur* and *Lifes Rich Pageant*. I hope I have captured something of the giddiness and yearning of those days. Remember every moment.

Victor Gagnon and Patrick Rose graciously allowed me to tap into their archives of rare recordings—again. I am so lucky to have them as resources.

The following friends and colleagues provided immeasurable support throughout the journey: Jeremy Beer, Eric Black, Emma Bolden, Pam Brannon, Bob Clay, Ben Guterson, David Guterson, Stanton Hall, Paul Harasha, Stephen Judge, Bill Kauffman, Richard Kaczynski, Steve Kilbey, Peter Koppes, Paul Lickteig, Daniel McCarthy, John J. Miller, Fred Mills,

Margaret Obuch, Christopher Sandford, Vaughn Sterling, Serge van Neck, and Ernie Ward.

The University of North Carolina Wilmington MFA program continues to be a source of encouragement and assistance. I owe a special debt to Wendy Brenner, Phil Furia, Philip Gerard, David Gessner, and Rebecca Lee.

I'm not sure I can adequately thank Nova Chase, Scott Fothergill, Mike Monk, and EnvisionWare, Inc.—my non-writing employers—for their continued support and understanding. I would say Mike is fairly unique among employers in that he has always encouraged my creative pursuits and has never viewed them as an encroachment on the work I do for his company. If more bosses were like this, there likely wouldn't be so much tension between artists' creative aspirations and their daytime careers.

Last and most important, all thanks to my wife, Harper Piver, and our two beautiful children, Dolly and Dean. You are the everything.

Notes

Wherever possible, I have attempted to cite the sources for my information within the text. What follows are supplemental notes on the primary and secondary sources used in the composition of each chapter. A list of those sources follows these notes.

PROLOGUE

This section is derived from personal memories overlaid with the trace imprint of the "old" Athens as described in Rodger Lyle Brown's *Party Out of Bounds*.

CHAPTER ONE

The descriptions of Reed Hall come primarily from Kathleen O'Brien (personal interview) and Rodger Lyle Brown (via *Party Out of Bounds*) supplemented by my own vivid memories of a virtually unchanged fourth floor and subwastement in the early 1990s.

"The girls were rowdy." Brown, *Party Out of Bounds*, p. 107

"I'd like to say that playing the drums..." Santelli, "The Back Door of Success." *Modern Drummer*

"wrong side of the law." Buckley, *Fiction*, p. 31

"clean-living, hard-working lad..." Black, *Reveal*, p. 25

"I was five or six when my older brother bought *Meet the Beatles*... " Rossiter, "R.E.M. in the Hall." *Online Athens*

"not ashamed of being Southerners." Santelli, "The Back Door of Success." *Modern Drummer*

"[She and I] would sit around the lunch room discussing things..." Gray, *It Crawled from the South*, pp. 19–20

"heartily sick of the Capricorn roster's..." Gray, *It Crawled from the South*, p. 21

"Get this [...] the Back Door Band's guitarist's girlfriend's..." Brown, *Party Out of Bounds*, p. 101

"I would have paid to do it." Brown, *Party Out of Bounds*, p. 102

"[He] explained that he was not only Paragon's chauffeur..." Copeland, *Wild Thing*

"We would play along to the Ramones' first record..." Black, *Reveal*, p. 26

"I want you to sign bands I can't stand." Copeland, *Wild Thing*

"Not to put too fine a point on it..." Copeland, *Wild Thing*

"Bill and Mike hung me upside down over a bridge..." Copeland, *Wild Thing*

CHAPTER TWO

My own experiences are to blame for the depiction of the Clermont Lounge, Atlanta's most notorious strip club.

The portrait of UGA Greek life is a composite of Brown's descriptions in *Party Out of Bounds* and my personal run-ins with that system.

The very brief romantic involvement between Kathleen O'Brien and Peter Buck surfaced publicly (albeit obliquely) in Buckley's *Fiction* (pp. 29–30) and was reiterated (without prodding) by multiple sources, but it's neither here nor there. Which of these people *didn't* date each other at some point?

"black water spilling from faucets…" Tagami, "Clermont Hotel Shut Down, Strippers Unaffected." *Atlanta Journal Constitution*

"a dozen guys in flannel shirts…" Brown, *Party Out of Bounds*, p. 32

"No, these people are not crazy…" Paulzonkey, "Rocky Horror at the Varsity Theater Late '70s Michael Stipe & Vladimir Noskov." *YouTube*

"unbelievably happy." Black, *Reveal*, p. 19

"My people…" Bollen, "Michael Stipe." *Interview*

"possess(ed) a romantic beauty and tenderness all their own." "Joel Chandler Harris." *Wikipedia.*

"What I've never told anyone…" Miccio, "Michael Stipe Amends 'When I First Heard Horses' Story, Acknowledges Foghat." *Idolator*

"tore my limbs off…" Buckley, *Fiction*. p. 25

"unorthodox sex and energy theories." "Wilhelm Reich." *Wikipedia*

"I have always referred to the Beatles as elevator music . . ." DeCurtis, "Michael Stipe Q&A," *R.E.M.: The Rolling Stone Files*, p. 185

"Not troubled, no." O'Hagan, Sean, "Michael Stipe: I Often Find Myself at a Loss for Words." *The Observer*

"Where I learned…" Stipe, Michael, "My 10 Favorite Books." *New York Times*

"all covers, from Tom Petty to Elvis." Brown, *Party Out of Bounds*, p. 119

"Hell yeah!" Brown, *Party Out of Bounds*, p. 100

"It has been romanticized beyond all belief." Pond, "R.E.M. in the Real World," *R.E.M.: The Rolling Stone Files*, p. 77

CHAPTER THREE

"It was a heavily sexual time." Brown, *Party Out of Bounds*, p. 127

"On a sliding scale of sexuality…" O'Hagan, Sean. "Michael Stipe: 'I Often Find Myself at a Loss for Words." *The Observer*

"Fag? Fag?…" Brown, *Party Out of Bounds*, p. 125

CHAPTER FOUR

"rotten cocksucker." Buckley, *Fiction*, p. 45

"incapacitated due to alcohol consumption…" Gray, *It Crawled from the South*, p. 24

CHAPTER FIVE

"my first love." Baldwin, "Michael Stipe on R.E.M. and Fear of Collage." *Here's the Thing*

"For years I've heard the rumor…" "R.I.P. R.E.M." *The Online Photographer* (reader comment)

"one of the nation's most liberal and politically correct…" Fletcher, *Perfect Circle*, p. 284

"There were absolutely no legal aid jobs anywhere…" Phillips, "Bertis Downs Fell into the Job of a Lifetime." *Online Athens*

"I remember liking R.E.M. a lot." Sullivan, *Talk About the Passion*, p. 10

"I recognized early that they were…" Sullivan, *Talk About the Passion*, p. 14

"I made use of what I had…" Brown, *Party Out of Bounds*, p. 152

"R.E.M. had no idea…" Sullivan, *Talk About the Passion*, p. 20

"asshole henna heads…" Brown, *Party Out of Bounds*, pp. 171–172

CHAPTER SIX

"footnote to rock history." Ingrid Schorr, "Rockville Girl Speaks," http://hilobrow.
  com/2011/09/23/rockville-girl-speaks/
"We were driving at night..." Berry, *And I Feel Fine... The Best of the I.R.S. Years
  1982–1987*
"Michael is so unpredictable..." Walters, "Visions of Glory." *Spin*
"I kind of agree with Burroughs..." Gray, *It Crawled from the South*, pp. 106–107
"Even if I could have sold..." Starrs, "R.E.M. In the Hall: Producer Remembers First
  Recordings With R.E.M." *Online Athens*
"tremendous amount of raw energy." Gray, *It Crawled from the South*, pp. 91–92
"flat and dull." Fletcher, *Perfect Circle*, p. 50
"Pop songs as false emotional advertising..." "Jon King." *Wikipedia*.

CHAPTER SEVEN

"one of the few great American punk singles." Fletcher, *Perfect Circle*, p. 61
"We're not so versatile..." Pond, *R.E.M.: The Rolling Stone Files*, p. 79
"head injuries sustained in a bicycle accident." "David Huber Healey '81." *Princeton
  Alumni Weekly*
"Copeland is a sort of right-wing fascist." Buckley, *Fiction*, pp. 141–142
"This EP is so arcane..." Hull, "R.E.M.: *Chronic Town*." *Creem*.

CHAPTER EIGHT

Lance Smith's "Green Light Room" reference is from *Talk About the Passion*.
Mike Mills's water-tower story is something of a legend in Athens. Formally appeared
in print in Fletcher, *Full Circle*, p. 112: "Mike Mills had been arrested for 'cavorting
nude with a young lady on a water tower.'"
Bill Berry's cocaine use: "Bill has confirmed that he was using cocaine in the 1980s."
Black, *Reveal*, p. 106
"Some musicians need to reject..." Dombal, "R.E.M." *Pitchfork*
"I was standing in the City Gardens..." Fletcher, *Perfect Circle*, p. 93
"the crazy Athens music lifestyle..." Butchart, "30 years ago..." Facebook post
"disdain for the easy and obvious." Keenan, "To Live and Shave in LA." *The Wire*
"I stopped taking drugs..." Bollen, "Michael Stipe." *Interview*
"bovine prosthetics or such." Considine, "R.E.M.: Subverting Small Town Boredom
  (1983)." *The R.E.M. Companion*, p. 22
"Why do they need to preserve it?" McWhirter, "For R.E.M. Fans..." *Wall Street
  Journal*
"Art isn't something that happens..." Daley, "Peter Buck..." *Salon*
"R.E.M. is clearly the important Athens band." Pond, "*Murmur* Album Review."
  R.E.M.: The Rolling Stone Files, p. 28
"We're not a party band from Athens." Slater. "R.E.M.: Not Just Another Athens,
  Georgia, Band." *R.E.M.: The Rolling Stone Files*, p. 26
"out of a misbegotten display of group solidarity." Keenan, "To Live and Shave in LA."
  The Wire
"the most wretched and abysmal experience of our lives." Black, *Reveal*, p. 85
"kinda neat." Black, *Reveal*, p. 85
"The songs have obviously been chosen..." Gray, *It Crawled from the South*, p. 55
"didn't sell one record." Black, *Reveal*, p. 87
"Those shows were probably a lot more successful..." Boberg, *Reveal*, p. 87

"We'd much rather play for fifty people…" Azerrad, *Our Band Could Be Your Life*, p. 218

"Of course I moved down there and promptly blew off school." Cost, "Sweet Emotion." *The Bob*

"The 'Trolls,' as no one refers to them ever…" Guthrie, "30 Things You'll Never See in Athens, GA Again." *Movoto Real Estate*

"machinations…the beginning of the next era…" Brown, *Party Out of Bounds*, pp. 211–212

"The guy wanted to make records." Gray, *It Crawled from the South* (Revised Edition), p. 204

"began being self-conscious." Fletcher, *Perfect Circle*, p. 103

"Everybody thought Michael didn't want to talk." Daley, "Peter Buck…" *Salon*

"The weather report was, 'South central rain…'" Rosen, *R.E.M. Inside Out*, p. 37

"With that one we had to make him work a bit…" Buckley, *R.E.M. Fiction*, p. 104

"He didn't have to scream it…" Buckley, *R.E.M. Fiction*, p. 100

"So many of the early songs…" 29caps, "R.E.M. – Harborcoat…" *YouTube*

"Like much of the band's early '80s material…" Perpetua, "Harborcoat." *Pop Songs 07–08*

"'7 Chinese Bros.' was about me breaking up a couple…" Perpetua, "7 Chinese Bros./ Voice of Harold." *Pop Songs 07-08*

"Part of it is rocks and part of it is the sun…" Fletcher, *Perfect Circle*, p. 106

"*Reckoning* proves that both Stipe's…" Sasfy, "Reckoning With R.E.M." *Washington Post*

"confirms R.E.M. as one of the most…" Snow, quoted in Lesemann, "R.E.M.'s Reckoning resurfaces." *Charleston City Paper*

"We are just beginning to see R.E.M. develop…" "Reckoning." *College Music Journal*

"Everyone was real nice to us…" Gray, *It Crawled from the South*, p. 144

CHAPTER NINE

"Chris asks how long I will need with the guys." Walters, "Visions of Glory." *Spin*

"I don't ever see us being a band that preaches…" Gray, *It Crawled from the South*, p. 194

"I guess I've tried to alter the idea of commodity…" Dieckmann, "R.E.M.'s Michael Stipe." *Musician*

"Have you ever been to London?" Black, *Reveal*, p. 104

"What did they expect to do in early March in the UK …" Buckley, *Fiction*, p. 117

"One of the best-documented side-effects of cocaine…" Black, *Reveal*, p. 106

"The first thing I noticed was that Michael had shaved the crown of his head…" Black, *Reveal*, p. 105

"I was just tired." Bollen, "Michael Stipe." *Interview*

"In the early Eighties, as a 22-year-old queer man…" Grow, "Michael Stipe Talks HIV Test Delay." *Rolling Stone*

"You all remember the Reagan-Bush internment camps, right?" Calabrese, "REM's Michael Stipe Delayed HIV Test…" *Herman Cain*

"51 percent of the respondents supported a quarantine…" "Poll Indicates Majority Favor Quarantine for AIDS Victims." *New York Times*

"one of our highest public health priorities." Cannon, "Ronald Reagan and AIDS: Correcting the Record." *RealClearPolitics*

"The tragedy lies in what he might have done." White, "Reagan's AIDS Legacy / Silence Equals Death." *SFGate*

CHAPTER TEN

"One could make an interesting argument…" Perpetua, "Life and How to Live It." *Pop Songs 07–08*

"You confused and injected me [real Michael] in the work," Perpetua, "Ask Michael Stipe: Finale!" *Pop Songs 07–08*

"Oh my God… He's so sappy and thick, I'm embarrassed." O'Hagan, "Another Green World." *The R.E.M. Companion*, p. 119

"R.E.M. undermines our certitude in reality…" Puterbaugh, "*Fables of the Reconstruction* Album Review." *R.E.M.: The Rolling Stone Files*, p. 45

"It's a progression along existing lines…" Platt, "R.E.M.: *Fables of the Reconstruction.*" *The R.E.M. Companion*, p. 40

"One senses that something great is brewing." Defendorf, "R.E.M." *Orlando Sentinel*

"Forty-five years ago, maybe Athens, Georgia…" Isler, "History of R.E.M." *Musician.*

"The guy who yelled 'Fuck you' during 'Moon River'…" White, "1985 Concert Chronology." *R.E.M. Timeline*

"Natalie was really the reason my work became politicized in the late Eighties." McNair, "How We Met: Michael Stipe and Natalie Merchant." *Independent*

CHAPTER ELEVEN

"Loved Mystery Date." Walls, Facebook post ("Athens Music History" group)

"The offices are run on an 'environmentally conscious' basis." Gray, *It Crawled from the South*, p. 190

"The girl I've been dating for six years broke up with me last Saturday." Walters, "Visions of Glory." *Spin*

"But the last thing he said to me before he died…" Black, *Reveal*, p. 130

"The greatest time here was from '77–'81…" Sullivan, *Talk About the Passion*, p. 117

"musical carpetbaggers." Sullivan, *Talk About the Passion*, p. 117

"crazed-looking…" Maslin, "'Athens, GA' on Rock Bands." *New York Times*

"I never planned on being a musician…" *Athens, GA: Inside/Out*

"Guitars as malfunctioning lawn equipment…" Voegtlin, "Bar-B-Q Killers – Comely." *Stylus*

"There was no one like her." Jordan, "'Barbecue Killers' Musician Laura Carter Dies at Age 37." *Athens Banner-Herald*

"I was interested in doing something in my career…" Coley, "REM Producer Don Gehman Full Interview." *SoundCloud*

"[Gehman] made life hell for me…" *R.E.M. by MTV*

"This is a song that means a huge amount to me…" Stipe, "These Days." *R.E.M. Live at the Olympia in Dublin*

"This may well be my favorite song…" Stipe, "Fall on Me." *Unplugged 1991/2001: The Complete Sessions*

"played the living shit out of ['Fall on Me']. . ." Bollen, "Michael Stipe." *Interview*

"It's one of my great regrets…" Hyden, "Bittersweet Me." *Grantland*

CHAPTER TWELVE

"There's a live R.E.M. recording…" Goldman, "Michael Stipe Is Not Grumpy." *New York Times*

"The freshmen at the University of R.E.M…." Cummings, "R.E.M: Lifes Rich Pageant." *Spin*

"always fairly strange." Wilkinson, "The Secret File of R.E.M." *The R.E.M. Companion,*
p. 80
"I don't think the mainstream is ready for us." *R.E.M. by MTV*

CHAPTER THIRTEEN

"incredibly violent ... about using people over and over again." Sullivan, "The One I
Love – R.E.M. | Song Info." *AllMusic*
"the whole 'The One I Love' scenario was a very Stipe-type thing..." Sullivan, *Talk
About the Passion,* pp. 122–123
"STIPE SAYS / DON'T GET BUSHWHACKED..." DeCurtis, "R.E.M.'s Brave New
World." *R.E.M.: The Rolling Stone Files,* p. 101
"I couldn't not be political in that environment." McCormick, "Citizen Stipe." *Daily
Telegraph*
"We're pigs! Americans are pigs!" Sutherland, "R.E.M.: Peter Buck's American
Nightmare." *Melody Maker*
"Stipe playing a guitar drone, while other musicians..." White, "1987/88 Concert
Chronology." *R.E.M. Timeline*
"I think injustice occurred." Fletcher, *Perfect Circle,* p. 163

Sources

INTERVIEWS
Much of the material in this book derives from interviews with:

Diane Loring Aiken
T. Patton Biddle
Paul Butchart
William Orten Carlton
Mike Doskocil
Chris Edwards
Craig Franklin
Jonny Hibbert
Billy Holmes
Keith Joyner
T. Kyle King
William Mull
Kathleen O'Brien
David Pierce
Mike Richmond
Jeffery J. Rogers
Ingrid Schorr
Nick Searcy
Velena Vego
Jeff Walls
Kurt Wood

CONCERTS
Concert chronology has been based on the latest information available on *The R.E.M. Timeline* (www.remtimeline.com). Unless otherwise noted, all direct quotes from concerts are sourced from T. Patton Biddle's extensive audio archives (including 1987 tour tapes made by Buren Fowler) and the archives of Victor Gagnon and Patrick Rose.

LYRICS
Most readers will be aware that the official lyrics for R.E.M.'s IRS albums remain unpublished. In the instances where I have quoted from songs, I have relied on my own ears as well as the crowd-sourced efforts at The Complete R.E.M. Lyrics Archive (http://www.retroweb.com/rem/lyrics/).

BIBLIOGRAPHY

29caps. "R.E.M. - Harborcoat / Lillian Hellman Intro – Dublin 2007." *YouTube*, YouTube, Sep. 1, 2008, www.youtube.com/watch?v=2eIyA9AgVXI.

Azerrad, Michael. *Our Band Could Be Your Life*. Little, Brown and Company, 2001.

Baldwin, Alec, host "Michael Stipe on R.E.M. and Fear of Collage." *Here's the Thing*, iTunes app, Nov. 7, 2016.

Berry, Bill. Liner notes. *And I Feel Fine… The Best of the I.R.S. Years 1982–1987*, R.E.M., 2006. CD

Black, Johnny. *Reveal: The Story of R.E.M.* Backbeat, 2004.

Bollen, Christopher. "Michael Stipe." *Interview Magazine*, May 4, 2011, www.interviewmagazine.com/music/michael-stipe.

Brown, Rodger Lyle. *Party Out of Bounds: The B-52's, R.E.M., and the Kids Who Rocked Athens, Georgia*. Everthemore, 2003.

Buckley, David. *R.E.M. Fiction: An Alternative Biography*. Virgin, 2011.

Burroughs, William S. *The Adding Machine: Selected Essays*. Seaver, 1986.

Butchart, Paul. "30 years ago on the morning of April 14, 1983…" Apr. 15, 2013. Facebook post.

Calabrese, Dan. "REM's Michael Stipe Delayed HIV Test to Stay out of the, Um, Reagan-Bush Internment Camps." *Herman Cain*, Jun. 30, 2014, www.hermancain.com/rems-michael-stipe-kept-gay-se.

Cannon, Carl M. "Ronald Reagan and AIDS: Correcting the Record." *RealClearPolitics*, Jun. 1, 2014, www.realclearpolitics.com/articles/2014/06/01/ronald_reagan_and_aids_correcting_the_record_122806.html.

Coley, Sam. "REM Producer Don Gehman Full Interview." *SoundCloud*, May 29, 2011, www.soundcloud.com/samcoley/rem-producer-don-gehman-full.

"Coors Brewing Company." *Wikipedia,* Wikimedia Foundation, Apr. 30, 2018, en.wikipedia.org/wiki/Coors_Brewing_Company.

Copeland, Ian. *Wild Thing: The Backstage, On the Road, In the Studio, Off the Charts Memoirs of Ian Copeland*. Simon & Schuster, 1995.

Copeland, Miles. "The Copeland Chronicles." *AND Magazine*, andmagazine.com/us/the_copeland_chronicles.html.

Cost, Jud. "Sweet Emotion." *The Bob Magazine*, Sep. 1993.

Cummings, Sue. "R.E.M.: Life's Rich Pageant." *Spin*, Oct. 1986.

"David Huber Healey '81." *Princeton Alumni Weekly*, 1998, paw.princeton.edu/memorial/david-huber-healey-'81.

Daley, David. "EXCLUSIVE: R.E.M.'s Mike Mills Remembers Band's David Letterman Appearances, How He Broke the News of His Retirement." *Salon*, May 20, 2015, www.salon.com/2015/05/20/exclusive_r_e_m_s_mike_mills_remembers_bands_david_letterman_appearances_how_he_broke_the_news_of_his_retirement.

———. "Peter Buck: 'I Think We Were All Really Ready for a Change.'" *Salon*, Oct. 9, 2013, www.salon.com/2013/10/09/peter_buck_i_think_we_were_all_really_ready_for_a_change.

Defendorf, Richard. "R.E.M." *Orlando Sentinel*, Jul. 7, 1985, articles.orlandosentinel.com/1985-07-07/entertainment/0310240193_1_rem-wendell-gee-reconstruction.

Delany, Samuel R. *Dhalgren*. Bantam, 1975.

Dieckmann, Katherine. "R.E.M.'s Michael Stipe." *Musician*, Sep. 1, 1990.

Dombal, Ryan. "R.E.M." *Pitchfork*, Nov. 20, 2011, pitchfork.com/features/interview/8712-rem.

Durrell, Lawrence. *The Black Book*. Faber, 2012.

Fletcher, Tony. *Perfect Circle: The Story of R.E.M.* Omnibus Press, 2013.

Gayton, Tony (director). *Athens, GA: Inside/Out*. Eclectic DVD Dist., 1987.

Goldman, Andrew. "Michael Stipe Is Not Grumpy." *New York Times*, Dec. 16, 2011, www.nytimes.com/2011/12/18/magazine/michael-stipe-is-not-grumpy.html.

Gray, Marcus. *It Crawled from the South: An R.E.M. Companion*. Da Capo Press, 1993.

Gray, Marcus. *It Crawled from the South* (revised edition). Da Capo Press, 1997.

Grow, Kory. "Michael Stipe Talks HIV Test Delay." *Rolling Stone*, Jun. 26, 2014, www.rollingstone.com/music/videos/why-michael-stipe-waited-five-years-to-get-an-hiv-test-20140626.

Guthrie, Blake. "30 Things You'll Never See In Athens, GA Again." *Movoto Real Estate*, 2014, www.movoto.com/guide/athens-ga/never-see-again-athens.

Hull, Robert A. "R.E.M.: *Chronic Town.*" *Creem*, Jan. 1983.

Hyden, Steven. "Bittersweet Me." *Grantland*, Jun. 6, 2015, grantland.com/features/michael-stipe-rem-career.

Isler, Scott. "History of R.E.M." *Musician*, July 1985.

"Joel Chandler Harris." *Wikipedia*, Wikimedia Foundation, Mar. 28, 2018, en.wikipedia.org/wiki/Joel_Chandler_Harris.

"Jon King." *Wikipedia*, Oct. 23, 2017, en.wikipedia.org/wiki/Jon_King.

Jordan, Julie Phillips. "'Barbecue Killers' Musician Laura Carter Dies at Age 37." *Athens Banner-Herald*, Dec. 7, 2002, onlineathens.com/stories/120702/roc_20021207054.shtml#.WjEicVWnHIU.

Jovanovic, Rob. *Michael Stipe: The Biography*. Portrait, 2007.

Keenan, David. "To Live and Shave in LA." *The Wire*, no. 222. Aug. 2002.

kenjames64. "R.E.M., 2 October 85 (Complete and Unedited Show, HQ)." YouTube, Apr. 3, 2015, www.youtube.com/watch?v=jckCwlAw6y8.

Larson, Kay. *Where the Heart Beats: John Cage, Zen Buddhism, and the Inner Life of Artists*. Penguin Books, 2013.

Lesemann, T. Ballard. "R.E.M.'s Reckoning Resurfaces." *Charleston City Paper*, Charleston City Paper, May 22, 2009, www.charlestoncitypaper.com/charleston/rems-reckoning-resurfaces/Content?oid=1195610.

Martin, Douglas A. *Outline of My Lover*. Soft Skull Press, 2000.

Maslin, Janet. "'Athens, GA' on Rock Bands." *New York Times*, May 29, 1987, www.nytimes.com/movie/review?res=9D03E4DF153AF93AA15756C0A961948260.

McCormick, Neil. "Citizen Stipe." *Daily Telegraph*, Oct. 20, 2001, www.telegraph.co.uk/culture/4726176/Citizen-Stipe.html.

McNair, James. "How We Met: Michael Stipe and Natalie Merchant." *Independent*, Nov. 8, 1998, www.independent.co.uk/arts-entertainment/how-we-met-michael-stipe-and-natalie-merchant-1183710.html.

McWhirter, Cameron. "For R.E.M. Fans, Tunes May Linger But Trestle Faces Day of Reckoning." *Wall Street Journal*, Feb. 6, 2012, www.wsj.com/articles/SB10001424052970204624204577180660673324908.

Miccio, Anthony J. "Michael Stipe Amends 'When I First Heard *Horses*' Story, Acknowledges Foghat." *Idolator*, May 16, 2008, www.idolator.com/391149/michael-stipe-amends-when-i-first-heard-ihorsesi-story-acknowledges-foghat.

MikeMillsTribute. "R.E.M. WEA Presentation 1988." YouTube, Apr. 22, 2010, www.youtube.com/watch?v=TwZkYc7GCL8.

Monty. "Drunks With Guns Interview." *The Termites Always Follow*, Oct. 5, 2011, thetermitesalwaysfollow.blogspot.com/2011/10/drunks-with-guns-interview.html.

O'Hagan, Sean. "Michael Stipe: 'I often find myself at a loss for words' – interview." *Observer*, Mar. 5, 2011, www.theguardian.com/music/2011/mar/06/michael-stipe-rem-collapse-interview.

Paulzonkey. "Rocky Horror at the Varsity Theater Late '70s Michael Stipe & Vladimir Noskov." YouTube, Apr. 23, 2010, www.youtube.com/watch?v=nvG6LeGWU2g.

Perpetua, Matthew. "7 Chinese Bros. / Voice of Harold." *Pop Songs 07–08*, Mar. 23, 2008, popsongs.wordpress.com/2008/03/22/7-chinese-bros-voice-of-harold.

———. "Ask Michael Stipe: Finale!" *Pop Songs 07–08*, Sep. 28, 2008, popsongs.wordpress.com/2008/09/28/ask-michael-stipe-finale.

———. "Harborcoat." *Pop Songs 07–08*, Apr. 25, 2007, popsongs.wordpress.com/2007/04/25/harborcoat.

———. "Life and How to Live It." *Pop Songs 07–08*, Jul. 22, 2008, popsongs.wordpress.com/2008/07/22/life-and-how-to-live-it.

Phillips, Julie. "Bertis Downs Fell into Job of a Lifetime." Online Athens, Feb. 2007, onlineathens.com/rem-hall/stories/downs.shtml.

Platt, John, ed. *The R.E.M. Companion*. Schirmer, 1998.

"Poll Indicates Majority Favor Quarantine for AIDS Victims." *New York Times*, Dec. 19, 1985, www.nytimes.com/1985/12/20/us/poll-indicates-majority-favor-quarantine-for-aids-victims.html.

Radford, Chad. "The gospel according to Romeo Cologne." *Creative Loafing Atlanta*, Feb. 24, 2011, creativeloafing.com/content-165796-The-gospel-according-to-Romeo-Cologne.

"Reckoning." *College Music Journal* 38, April 9, 1984

REMchout. "R.E.M. 1st TV Appearance 1983 Complete Version, Better Sound." YouTube, Nov. 4, 2011, www.youtube.com/watch?v=rQo0cR1onRM.

REMVEVO. "R.E.M. – Radio Free Europe." YouTube, Mar. 4, 2009, www.youtube.com/watch?v=kI5P5VeewyE.

R.E.M.: The Rolling Stone Files. The Ultimate Compendium of Interviews, Articles, Facts, and Opinions from the Files of Rolling Stone. Hyperion, 1995.

Richardson, Andy. "REM Rewind." *Northern Echo*, Oct. 6, 2011, www.thenorthernecho.co.uk/news/9292700.display.

"R.I.P. R.E.M." *Online Photographer*, Sep. 23, 2011, theonlinephotographer.typepad.com/the_online_photographer/2011/09/rip-rem.html.

Rosen, Craig. *R.E.M. Inside Out: The Stories behind Every Song*. Carlton, 2005.

Rossiter, Erin. "R.E.M. In the Hall – Frenzy of fame contributes to former drummer's shyness." *Online Athens*, 2007, archive.li/95b0A.

"Samuel R. Delany." *Wikipedia*, Apr. 30, 2018, en.wikipedia.org/wiki/Samuel_R._Delany.

Santelli, Robert. "The Back Door of Success." *Modern Drummer*, Sep. 22, 1987.

Sasfy, Joe. "Reckoning With R.E.M." *Washington Post*, May 10, 1984, www.washingtonpost.com/archive/lifestyle/1984/05/10/reckoning-with-rem/bb929767-c59c-4ca9-ac56-3338bb5f9824/?utm_term=.b56e34676db0.

Schaller, Michael. *Reckoning with Reagan: America and Its President in the 1980s*. Oxford University Press, 1995.

Smith, Patti. *Just Kids*. Ecco, 2010.

Starrs, Chris J. "R.E.M. In the Hall: Producer Remembers First Recordings With R.E.M." *Online Athens* 2007, onlineathens.com/rem-hall/stories/beginning.shtml.

Stipe, Michael. "My 10 Favorite Books: Michael Stipe." *New York Times*, Aug. 14, 2015, www.nytimes.com/2015/08/14/t-magazine/my-10-favorite-books-michael-stipe.html.

———. "Fall on Me." *Unplugged 1991/2001: The Complete Sessions.*

———. "These Days." *R.E.M. Live at the Olympia in Dublin.*

———, and Jonathan Berger. *Volume 1.* Damiani Srl, 2018.

Sullivan, Denise. *R.E.M. Talk About the Passion: An Oral History.* Da Capo Press, 1998.

———. "The One I Love – R.E.M. | Song Info." *AllMusic,* www.allmusic.com/song/the-one-i-love-mt0007796547.

Sutherland, Steve. "R.E.M.: Peter Buck's American Nightmare." *Melody Maker,* Nov. 5, 1988.

Tagami, Ty. "Clermont Hotel Shut down, Strippers Unaffected." *Atlanta Journal-Constitution,* Oct. 19, 2016, www.ajc.com/news/local/clermont-hotel-shut-down-strippers-unaffected/Sfow8X8UHwnLFbMv14efrO.

Teague, Kipp. *The Complete R.E.M. Lyrics Archive,* www.retroweb.com/rem/lyrics.

Voegtlin, Stewart. "Bar-B-Q Killers – Comely." *Stylus,* Aug. 28, 2006, www.stylusmagazine.com/articles/on_second_thought/bar-b-q-killers-comely.htm.

Walls, Jeff. "Loved Mystery Date." Dec. 4, 2014. Facebook post.

Walters, Barry. "Visions of Glory." *Spin,* Oct. 1986.

White, Allen. "Reagan's AIDS Legacy / Silence Equals Death." *SFGate,* Jun. 8, 2004, www.sfgate.com/opinion/openforum/article/Reagan-s-AIDS-Legacy-Silence-equals-death-2751030.php.

White, Darryl. *R.E.M. Timeline,* www.remtimeline.com.

"Wilhelm Reich." *Wikipedia,* 1 May 1, 2018, en.wikipedia.org/wiki/Wilhelm_Reich.

Young, Alex, director. *R.E.M. by MTV.* Anderson Digital, 2015.

ALSO AVAILABLE FROM VERSE CHORUS PRESS

NO CERTAINTY ATTACHED
Steve Kilbey and The Church: A Biography
Robert Dean Lurie
Based on extensive interviews, *No Certainty Attached* is the first biography of Steve Kilbey and his band, the Church. It charts their personal and musical ups and downs: the commercial heights of "The Unguarded Moment" and "Under the Milky Way," the creative breakthroughs of the *Priest=Aura* album and Kilbey's solo work, followed by the Church's struggle to survive in the wake of bad business decisions and Kilbey's drug indulgences, and their reemergence as an underground band with a worldwide cult following. [paper, 320 pages, 71 photos]

THE GO-BETWEENS
David Nichols
When Robert Forster and Grant McLennan formed the Go-Betweens in Brisbane in 1977, they were determined to be different. They were angular, spare and poetic when crashing directness was the prevailing style. Their heroes were Dylan, Creedence and Television when it was more fashionable to cite the Stooges and the New York Dolls. Their attitude was as punk as anyone's, but their lyrical guitar pop stood in sharp contrast to the trends of the day. The Go-Betweens earned a reputation as "the ultimate cult band" – they never had hits, but their music was greatly admired by peers from R.E.M. to Sleater-Kinney, and their influence has continued to grow over time. David Nichols relates their story with wit and verve, through to its sad conclusion, with the death of Grant McLennan in 2006. With many rare photographs. [paper, 288 pages, 85 photos]

DIG: AUSTRALIAN ROCK AND POP MUSIC, 1960-85
David Nichols
Dig tells the story of Australian rock and pop music over a crucial quarter century from 1960 to 1985—formative years in which the nation cast off its colonial cultural shackles and took on the world. Generously illustrated and scrupulously researched, it combines scholarly accuracy with populist flair. Nichols is an unfailingly witty and engaging guide, surveying the fertile and varied landscape of Australian popular music in seven broad historical chapters, interspersed with shorter chapters on some of the more significant figures of each period. The result is a compelling portrait of a music scene that evolves in dynamic interaction with those in the United States and the UK, yet has always retained a strong sense of its own identity and continues to deliver new stars – and cult heroes – to a worldwide audience. Those whose knowledge of Australian music doesn't extend far beyond the Easybeats, AC/DC, Little River Band, and Nick Cave will discover a wealth of music beyond those acts; and even those familiar with the work of the Missing Links, Pip Proud, Radio Birdman, and the Moodists will learn much about the scenes and connections that produced these bands and dozens more. [paper, 604 pages, 135 illustrations]

KILL ALL YOUR DARLINGS
Luc Sante

"Burning passion and a prose style to die for."—William Gibson

In his books (*Low Life*, *The Factory of Facts*) and in a string of wide-ranging and inventive essays Luc Sante has shown himself to be both a critic of uncommon power and range and one of America's pre-eminent stylists. *Kill All Your Darlings* is the first collection of his articles—many of which first appeared in the *New York Review of Books* and the *Village Voice*—and offers ample justification for this high praise. Alongside meditations on cigarettes, factory work, and hipness, and the critical tour de force, "The Invention of the Blues," Sante offers his incomparable take on icons from Arthur Rimbaud to Bob Dylan, René Magritte to Tintin, Buddy Bolden to Walker Evans, Victor Hugo to Allen Ginsberg, the Mekons to Robert Mapplethorpe. [paper, 300 pages]

ALSO AVAILABLE FROM VERSE CHORUS PRESS

INNER CITY SOUND
Punk and Post-Punk in Australia, 1976–85
Clinton Walker (editor)
The bands that spearheaded the late 1970s punk scene in Australia—the Saints, Birthday Party, Radio Birdman, and the Go-Betweens—are among the most important of their time. *Inner City Sound* is the classic account of the explosive development of that scene. Original articles from fanzines and newspapers, together with almost 300 photographs, vividly portray the creative ferment of the period and the dozens of bands that sprang up in the wake of the pioneers. First published in late 1981, *Inner City Sound* soon fell out of print. It became a lost classic, so sought after that it has been bootlegged like the rare singles listed in its discography. This new edition of "the bible of Australian punk" contains 32 extra pages of articles, photos, and discographic data, which take the story through to 1985, when Nick Cave, the Go-Betweens, the Triffids, and others began to break through internationally. [paper, 192 pages, 285 photos]

GREAT POP THINGS
The Real History of Rock'n'Roll from Elvis to Oasis
Colin B. Morton and Chuck Death, with an introduction by Greil Marcus

"A comic-book collection that brilliantly depicts the story of rock & roll."—Rolling Stone

The comic strips of Colin B. Morton and Chuck Death (aka Jon Langford), serialized over several years in LA Weekly, comprise a heartfelt and devastatingly funny history of rock. Like Monty Python, their version is surreal and ridiculous—yet somehow it all rings true. As they pinpoint the absurdities and oddities of rock history, the authors come closer to its truth than most conventional accounts—and they're much more entertaining. The caricatures—of rock figures from Mick Jagger to Captain Beefheart, Johnny Rotten to Courtney Love—are priceless. [paper, 232 pages]

WILD ABOUT YOU
The Sixties Beat Explosion in Australia and New Zealand
Ian D. Marks & Iain McIntyre
The astonishing outpouring of rock and roll in the 1960s in Australia and New Zealand gave birth to iconic bands like the Easybeats, the Masters Apprentices, Billy Thorpe and the Aztecs, the Purple Hearts, and the Missing Links, as well as launching the careers of a generation of musicians who went on to greater fame with their later groups (the Bee Gees, AC/DC, Little River Band, and more). Heavily illustrated and with a detailed discography, *Wild About You* is essential for all fans of '60s garage and beat music, and for anyone seeking greater knowledge of an hugely creative period in rock and roll history. [paper, 384 pages, 120 illustrations]

HIGHWAY TO HELL
The Life and Death of AC/DC Legend Bon Scott
Clinton Walker
The definitive account of AC/DC's rise to fame, when the ribald lyrics and charismatic presence of singer Bon Scott, along with the guitar work of Angus and Malcolm Young, defined a new, highly influential brand of rock and roll. Drawing on many interviews and featuring a gallery of rare photos, Clinton Walker traces the band's career through the life of their original front man, from small-time gigs to international success, up to Scott's shocking death in 1980. AC/DC's undiminished superstar status, and their indelible influence on a succession of genres from metal to grunge to rap, ensure that Bon Scott's presence continues to be felt strongly. Despite competition, this remains the authoritative biography of this seminal rock figure, dispelling many persistent rumors and myths and setting the record straight. [paper, 312 pages, 40 photos]

ABOUT THE AUTHOR

Robert Dean Lurie is a writer and musician based in Tempe, Arizona. He received his MFA in Creative Writing from the University of North Carolina Wilmington and is the author of *No Certainty Attached: Steve Kilbey and The Church* and *We Can Be Heroes: The Radical Individualism of David Bowie.*